SWEET LOU

Lou Piniella:
A Life in Baseball

Melissa Isaacson

TRIUMPH
BOOKS

No part of this publication may be reproduced, stored in a retrieval system, or transmitted in any form by any means, electronic, mechanical, photocopying, or otherwise, without the prior written permission of the publisher, Triumph Books, 542 South Dearborn Street, Suite 750, Chicago, Illinois 60605.

Triumph Books and colophon are registered trademarks of Random House, Inc.

Library of Congress Cataloging-in-Publication Data

Isaacson, Melissa.
  Sweet Lou : Lou Piniella, a life in baseball / Melissa Isaacson.
    p. cm.
  Includes bibliographical references and index.
  ISBN 978-1-60078-201-5
  1. Piniella, Lou, 1943– 2. Baseball players—United States—
Biography. 3. New York Yankees (Baseball team) I. Title.
  GV865.P56I73 2009
  796.357092—dc22
  [B]
                                2009000692

This book is available in quantity at special discounts for your group or organization. For further information, contact:

Triumph Books
542 South Dearborn Street
Suite 750
Chicago, Illinois 60605
(312) 939–3330
Fax (312) 663–3557
www.triumphbooks.com

Printed in U.S.A.
ISBN: 978-1-60078-201-5
Design by Patricia Frey
Photos courtesy of AP Images unless otherwise indicated

For Rick, Amanda, and Alec.
For Everything.

Contents

INTRODUCTION   vii

CHAPTER 1: *Tampa Bay*   1

CHAPTER 2: *Early Career*   13

CHAPTER 3: *Temper? What Temper?*   21

CHAPTER 4: *Big Apple*   45

CHAPTER 5: *Good-bye George, Hello Marge*   117

CHAPTER 6: *The Wizard of the Emerald City*   149

CHAPTER 7: *Going Home*   197

CHAPTER 8: *Curses*   233

REFERENCES   293

INDEX   295

Introduction

"**L**ou's Lou."

Not long after I began interviewing the family, friends, coaches, players, and anyone else I could find regarding the life and career of Lou Piniella, I lost track of the number of times that one particular phrase was uttered.

Again and again, people said it, and depending upon the context at the time, I took it to describe everything from his managerial style to his temper to his sense of humor. But until the end of the process, I was never really sure. Was "Lou's Lou" exempting him from his poor behavior? Was it glorifying all of his best qualities?

It became almost a quest, certainly a dual objective of the book as I sought to trace the evolution of one of the most colorful characters and popular men of his baseball generation.

I approached Chicago White Sox manager Ozzie Guillen at the end of a brutal five-game losing streak and potentially playoff-breaking losing streak at the end of the 2008 season. Not the best timing to approach any major-league manager but, as always, Ozzie was Ozzie, which meant, in this case, talkative and effusive when it came to discussing his crosstown counterpart.

At one point, Ken Griffey Jr., who once played for Piniella, poked his head into our interview to point to Ozzie and tell me, "Same people, same animal." It was clear after talking to Guillen that he took it as a compliment.

"When you see Lou Piniella in the winter meetings, now you realize who is Lou Piniella," Guillen said. "The respect he has in baseball, the love he has in the game. That's why to me, you look around, you can laugh and joke with him, but all of a sudden you see him with the real baseball people and you see it.

"When Lou walks into the winter meetings, everyone knows who's walking in. I wish one day I'm like that. When I walk in, all the people I see are media. When he walks in, baseball people [flock] to him. I feel honored to know him and ask questions of him. I wish we could see each other more often because I could learn a lot from him. Every time I have a chance, I take something from him."

Piniella's integrity drew fans early, drawing raves even in Jim Bouton's discerning *Ball Four* as a 25-year-old rookie during his brief preseason stay with the Seattle Pilots in 1969.

Bouton, by then a 30-year-old veteran, was intending to report to the Pilots' spring camp as stipulated by his contract, despite plans for a players' strike. That was until he called Piniella, as he did the other players, to relay what had gone on at a meeting with players' representative Marvin Miller.

"I reached Lou in Florida and he said that his impulse was to report, that he was scared it would count against him if he didn't, that he was just a rookie looking to make the big leagues and didn't want anyone to get angry at him," Bouton wrote. "But also that he'd thought it over carefully and decided he should support the other players and the strike. So he was not reporting.

"That impressed the hell out of me. Here's a kid with a lot more at stake than I, a kid risking a once-in-a-lifetime shot. And suddenly I felt a moral obligation to the players. I decided not to go down."

Lou Piniella knows how to handle people, always has. Most of all, he knew how to handle George Steinbrenner at least some of the time. His early days with the Yankees and ability to navigate the Bermuda Triangle of management, manager, and player in Steinbrenner, Billy Martin, and Reggie Jackson, illustrate Piniella's unique people skills as well as anything.

One of Piniella's favorite stories involves the infamous red phone in the Yankees dugout, which the Boss used to call his managers during games, make various suggestions, and generally drive them insane.

Piniella, then a first-time big-league skipper, recalled the time Hall of Famer Don Sutton was pitching against the Yankees and Steinbrenner, watching from his box, was sure Sutton was scuffing the ball. Sure enough, the dugout phone rang.

"What are you waiting for?" the Boss bellowed. "You see what he's doing to us. Why aren't you doing something about it?"

"Who's winning the game?" Piniella responded.

"We are, 4–2," said Steinbrenner.

"And who's pitching for us?" asked Piniella.

"Tommy John," sputtered Steinbrenner.

"Who the hell do you think taught Sutton? We got the master," said Piniella and hung up the phone.

Even as a player, Piniella was seemingly the only person in the entire Yankees organization who got away with riding Steinbrenner, like his infamous cry of "Hide the Hershey bars," when Steinbrenner walked into the clubhouse, drawing laughter from players and the Boss alike.

"Lou has a way of finding the good in people," said White Sox owner Jerry Reinsdorf. "Obviously Billy Martin had some bad things about him, and Lou found the good in Billy and George Steinbrenner, who fired him twice. Even Marge [Schott]. Lou's not a Pollyanna. He recognizes the foibles of some people, but he also finds the good in them."

The day before the 2008 All-Star Game in New York, as players warmed up for the Home Run Derby, I asked Reggie Jackson about Piniella. I asked how Piniella was able to "walk the line" in a Yankees clubhouse in which Jackson, Steinbrenner, and Martin were so often at odds and how he did it on a team with players like Piniella's close friend Thurman Munson, who drew lines of loyalty between them all.

"Because Lou *didn't* walk the line," Jackson said emphatically. "Lou was himself and he got along with people and he liked people. The line that Lou walked was all over the place. He would walk a mile to get to the center-field fence 400 feet away. That's the line Lou walked. Lou walked his own natural line."

Which is why, Jackson said, he both liked and admired him.

"You loved Lou; you loved him," he said effusively. "He was a very practical guy and believed in results and any thinking manager is the same way. You could say he was crazy or whatever when he played. But he was fun and exciting to be around, a good player, and he's turned into being a great manager.

"One of the things I didn't do that I wish I could have done was to be on his coaching staff because he's a great guy and a great baseball man and I love baseball and so does he."

The New York writers liked Piniella as well. And not just because he was quotable and funny and treated them like human beings rather than sewage, as athletes were starting to do when Piniella was a player. But that helped.

"One thing about Piniella is that he was a very honest guy and people appreciated that," said Murray Chass, the longtime baseball writer for the *New York Times*. "He was the kind of guy who, the day before the All-Star break, [writers] would go to him for the state-of-the-Yankees view and he was always willing to do that and be forthright in what he had to say.

"When all the stuff was going on with George, Billy, Reggie, and any other controversy, I remember going to him. To a great extent players didn't want to be quoted because they didn't want to get involved. They'd speak, but not for attribution. Once, I spoke to Piniella, he gave his view on what happened and I said, 'Do you want to be quoted?' and he said, 'Yeah, if you don't quote me, don't use it.'"

Piniella's temper is legendary, which only makes his enduring popularity that much more interesting. How does a guy who broke bats, threw helmets, tossed bases, and kicked his hat, among other things, still manage to have the respect of the teammates, coaches, managers, and umpires who were often in the middle of the hurricane?

Stan Williams, a loyal assistant to Piniella in Cincinnati and Seattle, tried to explain.

"You had to be kind of amazed," said Williams, who called Piniella Louie P. "He wore his heart on his sleeve and he has never changed. When we were at Seattle together, he was thrown out of one game after kicking a base around. He came in the clubhouse and I had to walk him around like a racehorse to keep him from having a heart attack because he was panting so hard. That's how intense he is. When he's out kicking bases, it's not to put on a show; it's his heart and soul.

"I once told Lou, 'I never realized how intelligent you are because you hide it so well with your temper.'"

Even the umpires, while most abhorred the volatile Earl Weaver and respected but did not necessarily like Billy Martin, had genuine affection for Piniella.

"He's a man's man and a damn good manager, too," said retired American League ump Larry Barnett. "That's the easiest way to describe Lou. At the time, you didn't like [the arguments], but as you sit back and reflect back on your career, it wasn't a bad thing. There are people I've run across in my career that were seven gazillion times worse than Lou Piniella as far as being a bad person. Lou is not a bad person. I have the utmost respect for him."

Piniella's anger, ferocious and uncontrollable as it might have seemed, was always short-lived and usually directed inward. And he was almost always apologetic afterward, worried what his wife Anita would think when she saw the invariable replays.

Even Rob Dibble, maybe especially Rob Dibble, understood this. Dibble, whom Piniella, as Cincinnati's manager, famously tackled in the Reds' clubhouse after Dibble essentially called Piniella a liar to reporters, still fondly recalls the talks the two had as Lou would bum cigarettes off of him.

"I've never been closer to any manager or coach in my life," said Dibble in a 2008 interview. "He's a wonderful guy; I respected him. He was a second father to me.

"Lou would hold a bat while a guy was hitting; he'd live and die with every pitch you threw. I've never seen anybody like him. Some people don't understand why former players like me love him. Well, some of my managers didn't even like me, didn't want me in their organization. They could care less about me as a person. Lou understood me."

Piniella stayed in Cincinnati for only three seasons and didn't take the team back to the postseason after the world championship in 1990. The Reds have yet to come close to that success since, reaching the playoffs just once in the next 18 seasons.

"This is most provincial city on earth," said longtime team broadcaster Marty Brennaman. "In this town, if you don't live here, if you pack up and leave when the season's over, people know that. If you live here year-round and suffer through the bad winters, they have a different respect for you. And once they determine you're one of them, even if you were not born here, they will go to the mat for you. But it takes a while. They have to embrace you, you can't embrace them.

"They knew of Lou's background [born and raised in Tampa], and he never did live here year-round. The fact that people loved him so much was even more impressive because they knew he packed up and left. But they still love him here. Nobody ever has a bad thing to say about Lou."

Even the former players who couldn't stand him as a manager grudgingly admit he probably made them better or at least tougher.

Jeff Cirillo, who played one season under Piniella in Seattle, did not like Piniella's particular brand of in-your-face managing, which demanded an aggressive response.

"I'm not a big guy," said Cirillo, "and I didn't hit home runs in batting practice. One day I heard [Piniella] and I looked back, and he was standing on the raised net at the back of the batting cage and he's going, 'Fucking Cirillo, just hit a home run in BP or I'm going to have a heart attack.' If you played well for him and you had the ability to stand up to him, you were king of the hill.

"But one thing I do admire in him and one thing I take from him is a stubbornness, 'I will show you.' It's not a mean streak but a chip, and a lot of his players play with his chip.

"Whatever emotion he gives you, it's not phony."

While Piniella has altered his approach depending on the makeup of his teams, said Billy Hatcher, a former player and coach under Piniella in Cincinnati and Tampa, he has always appreciated the guy who would kick a water cooler occasionally.

"He loved that," said Hatcher. "He hated passive people. He wanted you to show that you cared. If an umpire called a pitch on you a strike that you thought was a ball and you came back, he'll call you a sissy. 'You thought it was a ball?' he said. 'Let him know. There's a time and a place where you can get kicked out of a game. You start arguing; I'll come out there. I don't want you to think [you're alone]. I'll get kicked out of a game, but let me know you care.'"

Piniella unquestionably went too far in that regard with one of his players in Tampa, Ben Grieve. The player never responded and Piniella, from all accounts, never totally got over it.

"I've always told players who play for him that you're going to have a love-hate relationship playing for him, but once you step back and realize all he wants to do is win, you love him," said catcher Toby Hall, who played for Piniella in Tampa. "That's what some guys are going to soak in."

If Piniella evolved as a manager, his intense attention to statistics and matchups giving way to more shrewd, instinctive decisions, then he also changed as a man.

Always concerned about what his family would say after one of his televised outbursts against an umpire, he cut down the histrionics as he got older. Weight was always a struggle, but each off-season he would work at it, sometimes employing a trainer, and always coming back the next spring a little fitter, a little more dedicated to calming down.

He quit a pack-a-day smoking habit after being diagnosed with Type 2 diabetes when he came back to Tampa to manage in 2003. But it was not before years of trying. Chris Bosio, a former pitcher who would later serve as Piniella's pitching coach, recalled one particularly galling loss in spring training when they were with Seattle, after which Bosio was called into the manager's office.

"I sit down and Lou has like five Nicoderm patches all over his back and he's yelling, 'What the hell is going on with this team?' and suddenly I hear a click and a puff of smoke goes up and he's smoking a cigarette. And I go, 'Lou, that's going to kill you.' And he goes, 'Shut up, it's not going to kill me. It's you guys who are going to kill me.'"

While those present at Wrigley Field on June 2, 2007, the day Piniella was ejected for his tirade against the third-base umpire, might question how much Piniella has evolved, those who have been with him say it has been dramatic.

"Lou was a psycho in Cincinnati," said Bosio. "There was an urgency there, and he took a bunch of kids and turned them into winners. He went against [highly favored] Oakland and beat them when the Reds had no business being on the field with them. The A's look up the day before Game 1, and Lou has his players running the stairs in the stadium. They all thought he was nuts."

The Mariners teams that Piniella directed did not merely rise to respectability, but the franchise emerged from obscurity, survived a near move, and Piniella is still credited by many there with literally saving baseball in Seattle.

Family illness and differing philosophies with ownership drove him out after 10 seasons, and his return home to Tampa did not turn out the way he planned. Ownership did not fulfill the financial commitments it had made to Piniella to improve the team, and he left after three seasons. But the Rays improved under him, and the culture began to change.

"We can still feel Lou around here," outfielder Carl Crawford, one of the Piniella originals, said prior to the 2008 World Series. "I know I can."

Piniella's low point as a manager may have actually been the turning point.

"I think managing in Tampa and what he went through," said Hall, "actually helped him mature. What was nice, I think, was it helped him take a step back and made him concentrate on why he is one of the best managers in the game and what he does to be successful. I think it also made him step back health-wise because managing there for three years seemed to take 10 years off him."

In Chicago, although Piniella has displayed the full gamut of his personality—from snapping at reporters to kicking dirt on an umpire—his players have gotten the calmer Piniella who seems to recognize he is in the final innings of a fine career.

"He's easygoing, easy to get along with," said Jim Edmonds. "He doesn't bring the game into the clubhouse too often, and he doesn't bring it back the next day. That's what you're looking for, someone you can relate to. Baseball is a job; it's not life and death. It's secondary to the problems we have in the world and you have to remember that and some people need to be reminded that from time to time, but Lou separates that well."

Gene Michael, who was a teammate, coach, manager, and general manager during Piniella's tenure with the Yankees, said he didn't think Piniella was up to the task of managing in his first days with the Yankees, that he was too volatile.

"He changed, and he knew he had to do it and he finally did it," said Michael. "He has changed more in the last two years than probably all the other years he has managed. And he's better for it. He's outstanding during the game and preparing for the game, but his one little blemish was that he was still too critical, he showed his feelings too much. But I've seen the difference in the last two years and I've heard about it.

"It's different today, he's different today, and maybe he should've picked it up earlier, but now he is one of the best managers in the game because he's gotten smarter. He's a future Hall of Famer."

He's also a Tampa boy at heart, always will be. When the stresses of each Major League Baseball season make him look like Dorian Gray's portrait, it is Tampa that beckons Piniella back home to his family. To the beach. And the stone crabs. To the buddies he has had since childhood.

It is there where longtime *Tampa Tribune* columnist and friend Tom McEwen said Piniella's "cosmopolitan" air belies an unpretentious nature.

"In Tampa you might hear people say, 'Here comes Lou,'" said McEwen, "but you will never hear them say, 'Here comes Lou Piniella.'"

One of my favorite stories I have ever reported was one on Piniella that I did shortly after he was named the Cubs' manager in 2007. I traveled to Tampa, saw his childhood home, the parks where he played, his high school, his old haunts.

But what drew me in and stayed with me were his friends. While I went to Florida to try to get to know the new Cubs manager, the story became the people he surrounded himself with because—as I learned—they *were* him.

Mondy and Pauly and Tony and Benny and Carmine and Malio. His neighborhood buddies, his friends for life. All with parents and grandparents from Italy or Spain, some from the same region as his grandparents, many who worked in the same cigar factories in West Tampa as his parents, all who appreciate how hardworking their ancestors were. And all who embrace the concepts of giving their children a better life, of loyalty to their friends.

When I left, I felt like I had a new set of uncles and maybe a new way of looking at my own life.

"See those guys?" Carmine Iavarone said, pointing to a group of men at the bar of his restaurant. "They're not that close to Lou, but they all think they are because he'll come in here and sit at the bar and have a drink with them. That's Lou."

I eventually understood what it meant, what they meant, when they said "Lou's Lou," and it was more than just a catch-all explanation for why he called a squeeze play in the ninth or why he kicked dirt on the nearest umpire. It was more than a convenient crutch for those who couldn't think of anything clever to say.

"Lou's Lou," without exception, is said with the highest regard for the man, for his complexity, his quirkiness, his integrity, and yes, his sentimentality. And there is a lot of that.

Talking to one Piniella pal, Paul Ferlita, like the others a powerful-looking man, tanned, well-dressed, successful, I had to laugh as he described this group of confidantes who greet each other with hugs and share tears at every family wedding, funeral, and maybe even confirmation.

"A lot of us are pussies at heart," Ferlita said with a grin.

Piniella readily admitted to tearing up down the stretch of the 2008 season as the Wrigley Field fans serenaded the team after each victory with the corny but catchy "Go Cubs Go."

More than once, he has cried with his players, hugged them, even kissed them in the case of A-Rod and Ichiro—and maybe others who have not yet stepped forward.

He has also yelled so loud and so close that they could feel his breath on their faces.

Most of Piniella's players have passed the official demarcation of being born before his final game as a player in 1984 or not long enough after to remember him, eyes blazing, jet-black hair flying as he turned every Yankees hater into a reluctant admirer.

The ones who care in the Cubs clubhouse say they catch him on ESPN Classic. Some have actually gone to the trouble to Google him, the modern-day equivalent of checking the back of the baseball card.

But it's not the same.

Nor is he.

And so the quest began.

CHAPTER 1

Tampa Bay

There was never any doubt that Louie Piniella would be a ballplayer.

"I knew it when he was three years old," said his mother Margaret. "My brother Joe had a broom and he cut the stick down and bought a tennis ball, and you could see, even at that age, how hard Louie hit that ball."

It wasn't long before little Lou was out in front of the house for hours at a time, bouncing the ball off the steps and fielding "fly balls," which he created by throwing the ball onto the roof and catching it as it rolled off.

By six, he was at the park with the other boys. "If there was any team playing, he would be there," said Margaret. "I never had any problem with my kids. I knew exactly where they were. They were always at the park."

Until Lou was seven, he lived with his parents and Margaret's brothers Joe, Mac, and Uncle Mac's wife, Gloria, in West Tampa in the three-bedroom home of Margaret's parents, Marcelinno and Beñina Magadan, who emigrated from Spain.

In 1950, about a year after the arrival of baby Joe, Lou's younger brother by six years, the family moved from the house on Conrad St. to Cordelia St., where the diamond across the street now resides in Piniella Park.

1

"We spoke Spanish in the house because I thought it would be good for the kids to learn Spanish," recalled Margaret. "I wish I would've learned Italian from the Italians in the neighborhood."

The neighborhood was as bustling as the house—Spaniards and Italians all comingling in one loud, rollicking, great-smelling couple of blocks where everyone was seemingly related. "This neighborhood was paradise," said Margaret. "There were no problems with the neighbors, everyone helped out. I miss all of that."

Margaret, a tall, strong woman, was an All-State center in basketball from 1936–39 and a standout in softball. In grammar school, she played first base for the boys' team. "I was the only girl playing," she laughed. "They begged me to play."

Louis Piniella was a pitcher, and he played in the highly competitive Intersocial League in West Tampa with Lou's uncles Joe and Mac. It could be compared to semi-pro level, though those who saw the senior Piniella pitch say it was probably closer to Double A level.

"It was very good baseball," recalled Lou's childhood buddy Tony Gonzalez. "I remember his dad was a great pitcher. Both parents were very good athletes. And his Uncle Mike Magadan [Uncle Joe is the father of former big-leaguer Dave Magadan] was also a great player, so Lou has the DNA."

By the age of two, little Lou was a regular, sitting next to his mother and watching the Tuesday or Thursday night games and Sunday doubleheaders in Ybor City and West Tampa. When he got a little older, he would serve as batboy, studying the older men, who would drum the fundamentals of the game into the boy's head.

The games were more than simple recreation but a way of life for the working folks of West Tampa, inciting a passion that would carry off the ballfield and into their kitchens afterward, where the smell of thick vegetable soup and yellow rice and chicken would intermingle with talk of baseball.

"You'd listen to Lou's dad and uncles talk baseball," said another boyhood pal, Mondy Flores, "and they knew every nuance of the game. They were baseball fanatics, and Lou's mom was too, and it never stopped, what they did right, what they did wrong. Lou would come home to Tampa in the winter when he was managing in Seattle and have a cup of coffee with his mother, and she'd say, 'Lou, how come in this situation, you left that pitcher in?' And 'I don't understand why this guy doesn't bunt.'

"Lou would say, 'Mom, this guy makes $8 million. He doesn't want to bunt.'"

But he didn't argue. You respected your elders in Lou Piniella's neighborhood, where everyone was a surrogate parent.

"None of us had a lot of money," said Gonzalez, "but we were rich in the love of our families, rich with friends from the neighborhood. Grandparents lived with the children. We ate a lot of rice and a lot of potatoes. It was a treat to get a piece of meat. But they were hard-working people."

Most worked in the cigar factories, Margaret as a secretary for Morgan Cigar Company, and Louis as a salesman of cigars, cigarettes, candy, and household drugs from store to store until buying his own distributorship. Margaret then went to work for her husband, handling the bookkeeping while Lou's grandparents stayed home and took care of the kids.

At night and on weekends, there was baseball.

"They were tough times and that's all there was," said Gonzalez. "The first time Lou and I ever saw a TV, we were probably about seven. We had an old DuMont, Lou had one, too. From time to time, we'd wrap tinfoil around the antenna and watch the Game of the Week."

They would learn to speak English from the Catholic nuns, descendants of the Salesian Sisters, who had traveled down from their headquarters in Haledon, New Jersey.

"There was no messing with them," remembered Flores with a shudder. "When they were ready to have discipline, when they had had enough, it was enough, and there was not a person who would try to cross them. They wouldn't stand for it."

By then, it was already obvious to Lou's friends who were the most gifted boys among them but more than that, who was the leader.

"He had a magnetism," said Joe Ficcorotta, a neighborhood kid a few years younger than Lou and his friends who watched Piniella in awe. "He was a down-to-earth guy, but certain people just have that magnetism where they can get people to do things and energize people around him and that was Lou."

Baseball players sprouted quicker than the grass in the sun-bleached outfield, boys like Tony La Russa and Ken Suarez and Al Lopez Jr., on neighboring playground teams. But everyone played and in the summer, Lou and his pals would start their day on their neighborhood diamond at 8:00 in the morning—home plate not 50 yards from the Piniellas' house—and get kicked out at 10:00 when the park closed.

"Someone's mom would yell 'It's dinnertime,' we'd all scatter, and within 15, 20 minutes, we'd be right back out there," said Gonzalez. "It was a wonderful childhood."

Piniella excelled at basketball and football too, but touch football was as close as Margaret Piniella's boy would ever come to any sort of serious involvement with a game in which some thought he could have made a great quarterback.

"Yes, he could've been good," Margaret Piniella said in a no-nonsense tone. "He was good in everything. But I wouldn't let him. Neither of my kids played football. Too rough. My brother Joe, the oldest, almost lost a kidney playing football at Loyola [University in New Orleans]. It almost killed him. So I told Lou, 'No football.' They could play touch but no tackle.'"

Little did she know then that it was a seemingly harmless hike during a trip to the Pony League national baseball championship that would nearly kill her son.

Lou Piniella was 13 in the summer of 1956 as his West Tampa team, with La Russa as a teammate, traveled to Ontario, California. It was Lou's first plane ride, his first trip outside of Tampa, in fact, and all the boys were awed by the experience and particularly by a side trip to Mount Baldy before the title game.

"My folks made the trip and my dad rented a car because we were going to take some of the guys to a mountain range nearby," said one of Lou's closest friends, Paul Ferlita. "We were Florida boys from the flatland, so some of the guys rolled a log down one side of the mountain, not knowing it could do any damage.

"Well, my father held them back to scold them and by the time he came back, to this day I'm not sure if Lou was walking fast or running down the side of the hill, but the next thing we knew, he started tumbling down, on all rock, toward a drop that went 1,000 feet down."

All Lou remembered was stumbling over a loose rock and going over the cliff. La Russa remembered him catching up to the group from behind and then disappearing over the edge.

"I thought I saw him land on his back," the Cardinals' skipper recalled. "I thought he was crushed."

"The only thing between him and the bottom," said Ferlita, "was a big boulder about five to six feet around, and that stopped him. If that hadn't stopped him, he would have been hurt a lot worse and possibly killed.

"We rushed him to the hospital. My dad was driving a rented vehicle so he wasn't used to it and I remember he kept putting the brakes on and I was thinking we would get in a car wreck before we got to the hospital."

Doctors kept Piniella overnight with a minor concussion, cuts and bruises, and a sore ankle. It was broken, but X-rays, or the X-ray technician, didn't pick up the fracture.

"Lou played the next day but he couldn't pitch so he played outfield and he felt really badly because he was our best pitcher," said Ferlita. "But he was so grateful he was still alive, he said, 'I'm going to church every Sunday.'

"Then, after we got beat two days later, Lou was so angry he threw the baseball as high as he could, and it landed right in the middle of the winning team's prayer meeting."

The ankle injury would affect Piniella for years to come, in his mind effectively ending his basketball career in college. But it was his first true love, and some argue, his greatest talent.

When the boys played CYA basketball in grade school, they christened Piniella with the nickname "Louie, the Hook" because he wasn't much of a passer. "He got razzed about it all the time," said Ferlita.

In junior high, Piniella developed a reputation as one of the best up-and-coming basketball players in Tampa and fulfilled those expectations in high school, raining hook shots and one-handed jumpers over the competition as rival high schools packed the gym to boo the star from Jesuit High.

"He was at least equal in basketball to baseball," said Gonzalez. "He could shoot; his jumping ability was incredible; he had high, high energy."

"He was one of the best athletes to come out of Tampa," said Piniella's basketball coach at Jesuit, Paul Straub. "I really wanted to make a quarterback out of him, but his mother wouldn't let him play."

For close to 40 years, Piniella's single-game Tampa scoring record of 54 points stood. "And in his day, buckets that went for two points now go for three," Straub pointed out. A 50-percent shooter, Piniella scored 1,716 points in three years, another record.

"And one of the outstanding games he played, the other team put two men on him, and he scored one field goal," said Straub. "But the rest of the kids scored 55, and we won."

Among the schools that came calling for him in basketball was Louisville, but recruiters were concerned about his temper.

"I wasn't a bad kid," he said, "maybe just a little mischievous."

In high school, Lou and his friends would skip class to go watch the Reds in spring training at Al Lopez Field, less than a mile from their school. "We'd hang around the outfield trying to steal baseballs," Ferlita recalled. "Then we'd write notes [excusing their absences], and Lou would sign mine and I'd sign his."

It never worked.

The prefect of discipline obviously had an imagination and a sense of humor. "If you got caught smoking, you'd have to roll his cigarettes," recalled Piniella. If you acted the fool, "you'd have to draw pictures of donkeys, cut them out, and write 'I am a jackass,' on them."

And if you cut class to goof off at spring training, you'd have to draw two palm trees with a man sleeping on a hammock in between or write the school rules backwards 100 times.

"Either that," said Ferlita, "or he'd hit you on the head with his key ring."

Asked how often they got in trouble, Ferlita did not hesitate. "Quite often," he said. "Once, we compared our [excuse] notes, and we didn't even know where we were."

When they got home, there would probably be some yelling. "But our parents weren't too hard on us," said Ferlita. "We made decent grades, and we were pretty good kids."

Well, except for the time Lou hit the accelerator instead of the brake when his father was teaching him to drive and put a big hole in the chain-link fence that surrounded the ballfield across the street. But then, that was an accident.

* * *

One of the boys' strongest influences was Coach Straub, who lost both legs and was left with a permanently disabled right hand from injuries sustained during training maneuvers at Guadalcanal as a Marine corporal in WWII, and who showed them what winning was really about.

Straub once scared a kid who thought he was tough and was unaware of the coach's injuries by throwing a dart into his wooden leg.

At age 85 in the fall of 2006, shortly after Piniella was named manager of the Cubs, the old coach sat at his kitchen table with the yellowed newspaper clippings and black-and-white photos fanned out before him, his memory as sharp as his outlook was sunny.

Louie, he explained, invited him and some of his other former coaches to his retirement ceremony, brought them onto the field and had them introduced to the Yankee Stadium crowd. "Only time I've ever seen my dad cry," said Steve Straub, Paul's son.

They all genuflect at Coach Straub's name. "He's a marvelous man," said Piniella. "What an influence he had in my formative years. I've always quietly thanked him for all the time he put in with me and the values he set.

"In sports, the will to win, to compete, it all starts earlier in life. And he was tough on me, which was good because I had a hot temper. He started to try to change that process."

Straub said it wasn't easy, on him or on a young Lou Piniella.

"Every time he took a shot, they fouled him," said Straub, shaking his head. "They'd often try to start a fight with him, and officials would call fouls on him. They wanted him to get a technical. Lou would get very upset, and he'd come over and talk to me and I'd say, 'You've got to calm down. You can't let them do that to you. You're playing for a team, and they're the ones who are most important, not those people.'"

* * *

It wasn't necessarily his temper that cost him his senior season on the baseball team, though the big-league scouts heard that it was.

Either way, it resulted in part from Lou butting heads with Jesuit baseball coach Jack O'Connell in the spring of 1961. As Piniella remembered it, after losing in the regional finals in basketball, he reported to O'Connell for baseball season, at which point the coach told him he wanted him to be his starting pitcher in their first game against Jefferson three days later.

Piniella said he couldn't, that his arm wouldn't be ready, and O'Connell told him that if he didn't pitch, he was off the team.

Margaret Piniella recalled a slightly different version of the story.

"He would pitch, then next time someone else would pitch and then in the first or second inning, they'd put Lou in again," she said. "I said, 'Louie, you have a very promising career.' I told him, 'If you hurt that arm, then what happens? If you ruin that arm, you ruin your career. You're not going to be able do anything. You tell that coach you'll be ready to pitch when the time comes, but don't think you're going to pitch every game.'

"Well, the coach didn't like that, so Louie didn't play that year. The coach said, 'If you don't want to pitch like that, don't play,' so Louie said, 'I don't play.'"

Piniella's friend Kenny Suarez urged him to swallow his pride and ask to be back on the team but Lou wouldn't do it.

"Lou Piniella was too stubborn, too proud, and probably too dumb to apologize," Piniella wrote in his 1986 autobiography. "I sat there all spring watching my friends and eating my heart out."

Piniella figured his stubbornness cost him about $75,000, which is what the scouts had told him he could sign for out of high school. The next year, Tony La Russa signed for $100,000 out of the neighboring Jefferson High School.

Instead, Piniella was headed to the University of Tampa on a basketball scholarship where he would also play baseball.

The basketball part, unfortunately, didn't last very long.

Piniella recalled a game his freshman year at Louisville, a school that had once recruited him. It was a big game for Tampa, a chance to put the smaller school on the basketball map, and Piniella, playing guard, was called into the game before the half.

He was fouled three times, attempted four free throws and missed them all. In the locker room at halftime, Tampa coach Bob Lavoy called him out. "All-American high school basketball player, my ass," the coach bellowed.

Piniella couldn't help himself.

"You can't be so smart either," he yelled back. "You recruited me."

If his basketball career wasn't over by then, it would be soon enough. That same year, he jumped from the roof of a college bar in order to escape from the police, who were presumably looking for underage drinkers, and landed on the ankle he injured falling on Mount Baldy.

It had bothered him all through high school, but mostly in basketball when he would come down hard after shooting, and when he landed on the ground in the alley behind the bar, the pain was excruciating.

His father let him sit in jail that night, and when he hobbled out the next morning, it was clear the ankle would not allow him to play basketball for the rest of the season.

His baseball coach and the athletic director at the University of Tampa, Sam Bailey, said his star slugger wasn't meant for basketball anyway.

"I remember the injury, but he didn't have it when he was playing baseball," Bailey said. "He just didn't fit in basketball like baseball. He was a heck of a lot better basketball player than he showed at the University of Tampa, but the coach couldn't handle him. He didn't play as well for the basketball coach as he played for me. Lou was a special case."

The temper was already an issue, but Bailey clearly had a soft spot for the young man with the sweet swing. The coach also had a sense of humor and still laughs about the time Lou's grandfather came to a game in Miami and asked his grandson if he had had lunch.

When Lou said he hadn't, his grandfather slipped him a Cuban sandwich through the outfield fence, and Lou shoved it into his glove until a line drive suddenly came toward him, lettuce flying one way, tomatoes the other as he made the catch.

"That's a favorite story," said the 85-year-old Bailey.

Piniella was never known as a lover of exercise, so while the team did attend to fitness, Bailey slipped a little extra running in for Lou.

"All he wanted to do was hit, so sometimes I'd run him out to the outfield, then I'd wave him in and he'd think he was going to bat, so he'd run in," said Bailey. "Then I'd say, 'Lou, you're playing in too close' or something else and send him back out to the outfield.'"

During a solid freshman season, the scouts returned to see the kid they had shunned the year before. "Even though we were a small school, we played Florida, Florida State, Miami, so we got good exposure," said Bailey, "and after about three, four games, the scouts were in our dugout all the time to see Lou. He was such a great natural hitter.

"He had the talent, a great eye, a natural swing. He never carried the bat awkwardly or swung awkwardly. The only thing I told him was to lay off the first pitch and watch it into the catcher's mitt and then to look for what you want. I thought he'd be an outstanding player in the majors if he controlled his temper and got the right manager."

Piniella was ready, and that summer he came home one day to find a scout representing the Cleveland Indians waiting for him on Cordelia Street. The Indians, the scout told him, were prepared to offer him a signing bonus of $10,500—a $7,500 progressive bonus and $7,500 against his education if he signed with the Indians—$25,000 in all.

Piniella never blinked. He signed on the spot and became a professional baseball player. He was on his way.

CHAPTER 2

Early Career

Professional baseball careers don't usually begin with big signing bonuses and a heralded arrival in the big leagues. It happened even less frequently in the summer of 1962. For 18-year-old Lou Piniella, it began in Selma, Alabama, home of the Cloverleafs, the Indians' Class D team.

After a tearful goodbye with his mother, Piniella's adulthood officially began, and at least for the first leg, he took his Uncle Mac along for the ride. The two drove the full day's trip from Tampa, arriving in Selma the same night.

The next night, after being told by his new manager, Pinky May, that his old spikes were not fit for a professional ballplayer, Piniella played right field and hit leadoff in his first game.

Before the game, Uncle Mac had a seat beside May, father of future major league catcher Milt May, in the dugout.

"He told me, 'You have a big leaguer there, my friend,'" Mac Magadan recalled.

It wouldn't be quite that simple. But it would work out in one way. Piniella was the only member of the 1962 Selma Cloverleafs to ever even sniff the big leagues. No one else had so much as the proverbial cup of coffee.

Piniella was the big prospect, and they paid him a team-high $650 a month that summer in Selma. He began his career by rapping a double in his first at-bat, but he struck out the next time up, and after his first three weeks in professional baseball, he had failed to crack .200. And worse, he had no idea what he was doing wrong until he mentioned to May that his Uncle Mac had advised him on the drive up to Selma to close his stance and protect the plate against those big curves he was about to see in professional ball.

May told him to go back to his old stance, to worry about the fastball first, start pulling the ball again, and drive it with the power they had heard about. The next night, he hit a home run deep and finished the season at .270 with eight home runs and 44 runs batted in.

That November, the Washington Senators made Piniella the first player chosen in the minor league draft with a new contract that didn't raise him a nickel from the $650 per month he had made in Selma. It was his first lesson in the business of professional baseball.

But at age 19 and brimming with confidence after his first season, he fired off a letter to general manager George Selkirk, which Piniella recalled in his autobiography:

Dear Mr. Selkirk,
I received your contract and it must be the wrong one. It calls for six-fifty a month and that is the salary I made last year. I showed I could play professional baseball in 1962 and I expect a raise, a substantial one, for 1963.

A few days later, he got his reply:

Dear Lou,
Your contract calls for six-fifty and that is what you will be paid. You are only a Class D ballplayer and you haven't proven yourself yet. I am enclosing these scouting reports, which indicate that several of our scouts believe you will never be more than a Triple A player. If you want any chance at all in this organization, sign this contract and send it back to me by return mail.

Piniella believed it and was more than a little scared by it. Only years later did he realize that there were probably a half-dozen other scouting reports that raved about his potential but that Mr. Selkirk did not bother to send those.

It would not be the last time Piniella was unhappy with his contract, nor was it the first lesson in how to never count on anything in professional sports.

In his first three years as a pro, he played for three different organizations. His third, the Baltimore Orioles, who obtained him in a trade with Washington, would turn out to be the most agonizing yet.

*   *   *

After starting out in Class C ball upon his return from National Guard duty, a demotion after hitting over .300 in two years in Class B, Piniella wasn't thrilled. But the team promised he would be called up to Baltimore in September.

The manager at Class C in Aberdeen, South Dakota, was a warm, gentle man named Cal Ripken Sr. Piniella's teammates included a pitcher, Jim Palmer, a shortstop, Mark Belanger, and the manager's kid as their batboy, a cute little four-year-old tyke, Cal Jr.

Piniella had just turned 21 when, as they had promised, he was called up to Baltimore. Hank Bauer was the manager, a former Yankees star and a tough cookie who told him to keep his mouth shut and try to learn a thing or two.

Once, early on, Piniella pinch hit for future Hall of Famer Robin Roberts and grounded into the last out. In the clubhouse, Roberts snarled at him, "Young man, I could have done that myself."

That, however, would hardly prepare him for his next season and his next baseball tour of duty in Elmira, New York, under Earl Weaver whom Piniella called, "the first manager who really intimidated me."

Weaver was the classic drill sergeant, running his team through a two-a-day tryout that would rival the Marines. Weaver rode Piniella particularly hard, and Piniella snapped back.

Early in the season, after going into a game as a pinch-hitter, Piniella struck out for the second time to end a 24-inning game. Weaver told him he was "worthless" and Piniella, angry at being benched after two weeks, shot back, "How would you know? You haven't seen enough of me."

Weaver suspended him for a week but two days into the suspension woke him up and told him to get his ass to the ballpark, that he needed him after an outfielder was injured.

Piniella got along with Weaver reasonably well that season by staying as far away from his manager as possible—no card games, golf games, no sitting near him in the dugout. He realized the two were like a pair of combustible components, but he did not understand how Weaver could hold his temper against him when Weaver himself had all the self-control of a two-year-old.

The funny thing was that Weaver was actually very fond of Piniella and admired him as a ballplayer.

"He was my kind of ballplayer because he was a good ballplayer, he got the job done," Weaver said in a 2008 interview. "You could count on him to play every day, and you could count on him in the clutch, especially in the clutch.

"He was an outstanding prospect, he was an outstanding major-league ballplayer. A little short of the Hall of Fame but God darn it, he was a winner and he contributed a lot. Any manager in the big leagues would have taken him at any time."

Piniella's temper, said Weaver, didn't bother him personally.

"Because I was the same type of player, though not as talented," Weaver said. "We came out of the same mold. When I was a player, I'd break a watercooler here and there. Now, as a person in authority, I knew he had to be disciplined when he broke a door or helmets. In those days, that was a lot of money. He would break two, three, four helmets and the general manager would come to you and say, 'Listen, he's going to pay for those himself.' They took it out of his check.

"But he was a great talent and there wasn't a time I didn't turn in a prospect report on him and when I wrote them for the Baltimore

Orioles, I'd always say he's going to the major leagues with no doubt about it."

Grudgingly, Piniella would later admit he was one of the finest managers he had ever known and instilled in him a true passion for winning. But the two would continue their tumultuous relationship for years to come, well after Piniella left Baltimore.

After that first season in 1965, however, he would never play for Weaver again after being traded once more, this time to Cleveland.

* * *

It was with the Triple A team in Portland in 1966 where Piniella first met Stan Williams, who would later serve on his coaching staffs in New York, Cincinnati, and Seattle. Williams was seven years older; had already played eight years with the Dodgers, Yankees, and Indians; injured his arm; and had gone back to the minors.

Williams shared with the fiery young man from Tampa how to play gin rummy and shared his love of crossword puzzles, which Piniella would continue as a hobby. But it was not going to help him to relax.

"I remember him kicking the door off the wall and throwing trash cans," recalled Williams, a close friend since. "It was a penny a point, and I won all his money. He used to call it 'sale city,' when he had to sell all his sweaters to pay the bills.

"He had that intensity right from the beginning. He wasn't the most talented player in the world, but he was as good a player as you'd want to play for you because he got everything he could get out of his talent. He was an all-around good player because he pushed himself to the limit."

After a failed experiment at catcher, Piniella was back in the outfield at Triple A Portland, where he credited the manager there, Johnny Lipon, with not just teaching him how to hit the slider, which had become a real problem, but to become a professional hitter—to hit and run, hit to right with power, establish discipline at the plate, and to have bat control. Piniella was a contact hitter, not a home-run hitter, and it would serve him well the rest of his career.

After hovering around .200 the first half of his first season in Portland, Piniella came on strong in July, batting above .300 the rest of the way, then hit .308 the next season with eight home runs and 56 RBIs.

But it was after that 1967 season that life would change in a more profound way than hitting the breaking ball.

Anita Garcia had attended Hillsborough High School and had heard of the All-American basketball player at Jesuit named Lou Piniella, but had never met him until after she attended the University of Florida and the University of South Florida, where she majored in art and education and in 1962 won some notoriety herself as Miss Tampa.

Like most couples after they have been married for a while, the stories vary a little as to how exactly they met.

In his 1986 autobiography, Lou recalled spotting Anita in a Tampa bar on the arm of a friend, Ron Perez. Piniella described Ron's date as "a striking-looking girl, dark-haired, with a great figure and a warm smile."

He said his buddy introduced the two and that when he saw Perez a few days later, he asked about Anita and was told the two had broken up.

"I thought of those green eyes and that great smile and that wonderful figure," Piniella wrote, "and I said to Ron, 'Do you mind if I call her?'"

His buddy didn't have a problem with it, and Piniella called her the next night. He introduced himself, told her he had gotten her phone number from Perez, and asked if she would like to go out that Saturday night.

"I'm busy," she said, according to Lou's memory.

He told her he'd call her again and she responded, "If you want to."

"It wasn't the most encouraging phone conversation I'd ever had with a girl," he wrote.

It got just a little better on a second call for a date and a second rejection, after which Anita, as Lou recalled, asked him to "please" call again. But on a third call a few days later, Anita, according to Lou's recall, resulted in her telling him she might be busy; she'd have to check and call him back later in the week.

"Anita, I'm a professional ballplayer," he told her. "I'll be going to spring training in a few months and I won't be around. There is also something else about a professional baseball player. You get three strikes in this game and then you are out. I have called you twice and you were busy. This is my third call. If you turn me down again, that will be three strikes and you'll be out. I sure won't be calling again."

"Well, is that right?" she responded in his vision of the story.

"Yes, that will be it," he said. "Three strikes and you're out."

"She must have liked my determination or my ultimatum or something," he wrote. "She finally said, 'What time, Saturday night?'"

In Anita's version in a 2003 interview with the *St. Petersburg Times*, the two met at an exhibition football game.

"I think there was chemistry right away," she said.

When Lou called to ask her for a date, Anita said, "he kind of waited until the last minute, and I already had other plans. So he called again a week later, but I had another date.

"So the third time he called, he said to me, 'I just want you to know before you give me your answer that I play professional ball and in my game, three strikes and you're out. And you've got two.'"

Either way, the ending was the same, as they were married between spring training and the start of Lou's season with Portland.

By 1968, Piniella was sure he was going to get the big call-up. That winter, however, instead of working out, the newly married Piniella attended college classes at the University of Tampa and worked part time at E.F. Hutton.

Despite having a few solid years of Triple A ball under his belt, Piniella did not convince the stern Cleveland manager Alvin Dark he was ready for the big leagues.

Piniella thought Dark disliked him because during spring training, some of the veterans like Luis Tiant and Leon (Daddy

Wags) Wagner and Duke Sims took a liking to him and "horsed around" on the bus, in the clubhouse, and in the dugout.

When Dark informed him that indeed he would be spending another year in Triple A, Piniella stormed into Gabe Paul's office to complain, only to be reassured he was "only a phone call away."

"Here's a dime," Piniella shouted as he pulled the coin out of his pocket, "don't forget to call me collect."

He ended up going home to Tampa, refusing to report to Portland after demanding that Paul pay him the major-league minimum of $7,500 rather than the minor-league salary of $5,500.

Paul ended up "compromising" by offering him $1,500 more, and Piniella returned to Portland, where he would hit .317 that season. In September, he got the call and reported to Cleveland, where he got mop-up work under Dark and prayed he'd be picked up by Seattle or Kansas City in the expansion draft, which he was by the Seattle Pilots.

Piniella was to earn a whopping $10,000 for the 1969 season but didn't make it out of spring training before being traded to his fifth organization, the Kansas City Royals. With a $2,500 raise he wrangled from Royals GM Cedric Tallis over the phone, Piniella joined the Royals and in his first exhibition game, he hit a home run and double off Steve Carlton.

He broke camp with the big club, led off the season with four straight hits, and all of a sudden was an overnight sensation, a rookie phenom who hit .282 with 11 homers and 68 RBIs. And when the season was over, Piniella was the 1969 Rookie of the Year as voted by the Baseball Writers' Association (*The Sporting News* chose Carlos May, the outfielder from the White Sox who hit .281 with 18 homers and 62 RBIs).

It meant a sizable raise to $25,000 for the following season. Finally, he had earned some respect.

CHAPTER 3

Temper? What Temper?

At various times over the course of his playing and managing career, Lou Piniella would blame his Latin blood, his DNA, and sometimes, just plain ignorance, for his famous temper.

But he would never deny it. Nor does his mother Margaret.

"They say he has a temper," she said in a September 2008 interview. "Well, everyone has a temper. I have a temper too. But when the game's over, that's gone. I go home and I'm a different person. That's the way Lou is too. He just wants everything to be perfect."

Those who know Piniella best say that is where it all begins—a desire for him and, specifically referring to major-league umpires, for those around him to perform up to expectations.

Tony Gonzalez, a close friend since childhood, says it's simply a case of being fair-minded.

"He loves the team he's managing and he loves the competitiveness of sport, and he does not want an umpire's decision to affect the outcome of a game," Gonzalez said. "That ruins his idea of a perfect game. If he perceives an error, he gets extremely frustrated and he loses his patience. He wants everyone to be perfect in that arena

21

and if everyone's perfect, then the best team is going to win. All he wants is for it to be fair."

From his earliest memories of his father and uncles playing in their Intersocial League games in Ybor City and West Tampa, Piniella also remembered the legendary arguments that would ensue.

"People watch me play and think I get excited," he wrote in his 1986 autobiography. "They should have seen my family play."

Piniella recalled one game when his father was pitching against a local rival and kept shaking off his catcher's signals. When the catcher came out to ask what the hell he wanted to throw, Lou Sr. told him to get back behind the plate and he'd throw whatever the hell he wanted.

Well, the catcher did not much appreciate that, further words were exchanged, and, wrote Piniella, "All of a sudden, my father let go with a haymaker and the catcher was down. He rolled over and wrestled my father to the ground, the two of them whacked away at each other, all the other players ran over to break it up, the fans came down from the stands, and everybody was having a heck of a time."

This went on for about 15 to 20 minutes. "Finally, they all became exhausted," Piniella recounted, "the catcher went behind the plate, my father went to the mound, and the game continued as if nothing had ever happened."

Fights on the field, among the fans, with the umpires, were almost a staple of Piniella's youth.

"The Magadans [Lou's uncles], my father, they would argue over dominoes," laughed Lou's younger brother Joe.

Piniella said he takes after his mother in that department and indeed, Margaret Piniella was known to get involved in more than one argument with an umpire at one of her husband's or brothers' games, or with opposing fans heckling her at one of her son's basketball games.

"When we were kids," said close friend Paul Ferlita, "she wouldn't come into the ballgames oftentimes. She'd sit in her car behind the left-field fence so she wouldn't get too excited."

Once, the legendary *Tampa Tribune* columnist Tom McEwan recalled calling Margaret Piniella to interview her for a story he was writing on Lou. "She was a strong woman," McEwan said. "I said, 'I think Lou is a wonderful fella except for his temper, and she said, 'TEMPER? WHAT TEMPER?' She was wonderful."

There are various versions of one story that had Margaret on the basketball court at a high school game to argue a call or to defend the family's honor. "That's where Lou got his temper from," said Ferlita. "The old man got upset too. He had a temper too. But he wasn't as quick as she was."

Was Lou embarrassed? "Nah," said Ferlita, "he was probably arguing too."

At Jesuit High, other teams would key on Piniella in basketball, not just because he was so good, but knowing he had a quick temper, they would try to draw him into committing technical fouls.

"He'd be on that foul line all the time," said high school coach Paul Straub. "Every time he took a shot, they fouled him. They'd often try to start a fight with him, and then officials would call fouls on him. They'd hope he'd say something back to them so the officials could throw him out.

"I would take him out of the game, and he would cry and apologize and I'd say, 'Lou, they're after you because they want to get you out. You're playing for the team, don't worry about these people.'"

But it was as ingrained in Piniella as his height, his dark hair, and his square jaw.

As a kid, said buddy Carmine Iavarrone, Piniella "would never be mad at you, he was always just mad at himself. All the kids would tell you that. He would throw his glove, swing his bat. There are guys who are bullies and hotheads but he was just so tough on himself, he never took it out on others. His teammates loved him."

At least for mass public consumption, Jim Bouton, Piniella's Seattle Pilots' teammate in 1969, was the first to call Piniella a "red ass" in his book *Ball Four*. But Piniella was quite familiar with the term by then.

He had been cursed by it in high school, when differences with his baseball coach resulted in a boycott of his senior season and offered as a reason big-league scouts stayed away, delaying his signing until the following year.

At the University of Tampa, baseball coach Sam Bailey adored Piniella but worried that his temper would keep him out of pro ball if he wasn't careful.

"He didn't blame other people or the bat or the field or the weather; he'd just get mad at himself," Bailey said, echoing the others. "I don't remember him ever having any trouble with the umpires. And he didn't argue with me. As soon as he blew up, I'd wait for him to cool down, I usually got him to the side and talked to him for a bit. I didn't holler and scream. But I did tell him that his worst enemy was Lou Piniella. He thought he ought to bat a thousand. But he realized he had to control his temper or he wouldn't get anywhere."

While Piniella may have tried, he didn't exactly shake it after that, regardless of injury to property or himself. Once, while playing Class D ball in Selma, Alabama, for the Cleveland Indians organization, Piniella threw his glove and it landed at the bottom of a giant water barrel that the team used for drinking water. While trying to retrieve it, he slipped, fell in headfirst, and nearly drowned before being pulled out.

Another time, playing Class A ball for the Washington Senators in the Carolina League, Piniella hit into a double play in a crucial spot and took his frustration out on the trainers' bag, inadvertently breaking a bottle of acid, which burned through the bottom of the bag. When the trainer picked up the bag and everything spilled out onto the dirt, he actually began to cry.

"I felt bad," wrote Piniella in his biography. "I wasn't very mature."

Then, sandwiched around a stint with the Baltimore organization playing for Earl Weaver, where Piniella observed and more than occasionally butted heads with the all-time legend of temper tantrums, there was the outfield fence incident.

Back with Cleveland in a Pacific Coast League game in 1967, Piniella struck out in a critical situation, threw his helmet and his bat as he often did, then sprinted to his spot in left field, where he kicked the eight-foot high outfield fence. Being portable, however, it collapsed under the force of his kick and he once again had to be rescued—this time by the ground crew from under a pile of planks.

The next day, the manager attached a punching bag to the corner of the dugout for Piniella to vent his frustrations in a little safer manner.

"It's my personality," said Margaret Piniella. "Lou's got a lot of patience but he wants to win. I never want to lose either. Even now, I find myself talking to myself when I see certain things that happen [in a ballgame]. That's the way it should be. Some players, if they don't hit, they don't hit. But he doesn't accept that. He used to practice by himself, shooting baskets for hours to do it right."

As a big-leaguer, the passion fired just as hotly and no light bulb was safe in the tunnel leading from whatever dugout Piniella occupied to the clubhouse. Nor were the water coolers he dented, one of which he decided to buy and mailed home to Tampa, where he kept it for years in his garage.

Yankees teammate Fred Stanley remembered the image of Piniella standing on the steps of the Yankee dugout, screaming at the opposing pitcher and taking particular relish in trading barbs with Earl Weaver when the Yankees played the Orioles.

"He'd yell at the pitcher, 'Throw me a fastball,' and call him gutless," Stanley laughed. "Hopefully the pitcher would get angry and throw him a fastball next time he was up just to show him he could, and then Lou would smoke it."

Orioles pitcher Steve Stone, later a broadcaster for the Cubs and White Sox, remembered a similar exchange when he faced Piniella.

"I remember throwing him, as I threw most everybody, three or four straight curveballs," Stone said. "And I remember in Baltimore, he actually swung so soon that he fouled the ball up over our dugout on the third-base side. He guessed curveball and it was so slow that he yanked it way over the dugout into the upper deck, and he screamed out at me to 'throw the fucking fastball.' That's one of my vivid recollections of Lou as a player."

And if he guessed wrong and made an out? "Half of our bench would jump up and scatter, and then you'd look over, and their bench had jumped up to see if Lou was throwing things in our dugout," said Stanley.

The thing was, they all recalled, Piniella always calmed down shortly after a blowup, and he was always remorseful.

"I never saw him go crazy for even five minutes," said Stanley. "It was a five-second deal. He'd punch something, throw his helmet. Once he threw something near my locker and it hit a plate of spaghetti. He thought it was his locker, and he got a chunk of spaghetti sauce on my sport coat. I'm just sitting there and he's going, 'Oh no, I'm sorry. I'll get it cleaned. I'll get it cleaned.' You could laugh with him and at him. You had to."

Once, Piniella flung his helmet in the dugout and grazed the head of manager Bob Lemon. "But that was a ricochet," said Stanley defending him. "It bounced off two things first. It was not an all-out assault."

Just the same, Lemon took to wearing a batting helmet in the dugout after that just in case. "But once Lou saw him sitting there with the helmet," said Stanley, "he felt so badly he would go to the runway to throw his helmet."

"Lou had a very simple set of rules," said Dave Phillips, a major-league umpire for 32 years until he retired in 2002. "If he didn't swing at the pitch, it wasn't a strike. And if you abided by those rules, you seemed to get along with Lou pretty well."

Phillips laughed. He made his major-league debut in 1970, his first game in his first season involving Piniella as a player on the Kansas City Royals.

"Lou was certainly an above-average hitter, a guy who used to come to the park with a great deal of intensity," Phillips said. "I can remember looking at him and he was unshaven, which was not in fashion then, and I'd say, 'Hi Lou, how're you doing?' and he'd look at you real gruff-like.

"But I sincerely really like Lou. As difficult as he was as a player and as volatile as he could be, as a manager I thought he was extremely fair."

That said, one of Phillips' favorite stories involved Piniella in his playing days and an incident Phillips described as "the only time I ever thought a player was going to hit me in an argument."

The Yankees were in Baltimore for a four-game series with the despised Orioles and Piniella's antagonist, Earl Weaver. The teams were playing on a rain-soaked weekend in mid-August in a series marked by horrible field conditions, long delays, and the usual shenanigans involving Weaver.

On one occasion, Phillips, working first base, called a balk on Baltimore pitcher Mike Flanagan with Piniella at the plate.

"Earl came out to argue and we got into it good," Phillips said. "I ran him, but it was a long argument, a real beauty, typical of Weaver and it took a while to restore order."

On the first pitch after the ejection, Piniella guessed wrong and hit a slow roller to second baseman Rich Dauer, who dropped the ball before firing to first to get the out.

"He got him by a good step but as soon as I called him out, Lou flew into an absolute rage," Phillips recalled. "He comes running at me like nobody's business and I'm thinking, 'If this sumbitch gets loose, I'm running to right field.'

"He's pissed off he hit a slow grounder after waiting forever for Earl to leave the field, and then he thinks the only reason I called him out was to make up for Earl. Gene Michael was the first-base coach and Bob Lemon was the manager, and both of them are trying to restrain Lou and he's pushing and jumping and of course, I ejected him and I'm yelling, 'Just get him on the ground,' and they literally corralled him and three or four guys just dragged him out of there."

After the game, the entire crew, said Phillips, was exhausted, sitting in their dressing room adjacent to the New York lockerroom when Jimmy, the Yankees' clubhouse attendant, came in with food and a story for the umps.

"Jimmy told us that after Lou was ejected, he was the only one in the clubhouse when Lou came in," Phillips recalled. "Jimmy had seen the replay and didn't want the whole clubhouse torn up because he knew Lou. But as he started to leave, Lou called out, 'Did you see the replay, Jimmy?'

"Jimmy acted like he didn't hear him because he didn't want to answer, but Lou yelled this time, 'Jimmy, did you see the replay?' Well, Jimmy is stuttering and trying to get out of there and he says, 'Yeah Lou, I seen it.'

"Lou says, 'I was out, wasn't I?'

"And Jimmy says, 'Yeah Lou, you were out.'

"And Lou says, 'Yeah, I thought so.'"

That endearing side of Piniella was just as memorable to some.

Like most AL umpires, Terry Cooney, an 18-year veteran who retired in 1993, often saw the fiercely competitive Piniella. But when Cooney thinks back to the former Yankee's playing career, one memory of a particularly tranquil Piniella stands out.

"Lou came in as a pinch-hitter, they needed a baserunner, and when he walked up to home plate, he was swinging his bat and singing 'Chicago, Chicago, that toddlin' town,'" Cooney recounted. "And he kept on singing as the pitcher wound up. Then he immediately slapped it out to right field for a base hit, and as he left home, he was still singing.

"I looked at the catcher and I said, 'I thought when you're hitting, you had to have complete concentration on what the pitcher is doing but I guess that just disproved that theory.' He just laughed and he said, 'That guy is a heck of a hitter.'"

There were times Piniella could manage his rage, one of the most noteworthy instances occurring in the midst of a no-hitter by Yankees pitcher Dave Righetti, who remembered it as vividly as his own performance 25 years later.

A questionable call had gone against Piniella in the eighth inning, when he popped up in foul territory behind the screen. Red Sox catcher Jeff Newman dived into the first row of seats and came up waving his glove. But just as Piniella was about to erupt, he stopped himself and turned to go back to the dugout, aware that a prolonged argument might distract Righetti or at least disrupt his rhythm.

On his way, Piniella did, however, pause just long enough to say a few words to home-plate umpire Steve Palermo, who happened to be on the ground at the time, writhing in pain after falling down on the play and sustaining a knee injury that would require major surgery.

As the Yankees' training staff attended to Palermo, Piniella elbowed his way through the crowd and politely informed the ump, "When you get up and we're ready to play again, Newman didn't catch that ball."

Sitting in the visitor's dugout in Wrigley Field, Righetti, now the pitching coach for the San Francisco Giants, remembered it well. "The Yankee Stadium field went downhill and next thing you know, Palermo is gone, he just disappeared," Righetti said. "We're all jumping up in the dugout to see where he was, if he was hurt, and Graig Nettles goes, 'So, who's going to tell Lou he's out?'"

Piniella laughed when reminded, proud of his role in Righetti's day.

"I didn't argue; I remember that," he said.

Instead, said Palermo, "he just went into the tunnel and smashed a few bats against the wall."

But Righetti, like Piniella's friends, are protective of Piniella's image and unhappy with the perception of him as some sort of an out-of-control, crazy man.

"They show tirades of minor-league managers on ESPN," said Righetti, "and I just don't like it when he's involved in that and made to look that way. I'm sure there were times when he went out there early in his career [to argue with an umpire] going, 'What the hell am I doing out here? But as long as I'm out here, the fans will eat it up.' It got to that point with Billy [Martin], where it was okay. But I was always worried people were going to think that way about Lou because he's too good of a manager."

When he was named manager of the Tampa Bay Devil Rays, Piniella told reporters that he knew his volatile on-field behavior could be considered a fan attraction.

"I learned a long time ago from George Steinbrenner that I'm here to entertain," he said. "It's a business. So I kick my hat around a little bit."

Most of the umpires understood.

"I think it was a part of the game the fans liked," Phillips said. "I didn't go to acting school, but we could yell at each other and bob our heads and shake our shoulders and some of that is pageantry and Lou did it really well."

Former Cubs manager Lee Elia was almost wistful when talking about how times have changed between managers and umpires.

"It's a shame because baseball is entertainment, no matter how you cut the pie," Elia said. "It used to be where you could let it go with an ump and he'd let it go back and he didn't throw you out. He might take a little jeering from the fans, but the players respected it. Today, for whatever reason, a little piece has been lost.

"There was nothing more beautiful than Billy and Lou and Earl going at it with the umps. Doggone it, those were some great times."

In a 2006 interview with Frank Deford for HBO's *Real Sports with Bryant Gumbel*, Piniella acknowledged that in addition to entertainment, managerial meltdowns are necessary for their motivational effect.

"Sometimes a manager, you know, he needs to wake up his club a little bit," he said. "I've gone out to home plate, you can ask these umpires, many times, saying, 'Look, one of you guys is going to have to throw me out tonight. Now, who wants the honor?'

"Invariably, one of them will. And I remember this one game, the second-base umpire was supposed to kick me out. And I kept sending runners over there, and he kept calling them safe. And I'd say, 'For God's sake, call somebody out so I can go out and argue with you.'"

But Piniella had also known well before he got to Tampa that that sort of behavior was looked down upon by his wife and children, something his son Derek informed him in no uncertain terms when, at the age of nine, he told is father after one particular on-field tirade, "Gee, Dad, you're embarrassing the whole family."

On his wife Anita's 43rd birthday, family and friends gathered at the Piniella home to watch one of Lou's games when Piniella got into a wild argument with the umpires in which he kicked dirt, threw his cap, and otherwise created a spectacle.

When he returned to the hotel that night, he remembered it was his wife's birthday and called home.

"I'm 43 years old," she told her husband, "and I'm married to a four-year-old."

There have been times his friends could do little more than laugh. On the golf course one day, Piniella got so angry that he threw each club into the water and then finally, his entire bag, and then walked off the course. The story went that several minutes later, he walked sheepishly back through the clubhouse and when asked where he was going, he muttered, "My car keys were in my bag."

As a player, his tirades were most often directed at himself.

"It was always toward his performance," said Stanley. "He was never really satisfied. That's probably why he was such a good player. He had a tremendous drive."

That's why as a manager, not only has Piniella understood Cubs pitcher Carlos Zambrano, who has developed a reputation for his emotional displays on the mound and in the dugout, but he also has little patience for players he thinks lack passion.

Case in point was Ben Grieve, the Devil Rays' designated hitter who once looked at a called third strike to end a one-run loss, stranding a runner on third. When Grieve returned to the dugout,

Piniella, then Tampa Bay's manager, asked him why he didn't swing, and Grieve said the pitch was a ball.

Piniella was furious, asking Grieve why then, didn't he argue? When the player said it was because it didn't matter at that point, Piniella erupted, one eyewitness saying, "Yeah, it was bad, hard to watch."

On the flip side, Reds pitcher Tom Browning remembers being pulled early in a game and taking a bat to the dugout wall in frustration.

"I was pitching in Atlanta and we had like a 6–0 lead and they tied it up and Lou chewed my ass out," Browning said. "I took a bat out when I got back to the dugout and was beating it against the wall, swearing, when I saw Lou looking at me. I fully expected him to yell at me some more for acting like an idiot."

Instead, said Browning, Piniella just nodded.

"Yeah, I'd be pissed too," Piniella said, "if I'd just thrown that horseshit up there."

Tim Belcher, who played for Piniella in Cincinnati and Seattle, had a similar experience pitching for the Mariners during the 1995 season. "He asked me to walk someone early in a game at Yankee Stadium," Belcher recalled. "I was struggling, pissed off, he had to come get me in the [fourth] inning, and I was upset about getting the quick hook. I remember coming in and in a fit of rage, I took a bat and broke the phone in the dugout. I turned to Lou and said, 'There, now call the bullpen.'

"He started laughing and said, 'That Belcher, isn't he great?'"

Belcher felt that as a veteran, he got a "longer leash, so to speak."

"But young or old, Lou was pretty perceptive as far as identifying weakness from a player in terms of mental toughness and if he sees that, he's not going to treat you with kid gloves, he's probably going to go in the other direction," Belcher said.

Piniella's most famous outburst toward one of his players had nothing to do with a lack of passion on the player's part but in Piniella's opinion at the time, a lack of integrity.

The manager of the Cincinnati Reds at the time, Piniella's team had just defeated Atlanta 3–2 on September 17, 1992, a game in which Reds rookie Steve Foster was the closer. Piniella told reporters afterward that the team's star closer Rob Dibble had not been available.

"He couldn't get [his shoulders] loose warming up last night," said Piniella.

When Dibble was asked the same question and told what Piniella had said, Dibble responded, "There's nothing wrong with my shoulder. He's full of shit. He's not telling you the whole story. Go in there and ask him and then come back to me."

When Piniella heard about Dibble's remarks, he shouted, "The shoulder is *not* all right. That's not what he told me, and that's not what he told the pitching coach. If he was all right, he would have been in the game."

Piniella was still steamed minutes later in the hallway outside the clubhouse when he overheard Dibble snap at a reporter, "You guys are a joke."

At that point, Piniella charged past reporters and got Dibble in a bear hug, wrestling him into the locker next to his as reporters were hustled out of the clubhouse.

"After wrestling for a few seconds, I had two thoughts," Dibble recalled in a 2008 interview. "One, 'He's a lot older than me and I might hurt him and two, that's my boss and I respect people like that. The deacons in my church always taught us to respect our elders, and this was one of those moments where I knew this is one of the worst things that can happen."

Pitcher Tim Belcher helped break it up, getting his watch broken in the process.

"I'm sure Lou would like to have that instant back but Dibble brought it on," Belcher said. "My recollection was that Dibs went in [before the game] and Lou said, 'How are you feeling?' and Dibs said 'Okay, but if I could get a day, it would help.' And Lou said he'd see what he could do.

"If I remember correctly, Dibs was upstairs in shorts, so he knew by the seventh or eighth inning that Lou was going to stay away from him. Then after Steve got the save, everyone was congratulating him and giving him high fives and Dibs' ego was having a hard time seeing someone else get all the glory.

"When reporters said, 'Where were you in the ninth?' Dibs was like, 'I don't know, I could've pitched.' Lou said he had pitched his ass off and we wanted to give him a break. When they went back to Rob and told him, 'Lou said you wanted the day off,' Rob blew up. Then they went back to Lou, and in his mind, he was trying to protect Dibs and he was thrown under the bus."

When reporters returned a few minutes after the scuffle, Piniella was standing in the doorway of his office with his shirt off but still fuming.

"It's all over with," he said. "You guys saw it, write it."

The next day, Piniella and Dibble met with owner Marge Schott and general manager Bob Quinn for a half-hour, and afterward, it was announced that there would be no punishments for Dibble or Piniella.

"Believe me, I spent many days in the principal's office, and that was just like that," said Dibble. "It was the funniest thing getting scolded by Marge Schott."

Dibble, who had been suspended by the National League three times over the preceding two years for throwing at batters, throwing at a baserunner, and throwing into the stands, apologized to Piniella.

"It was wrong on my part," Dibble told reporters, referring to the obscenity. "I'm apologizing for that and I apologized to Lou... It's really a dispute between family members. Lou and I remain good friends. Something like this will not stand in our way on a professional level or a personal level. I used to fight with my brothers. The press just happened to be there."

Piniella's response: "I sort of lost my cool," he said. "When my integrity gets questioned, it's not that easy of a situation to deal with. Like I explained to Rob, it's my obligation when I get asked questions from the media about a player. I have integrity. I can't lie. Sometimes I can disguise it. But in this case, he couldn't get loose and wasn't available. That's it."

The next night, Dibble pitched and got the save and remembered clearly what happened on the last out.

"It was the end of the season, we were out of it but in front of 30,000 people, Lou runs out, throws a few fake punches at me and gives me a big hug," said Dibble.

"The crowd went crazy," said Belcher, "and at that point, it was over with."

Seventeen years later, the two remain bonded by the incident. Play word association using the word "Dibble" and "Piniella" will surely follow. But Dibble said the two "were always best friends and always will be. He was like a second father, like another teammate. Seventeen years ago, Lou and I had two seconds of WWE. To me, it was a second in our lives, but it's something we laugh about."

Ironically, said Dibble, he probably related to Piniella most when he lost his temper. "People get the wrong impression when anger boils over," Dibble said. "When you're in the game and you're a perfectionist, a base hit or a walk can set you off. One of my best friends and a role model off the field was [Reds teammate] Paul O'Neill and that [anger] was what made him a five-time world champion and a great player.

"He never swore, he was one of the best family men I've ever met, we'd be excited if we could ever get him to drink a beer. And there was no bigger competitor. Lou was the same way. A lot of us were cut from the same cloth. In baseball, you're judged day to day, out to out. One failure, one strikeout is very upsetting, and knowing Lou, I understood the mentality."

Dibble said he also felt close to Anita Piniella, considering her a "second mom."

"I had a lot of conversations with her, and she would explain to me, 'Lou takes every loss home with him. It hurts him personally.' Once you know that as a player, you think, 'Gee, he cares more than I realized he did.'"

Still, his image preceded him. And with each Piniella implosion dominating ESPN's SportsCenter highlights, the fire continued to burn as he moved on to Seattle, where base-throwing contests were soon staged in his honor.

* * *

As the Mariners skipper, Piniella scooped dirt onto home plate, pulled bases out of their moorings and hurled them, one time prompting the Mariners' Ken Griffey Jr. to suggest, "Maybe we should have a manager shot put contest."

Once, when the Mariners were playing a series with the Yankees, TV analyst and former big leaguer Tim McCarver remembered a pregame conversation between Piniella and former teammate Bobby Murcer.

"Bobby said, 'I notice you're not getting upset anymore,'" McCarver recalled, "and Lou said, 'All that stuff is overrated. Sometimes I'll do it just to rev up the players but I never bait the umpires.' That day he gets run in the seventh, and he looks up at Murcer in the booth and just shrugs his shoulders. It was hilarious."

Even in his fury, Piniella was almost always funny.

Once, with Seattle in 1998, Piniella kicked his hat a half-dozen times before finally flinging it into the stands during a game at Jacobs Field in Cleveland, where it was then thrown back at him. Umpire Larry Barnett said he ejected Piniella for pointing to the ground and showing him up after a disputed call at second base.

"Am I supposed to point to the sky?" Piniella said incredulously afterward. "Is my guy running in the sky? Is my runner Luke Skywalker or what? Look, all the frustrations of a long year came pouring out. I don't blame anyone for laughing. Everyone likes to see someone make a fool of themselves in front of 40,000 people."

The next season, in which he had a career-high five ejections, Piniella tried to pull third base out of the ground to toss it but couldn't, so he threw a bunch of bats on the field instead. "My back has been bothering me, so I didn't try too hard," he explained afterward.

Barnett, an American League umpire from 1969 to 1999 before becoming the Major League's supervisor of umpires in 2000–01, remembered the Cleveland incident well and appreciated his good humor.

"He threw his hat," said Barnett. "Then he tried to kick his hat and he kept missing, so I said, 'I can assume you weren't a place-kicker in high school.' He was mad walking off.

"But the next day there was a picture of him kicking the hat in the *Cleveland Plain Dealer*, and I sent it over to him and he signed it. I still have it. He's a good man and a good manager, and just watching him over the years, I think he's mellowed out a lot.

"The thing with Lou, I had him both as a player and as a manager, and you could get into some tremendously big arguments with him but he was a man about it. When it was over, it was over, and the next day was the next day. I think umpires respected that about Lou more than anything."

The umpires all made a point to say that Piniella was not to be compared to Earl Weaver on the list of confrontational managers. Although Piniella would get angry and argumentative, Weaver was more often abusive and disruptive. While Piniella was good-natured off the field, they said, Weaver was rarely charming.

Cooney said that on the field, "[Piniella] was quite a bit like Billy Martin in his attitude and fierceness. He'd do anything to win. But off the field, Piniella was a super nice guy."

Ted Hendry, a major-league umpire from 1978–1999, once ejected Piniella in a spring-training game when Piniella was managing the Mariners.

The season before, umpire John Hirschbeck had been spit at by Roberto Alomar, a game in which Hendry had been on the crew, and the word the next season was that the umps were going to be tougher than ever in clamping down on abusive behavior.

The next spring, in the eighth inning of an exhibition game between Seattle and Milwaukee on March 4, Hendry recalled that he said something to Mariners shortstop Andy Sheets and when Piniella had yelled out to Hendry, "I don't want you talking to my shortstop," Hendry ejected him.

Piniella said afterward that he said to Hendry, "Leave him alone. Let him concentrate," and Brewers manager Phil Garner concurred.

"There was no cursing, no nothing," Garner said. "It had nothing to do with an argument or with a play. We couldn't believe it. He didn't do anything."

There were repercussions for Hendry and unflattering reports in the media.

"I had to go see our boss, and the press made a big thing about it, that umps are going to run guys who aren't even arguing," Hendry said. "I ended up having a good talk with Lou and he went to the press and said, 'This had nothing to do with any feud' and stood up for me. He's a good baseball guy.

"I had some good run-ins with him, but one thing I like about Lou compared to a lot of other managers is that Lou would never hurt an umpire. Basically he's a guy that lets you work. He might not think you're a great umpire, but I don't think he would ever try to disrespect you. Deep down, he knows everyone is out there working hard. I wouldn't say that about a lot of other guys."

But if Piniella was mellowing, it was not yet evident, despite the fact that his family, coaches, players, and even umps wished it to be.

In May 2002, his last season with the Mariners, Piniella was tossed from a game in Tampa by umpire John Shulock for arguing the strike zone. Before family and friends, Piniella responded with a dramatic display that included covering home plate with dirt.

"My wife didn't think too much of my actions," he said later. "I knew she wouldn't."

Ichiro Suzuki, Piniella's All-Star center fielder, added, "I had never seen Lou get that angry before. But that was the image I had of him before I came over here, from the TV."

Later that season, Piniella picked up first base and threw it twice after an argument over a close call at first by umpire C.B. Bucknor. What really got Piniella mad was not the call, he said, but the smirk on Bucknor's face when he came out to argue. "I don't know about any eruption," said Piniella, "but I hurt my hamstring and my right shoulder."

In the midst of the outburst, veteran crew chief John Hirshbeck warned Piniella that he shouldn't get so "worked up."

"I'm a little old for that and John said that to me, and I understand," Piniella said. "I appreciate that."

Shortly after accepting the Cubs' job, Piniella again expressed regret at some of his actions.

"I don't like [the film clips of past outbursts] but they're part of me," he said. "I wish I could erase some of that junk out of my life. I don't like it. And I didn't win 1,500 games because I throw bases or because I have an argument with an umpire.

"But of all the organizations I've worked for, I could go back to any of them, and that should say something."

Derek Piniella said he resented the way in which his father was often portrayed.

"He has relaxed," he said in a 2006 interview. "What they put on ESPN [the clips of] him picking up bases, kicking dirt, it bothers you because that's not the way he is at home, and they portray him as this barbarian. He's an intense person but also very kind, very gentle, very intelligent. He just loses his cool every once in a while."

Derek Piniella recalled going to almost every home game when his father was managing in Tampa.

"If he did lose his cool, I'd be with him afterward, in his office after the game and it might take him a couple hours to cool down, but he'd talk about it, about a particular play and whether he was right or wrong," he said. "I wouldn't say he necessarily had regrets about his actions. He's a real smart guy, he knows how to motivate his team, and he picks and chooses his battles appropriately."

Did his father ever come home angry after games, he was asked.

"He wouldn't come home and take it out on family, but you can definitely tell the difference in his moods between winning and losing," Derek said. "He wouldn't be in a bad mood where he would take it out on us, but you could tell something was on his mind.

"I've seen him many a time over athletics and family things, little things like my niece winning a horse show, where he can get emotional. He definitely has a sensitive side. When his father passed away and when he got up to thank everyone for their support at his funeral, he really lost his composure. He has a big heart and is very sensitive. Those are two of the biggest things to know about him."

Mondy Flores and Carmine Iavarone, two more of Piniella's childhood buddies, trade off telling the story of the night in Cincinnati, when they had a valet hide Piniella's car at a restaurant after a game. "We thought we'd get a real rise out of him, but it didn't bother him at all. It was like he lost his cell phone," said Flores.

"Yeah," said Iavarone. "And that's a guy with a temper?"

After his first ejection of 2008, during a White Sox sweep of the Cubs at U.S. Cellular Field in June, Piniella complained that he was "ambushed" by the home-plate umpire on his way back to the dugout after arguing a checked swing call with the first-base umpire.

"You can't argue anymore," he said. "Anyway, I got a little frustration out. It's over with. They're still my buddies."

It was a far cry from his previous and only serious outburst as the Cubs manager.

On June 2, 2007, Piniella was ejected after a full-blown outburst that concluded when he covered third-base umpire Mark Wegner's shoes with dirt and had to be restrained by home-plate ump Bruce Froemming. Froemming also claimed Piniella made contact with Wegner with his foot.

That morning, Piniella had met with his pitcher Carlos Zambrano and his catcher Michael Barrett, a day after the two had come to blows in the Cubs' dugout. The team was about to lose its sixth straight game, its 10th of the last 12, it was eight games below .500 and seven and a half games out of first place in the National League Central.

"The umpire was correct; the guy was out," Piniella said after the ejection. "I was going to argue whether he was out, safe, or whatever. It didn't make a damn bit of difference."

So the move was orchestrated?

"Let's not talk about me," Piniella said. "You were all asking me [the day before] why I hadn't been kicked out of a game. Now you see that I got kicked out of one."

But this one, the 60th ejection of his career and one resulting in a four-game suspension, didn't sit well with Piniella. And kicking umpires or even kicking dirt on them was clearly not going to be laughed off as easily as it might have been in years previous. Now, on top of an umpire being sincerely pissed off, he heard words like "disrespected and demeaned." And when a crowd rained debris on the field, the manager "incited" them with his actions.

"He made physical contact with the third-base umpire," Froemming, one of the few umpires with whom Piniella did not get along, told a pool reporter from the *Chicago Tribune* that day. "He made physical contact with his foot, and he kicked dirt on [Wegner] several times, and the rest was show-and-tell.

"The whole world saw what he did. It was a terrible display of disrespect."

Piniella said he never made contact with Wegner.

"No, no, no," he said. "We kicked some dirt."

Froemming had put a hand on Piniella during the incident.

"We were trying to get him away to save him some problems," the umpire explained. "And he just wouldn't stop. It was just an absolute display of disrespect to the game and to the official."

A year later, Piniella's bench coach with the Cubs, Alan Trammell, was adamant that the move was "not premeditated.

I know that for a fact," Trammell said, "but sometimes he was frustrated because we weren't playing very well.

"But after that, he was embarrassed. He was. Wegner said he felt it was degrading and Lou said, 'You know what, I've done that a half dozen times in my career and nobody ever said that to me. I never realized it.' And he told me, 'I'll never do that again.'"

Piniella wrote a letter of apology to Wegner and for the rest of the 2007 and throughout the 2008 season, there were no more dirt-kicking, cap throwing, or otherwise theatrical displays by a man who turned 65 on August 28.

That same season, when the Cubs were playing in Cincinnati, the Reds wanted to tie a promotion into the night that Piniella famously threw first base into right field while manager of the Reds. Piniella politely said no.

"He's too old now to be kicking dirt," White Sox manager Ozzie Guillen said. "He's got to be tired. He might pull a hammy doing that, have a heart attack on the field. But people expect that from him. I guarantee you, people go to the ballpark and they can't wait to see a Lou argument. I can't wait. Every time we play against him, I'm like [to the umps], 'Come on, make one mistake, I want to see Lou come out.' Just to enjoy it and enjoy his passion for the game. Some people don't understand that, the passion for the game. That's the reason he manages for so many years. We need people like Lou in the game. He brings what he has. He's not a fake."

In October 2007, Aquafina Water came out with a commercial that spoofed the dirt-kicking episode. In it, Piniella came racing out of the dugout to confront the umpire on the third-base line:

Piniella (yelling): What a great call. You're doing a fantastic job, but people are expecting me to come out here and be upset so I'm going to kick some dirt, you understand?
Umpire (yelling back): Yeah, I understand that.
Piniella: Well, lately I've been feeling happy and content.
Voiceover of broadcaster: Lou is really giving it to him.

Piniella: You better kick me out of this game. I've got a reputation to uphold.

Ump: Fine, I can do that. (Screaming) You're out of here.

Lou (as he turns to storm back to the dugout): Fantastic. Say hello to the missus.

Ump: I will. You do the same.

Lou: All right.

Announcer: And there goes third base.

It was funny. And it captured Piniella's sense of humor, his relationship with the umpires, and the fact that underneath it all, no one could ever stay mad at him.

His childhood friends know this better than anyone.

"One time I said, 'Lou, why did you kick your hat?'" said his buddy Tony Gonzalez, "and he said, 'Because it asked for it.' Once he settles down and considers his actions, he meant it at the time but he doesn't mean it in a disrespectful way. He's a wonderful man. He's got a very sensitive side."

"Sometimes," said Mondy Flores, "I'd say to him [after a particular outburst he'd view on the highlights], 'What was with that last night, Lou? You have kids and a wife.' And he'd say, 'I know, wasn't it ridiculous?' But it wasn't at the time."

Paul Ferlita hopes Piniella never changes.

"It's just him, just a part of him," Ferlita said. "It's just his nature. He might look back and wish he hadn't done something, but he's not that embarrassed because it's who he is. If he had a season without an outburst, I'd think his intensity was gone. If he quits that sort of thing, I think that'll mean the fire has gone out."

CHAPTER
4

Big Apple

E arl Weaver. Alvin Dark. Charlie Metro. Jack McKeon. It was Lou Piniella's list of his least-favorite managers, McKeon was the latest member of the club.

"You're late, and you look out of shape."

Those were McKeon's first words to the Royals' former Rookie of the Year in the spring of 1973, the year McKeon took over for Bob Lemon as Kansas City's manager, as Piniella recalled.

"I'll be ready when the bell rings," he replied.

"You'd better be, or you won't be playing," said McKeon.

Piniella hadn't particularly liked McKeon before he got the job, when he felt McKeon had undermined Lemon with team executives the previous season while still the organization's Triple A manager.

And now, after Piniella had just missed winning the batting title by six points to Rod Carew the previous season, he did not appreciate the fact that his job was already being threatened by this guy.

Piniella had reported two weeks late, furious that after wrangling a $53,000 contract from Royals owner Ewing Kauffman he had to read about Amos Otis and his $100,000 contract and Freddie Patek's $70,000. Several pitchers had also signed contracts considerably higher than Piniella's.

Piniella considered the past few years.

In 1971, after a second big year—a .301 average with 11 home runs and 88 RBIs following a rookie season in which he hit .282 with 11 home runs and 68 RBIs—he had been offered only a $5,000 raise from the year before to $30,000.

But what really incensed Piniella was reading about Otis, a sensitive young outfielder the team had obtained from the New York Mets who signed a reported $50,000 contract after hitting .284, 11 homers, and 58 RBIs.

Piniella ended up signing for $33,000 but he was bitter about it, and what followed was a bad spring training and a worse season, marred by a broken thumb and ending with a respectable but below-par .279 with three home runs and 51 RBIs.

That winter, Piniella worked with batting coach Charley Lau in Venezuela and, exhibiting the transfer-of-weight hitting method that Lau preached, came back in the 1972 season with a vengeance. He hit .312 with a league-leading 33 doubles, 11 homers, and 72 RBIs and was named to his first All-Star team, the fourth-highest vote-getter in the American League.

Now Piniella looked toward 1973 optimistically. The previous year he had received a $3,000 raise to $36,000. That was understandable after the injury year, Piniella figured. But now, after his All-Star season and the fact that he had become one of the most popular players in Kansas City with the newly christened nickname "Sweet Lou," he felt he deserved far more than the $40,000 the Royals were offering initially.

Otis had signed for $100,000 pre–free agency, and Piniella was so steamed, he sat down and wrote a letter to management, telling them maybe it was time to just sell his contract to another club. Cedric Tallis, the club's GM, came back with a small increase to $42,000 and said they could go no higher. He would have to take it up with the owner himself.

More than a little nervous as he prepared to meet Kauffman at his home without an agent, Piniella recalled in his 1986 book that he decided he would ask for $70,000 and accept no less than $60,000.

The two had drinks and played liar's poker with Piniella winning $500. And when he went home at 1:00 AM, it was with a signed contract for $52,500. Well, $53,000 including the 500 bucks he won in poker. Kauffman also promised him $5,000 to build a pool or an addition to his home in Kansas City, where Lou and Anita had decided they wanted to settle.

That was okay until Piniella started thinking about it and reading more about Otis. Still angry, Piniella reported two weeks late, and now he had to deal with this McKeon character.

At 29 and a five-year veteran, Piniella was not ready for the leadership role McKeon demanded of him. Admittedly overweight and out of shape, Piniella was still miffed about his contract, hated McKeon's style, and struggled at the plate, finishing the season with a career-low .250 batting average along with nine home runs and 69 RBIs.

In the last few weeks of the 1973 season, Piniella was replaced in left field by McKeon favorite Jim Wohlford, whom McKeon had just brought up from Triple A Omaha.

It was the last season Piniella spent in Kansas City.

In late September, the Royals played a three-game set against the White Sox. The Sox were starting three lefthanders, so common sense dictated Piniella would play. But McKeon liked Wohlford, also a righthander whom he had managed in Omaha, and Wohlford played in all three games while Piniella saw no action.

Next up for the Royals was Texas with, as Piniella described, "Jim Bibby, a big, mean, hard-throwing righthander who wasn't afraid to pitch inside and didn't concern himself too much if one of those fastballs wound up in your ribs."

Piniella assumed Wohlford would be in again, and when he saw his own name penciled into the lineup instead, was both perplexed and annoyed. Confronting McKeon, he asked the manager why, if he hadn't played at all against the Sox and their righthanders, he was going against Bibby.

"Amos is scared to hit against him, he throws too hard for him and he tried to hit him," McKeon told him.

"You got this $100,000 outfielder and he's scared to play against this guy and you are going to do me the favor of letting me face him and letting me get hit?" Piniella said. "Is that it?"

"Damn it," said McKeon. "I'm the manager and I make out the lineup card, and you're playing."

And that was that. Except that Piniella refused to play. He told McKeon to get himself another left fielder and stormed out. He stayed in the clubhouse during batting practice, went to the dugout when the game began, and when the Kansas City players jogged onto the field, eight Royals took their positions looking like the missing man formation.

Piniella counted the minutes until the season was over, and when it was, he called Kauffman. Part of the conversation was to see where he stood, the other, to remind him of the $5,000 bonus for his house that he had not yet received. If the Royals didn't plan on keeping him, which Piniella thought was a distinct possibility with McKeon so enamored of Jim Wohlford, then he'd at least like to know so that he and Anita didn't build a pool or put a new addition on the house.

But as Piniella described it, Kauffman assured him that he was well-liked and part of the Royals future, and the Piniellas added on a den that winter, settling in for a long stay in Kansas City.

The good will would last until December 7. Piniella likened the phone call he received that day to a bomb falling on him, though perhaps not quite of the same proportion as Pearl Harbor.

It was Cedric Tallis. The Royals had traded Piniella and right-handed pitcher Ken Wright for reliever Lindy McDaniel.

"You're a New York Yankee," Tallis said.

After five years, Piniella was through in Kansas City and he wasn't sure how he felt about it. His family was settled. He and

Anita had friends there. He had a restaurant and a business partner to think about. There was the Honda dealership—and, oh yes, a house with a brand-new addition.

Then he started thinking about New York. There was new ownership under a guy named Steinbrenner. Bill Virdon had been hired to replace Ralph Houk as manager. Piniella didn't know him either. But there was that tradition. Ruth, Gehrig, DiMaggio, Mantle. Surely the Yankees would rebuild.

The more he thought about it, the more excited he became.

It was the New York Yankees, after all. And he was now one of them.

* * *

New York was everything Piniella thought it would be at first. Or at least Yankees spring training camp in Fort Lauderdale.

It was February 1974. Thurman Munson welcomed him to the club. Bobby Murcer kidded him. Bill Virdon seemed like a nice guy and asked only that they hustle. Piniella liked the team and the future. He told Anita he could see them winning a World Series before too long.

In his 1986 autobiography, Piniella described his first impressions of the man they would call "The Boss." Steinbrenner had spotted Bobby Murcer and shortstop Gene "Stick" Michael, a future coach, manager and GM for the Yankees, leaning casually against their bats at the batting cage without their caps on.

"Damn it," Steinbrenner yelled. "Put those caps on. Look like Yankees. And you, Michael. Get a haircut."

"Who in hell is this guy?" Piniella asked Munson of the husky man wearing the long-sleeved white dress shirt in the Florida heat.

"That," replied Munson, "is the new principal owner of the Yankees, George M. Steinbrenner III."

Steinbrenner had actually taken over the team the year before, but everyone was still getting used to him. One chief executive, Michael Burke, and one manager, Houk, had already quit. Piniella was concerned with his own situation, and he was okay with the $5,000 raise he had negotiated to play for $57,500 in his first season with the Yankees.

Piniella liked his new manager, who also believed in discipline like his new owner but preferred it be displayed on the field with solid defense and by being in better shape than the other team. Piniella credited Virdon, a former center fielder with the Pirates, with making him a better outfielder through endless fungoes and conditioning.

"Just off the top of my hat, not knowing him, I thought [Piniella] was a hard-noser," said Virdon some 34 years later, a special spring training instructor for the Pirates still best known for being the player whose ground ball took a bad hop and struck Tony Kubek in the throat in the 1960 World Series.

"I thought he needed work in the outfield," Virdon said of Piniella. "I thought he was a long way from being a good outfielder. I ran him along that route, and he became a very, very decent outfielder from his hard work. His talent was there. But I don't know if he had ever reached down and got it out of himself. Probably no one ever asked him to do it before."

Virdon believed that's where championships were won.

"We had a good crop that year," he recalled. "But I always said if you do not have a very decent outfield, you will not win. It doesn't mean you won't win some games, but you won't win the pennant unless you have a decent outfield. Not saying Mays and Clemente, but three decent outfielders out there."

Michael, in his last active season as a player, remembered being especially impressed at the way Piniella approached hitting.

"I remember he was dedicated to it, so into it, that he would share it with other people, sometimes even volunteer it, and I could tell then he would make a good hitting instructor," Michael said.

"He was a full-bown thinker at the plate, and before games, he'd visualize what the pitcher would do and he'd always be getting into his stance, usually without a bat. He'd make his little weight shift with his feet and hips, and you could tell he was so much more adept than other players."

It was a tough year for the Yankees, though they were in first place as late as September 24. Piniella called it "the year in exile" because that was the first of two seasons the Yankees had to share Shea Stadium with the Mets due to construction to Yankee Stadium.

It was a year of upheaval on many fronts.

Virdon moved Elliott Maddox from right to center and moved Bobby Murcer from center to right early in the season, putting Murcer in a funk that he was never really able to shake. Piniella would develop a strong friendship with Murcer and sympathized with a player who had been with the Yankees for so long and felt so emotional about the pinstripes and his association with all the great Yankee center fielders before him.

It got worse for Murcer. At the end of September on a road trip in Milwaukee, he broke a finger trying to break up a fight between catchers Rick Dempsey and Bill Sudakis. Because Murcer couldn't play, Piniella was moved to right field for the key series.

In the first game of the two-game set, the Yankees were ahead 2–0 in the eighth when Piniella misjudged a fly ball caught in the wind that went for a triple, allowing the Brewers to tie the game, which they eventually won in the tenth. The loss for the Yankees eliminated them from the race and gave the division title to Baltimore.

Piniella, who hit .305 that season with 70 RBIs, was convinced that his old nemesis Earl Weaver had jinxed him. Why? Because Earl had told him a week earlier at Shea that he was going to jinx him, and after the game in Milwaukee, Weaver sent him a telegram to rub it in further.

"Thanks," it read. "I knew you'd screw up someday."

Among the many reasons Piniella was popular with his teammates was his ability to take a joke as well as dish it out and a boyish manner that never ceased to crack them up. They made fun of his high-pitched voice, his temper, his odd habit of twirling his hair around his fingers and then smelling them—Hunter in particular teased him mercilessly about it.

They also found his forgetfulness amusing, as Piniella would often have to go shopping on road trips because he wouldn't bring enough clothes with him.

"We'd come off the road and Lou would just leave his suitcase in front of his locker," recalled Fred Stanley, who derived endless amusement in simply dressing next to Piniella during their years in New York. "The clubhouse guys would take his stuff out, clean it and put it back in and he'd take that thing back on the road. He was the only one to ever do that. It was just way less complicated for him, but you'd have to laugh because there would always be that suitcase with all of his clothes still at the ballpark."

Gene Michael recalled a similar scene.

"We'd be on the bus at the ballpark, waiting to leave to go on a road trip, and I remember Lou pulling up, pulling a suitcase from his car and repacking it right there on the pavement in the parking lot," Michael said, laughing. "I saw him open it up and lay it on the concrete and put in the dry cleaning he had picked up on the way.

"Sometimes the most intelligent people are not real organized."

But if he was scattered at times, Piniella was also remembered and admired in those days for an affable manner and willingness to help out a teammate, like the time he helped negotiate a new contract for pre-Nettles third baseman Celerino Sanchez.

The Yankees had signed Sanchez as a stopgap out of the Mexican League. When it came time to sign him to a new contract, it was Piniella who accompanied him into then-GM Gabe Paul's trailer, translated for Sanchez, and helped him through the negotiation.

When it came to negotiating his own contracts, it was seldom fun for Piniella but almost always interesting—his 1976 deal a prime example. The season before had not been a good one for him as inner-ear problems severely hampered him, and despite the fact that Paul had told Piniella that he would rather trade a player than cut his salary, he cut Piniella's salary by 20 percent for the 1976 season.

Soon after, on Opening Day, the *Daily News* printed a photo of players in the Yankees clubhouse, and in the background, stood an unclothed Lou Piniella. Catfish Hunter's attorney encouraged Piniella to sue the newspaper, and Piniella intended to do just that, thinking if nothing else, it would be a way to recoup his lost salary.

When Steinbrenner learned of the suit, he summoned Piniella to his office, where the Yankees owner told him that suing a newspaper was not a good idea, that it could provoke all the other papers into attacking the ballclub, and that above all else, it was just plain embarrassing for the Yankees.

Steinbrenner offered a solution. What if they paid him back the money Paul was going to cut from his contract, restoring his old contract of $66,000? Piniella agreed.

Steinbrenner was obviously a shrewd businessman, but at least, Piniella thought, he was fair. Or so he thought.

In 1977, Piniella signed a new Yankees contract for $80,000. But as the summer rolled on and with Piniella due to enter free agency, he was once again summoned to the owner's office.

Steinbrenner asked Piniella what he thought he was worth. Well, Piniella said, he wanted the security of a two-year deal (as was the norm for most players, he only had one-year deals up to then). Piniella said he thought one year at $110,000 and the next at $125,000 sounded fair, and they left it at that.

After the season, Steinbrenner asked him if he was ready to sign to the terms they had discussed.

"George, now wait a minute," Piniella told him. "When we talked this summer, I was hitting .280. I got hot, you know, hit .330 for the season and .333 in the Championship Series and had a good World Series. I think I deserve a lot more. Don't you?"

Steinbrenner did not. He challenged Piniella to "be a man of your word."

Piniella signed.

"George had a lot of respect for Lou, but there was one episode where Lou negotiated a contract with George over the dinner table on a napkin," recalled Steve Jacobson, longtime Yankee beat writer and later a columnist for *Newsday*. "Then when they got to the formalities the next day, there were things in there Lou hadn't agreed to the night before. George did that often where he'd sneak things into contracts."

Throughout his career, it always seemed like Piniella was surrounded by players making much more than he was—some situations he resented, some he didn't. One was former Oakland A's fireballer Catfish Hunter, who signed a landmark five-year, $3.75 million contract with the Yankees as a free agent on New Year's Eve 1974.

Piniella loved Hunter, a kind-hearted, sharp-witted country boy from Hertford, North Carolina, whom he had competed against since he was a rookie when he blasted a home run off of Hunter. And the give-and-take between the two, particularly their running comedy routine on the team bus, became legendary.

"Jim *Fucking* Wohlford," Hunter would hiss at Piniella. "You were replaced by Jim *Fucking* Wohlford."

Piniella would counter in any number of ways, relishing the rare bad outing by Hunter, after which nothing was out of bounds, recalled Fred Stanley.

"One of the finest lines I remember Lou getting off on Catfish," Fred Stanley recalled, "was when he said, 'A little boy goes into a convenience store, steals a candy bar and gets into huge trouble. And you've been stealing what, $3.7 mil from Steinbrenner?' Lou kept yelling, 'Do the right thing, give the money back.'"

But what truly bound Hunter and Piniella together was their mutual love and knowledge of the game.

Marty Appel, the Yankees public relations director from 1973–77, recalled the spring training that his hotel room in Fort Lauderdale was next to roommates Piniella and Hunter.

"One night I was trying to get to sleep, it was past midnight and the two of them came back from an evening out," Appel recalled. "They were loud and stayed loud and I thought, 'This is going to be a long night.' What were they doing? They were arguing with each other for hours over how to pitch everyone in the American League.

"It was funny, it was obscene, with Piniella trying to show that he knew more than Catfish. They're talking about how to pitch Sixto Lezcano with an 0–2 count and I'm thinking, 'I cannot believe I'm listening to this at three in the morning.'"

Hunter wound up going 23–14 with a 2.58 ERA for the 1975 season and Thurman Munson hit .318, but the season was a disaster. Bobby Bonds, who came to the Yankees from San Francisco in the trade for Bobby Murcer, had a decent year but was not an adequate replacement for Murcer, and the Yankees were beset with injuries to key players, including Piniella.

Piniella played just 74 games and hit just .196, his worst year in the big leagues, after puncturing his eardrum while bodysurfing during a Yankees spring training trip to Puerto Rico. The symptoms appeared after the team returned to Florida, when Piniella started experiencing headaches and dizziness. Surgery and medication never fully improved his coordination, and the season was a wash both for him and for the Yankees as the team finished in third place, 12 games behind the first-place Red Sox.

Except for one announcement in early August, it may have even been forgettable.

Bill Virdon learned about the hiring of new Yankees manager Billy Martin from reporters—before he was actually fired. And so began the Martin era. Five hirings. Five firings. One World Series title to go along with his four as a Yankees player. And more turmoil than Piniella had ever witnessed in his life.

Piniella remembered watching Martin on TV making his game-saving catch of a Jackie Robinson fly ball in Game 7 of the 1952 World Series. Piniella had liked Martin's spirit and energy from afar, liked competing against his teams when Billy was managing the Twins and the Rangers.

As 1976 dawned with Martin's first full season as the Yankees' manager, it also marked the return of Steinbrenner from a two-year suspension from baseball (shortened by nine months) following his guilty plea to making illegal campaign contributions to Richard Nixon.

For the team, it meant the return to Yankee Stadium. And for Piniella, it meant the real beginning of his baseball education. Baseball 101 taught by Professor Billy Martin was definitely a pass-fail proposition, in regard to both the students and the instructor.

A new aggressive playing style under Martin, propelled by new acquisitions Mickey Rivers and Willie Randolph, led the Yankees to their best start since 1958. And a brawl after a collision with Boston catcher Carlton Fisk at home plate on May 20 left Piniella with a cover shot on *Sports Illustrated* and the Yankees with a stamp on their new attitude.

Even Thurman Munson had stolen six bases to that point. And Rivers, who came from California in a trade for Bobby Bonds, was tied with Randolph with 14 steals each. Piniella was one of five Yankees hitters batting better than .300.

He had clear memories of the Boston fight.

"I was on [second] base and Dewey Evans makes a really, really nice throw to home on a fly ball and I got thrown out and Carlton, through a little meanness, stuck the ball right in my face and I didn't like it too much," Piniella recalled. "We got after it pretty good, and it turned into a nice fight."

Well, not that nice.

One consequence for the Red Sox was a separated shoulder for pitcher Bill Lee, who initially blamed Graig Nettles and later put it on Martin for encouraging the Yankees to be confrontational. After three straight 17-win seasons, Lee went 5–7 in 1976.

Piniella badly bruised his hand in the fight, and just when it had nearly healed, he punched a wall after making an out and reinjured it. "The first time the red-ass ever got me hurt," he wrote later.

Still, Piniella hit .281 in 100 games in 1976, platooning most of the season with Roy White. Like any competitor, Piniella wanted to play full-time, but he was okay with it, quickly learning what Martin and winning baseball were all about.

"I learned that a team can win without great individual stars," he wrote. "A ballclub wins when each player does what he can do to the best of his ability. You don't need to have someone hitting 40 home runs or knocking in 130 runs or winning 20 games. You do need each player contributing his own unique abilities to the entire ballclub.

"Earl Weaver taught me some important lessons about winning when I played for him as a kid, and now Billy taught me about team chemistry."

By late July, the Yankees, who had not finished first in 12 years, had a 14½ game lead in the East and ended up winning by 10½ games.

Now it was Yankees-Royals for the American League pennant and a matchup the Royals had won seven of 12 times during the regular season. Amos Otis was considered the best all-around player for Kansas City with a .279 average, 86 RBIs, 26 stolen bases, and a team-leading 18 home runs.

Otis, whose contract Piniella had once resented in Kansas City, had been under criticism in Kansas City for not delivering under pressure, but he had been ablaze in September, winning three games for the Royals.

"They're a lot like us," Piniella told *Sports Illustrated* of his former team. "Both teams rely on pitching and defense. We don't really have that much more power."

Two early throwing errors by George Brett staked the Yankees and Hunter to a lead they would not relinquish in a Game 1 victory in Kansas City. But in Game 2, the Yankees would return the favor with an American League playoff record five errors in a Royals win.

After New York took Game 3, Kansas City would get the best of Hunter and win 7–4 despite two Nettles homers to push the series to a decisive Game 5 at Yankee Stadium.

Piniella was on the bench for Game 5 with White in left for the Yankees against Kansas City's big right-hander Dennis Leonard, a scenario he once again understood under the Martin team-first regime. Piniella watched as the Royals' Jim Wohlford singled to put two men on in the eighth with the Yankees up, 6–3.

"Jim *Fucking* Wohlford," Hunter whispered to Piniella.

Moments later, Brett drove in Wohlford and Al Cowens, tying the score with a soaring home run to right.

With the pressure building in Yankee Stadium, fans who had littered the field with toilet paper upon every New York hit, unleashed their tension by showering the field with more debris, an exercise that delayed the game several minutes before the start of the bottom of the ninth.

Chris Chambliss would say later that he wanted to jump on the first pitch to possibly take advantage of reliever Mark Littell's loss of concentration. And sure enough he did, clocking Littell's first pitch, a high fastball, into the right-field stands. He barely made it past second base as he fought through the fans who rushed the field.

In the clubhouse, Martin cried, hugged Steinbrenner, and dedicated the victory to his old Yankees manager Casey Stengel. Then he told reporters that all the doubters could kiss his ass.

Oddly, the Yankees would be described as uptight by *Newsweek* magazine in the lead-up to the World Series against Cincinnati, while the defending-champion Reds and their Big Red Machine were called highly efficient but easygoing like their manager, Sparky Anderson.

"When you've won as much as we have, I guess it's like sex," Johnny Bench told *Newsweek* after Cincinnati's sweep of the Phillies in the NLCS. "It's great every time, but you don't have all those weird reactions like you did the first time."

The Yanks didn't exactly have weird reactions, but perhaps sapped from the emotion and energy expended in the Royals series were admittedly overtaken by the experience and the Reds, who swept them, 4–0.

The Reds became the first team ever to sweep both the playoffs and the World Series and the first NL team since the 1922 New York Giants to successfully defend its World Series title.

Martin, who was ejected in the final moments of the last game for hurling a ball from the Yankees dugout, griped that it was all the TV people's fault for rushing the start of the Series and throwing off his pitching rotation. Doyle Alexander, who had not pitched at all against the Royals, was his Game 1 starter instead of Hunter, who had pitched in Game 4 of the playoffs and wasn't ready.

Anderson christened his team one of the greatest of all time while Martin behaved more like a petulant child than the American League Manager of the Year, decrying the two-time champions.

"I'd like to say the Reds are awesome, but they aren't," Martin said. "Let them win five World Series in a row like we did. That's awesome."

The Reds were more experienced and a better team. But it hardly mattered to Steinbrenner or to Martin, who both took losing with a bitterness their players would come to know well in the coming years.

Piniella, meanwhile, felt for his buddy Munson, who hit .529 for the Series, including six straight hits. Munson had hit .302 for the year in being named the American League's Most Valuable Player after hitting .318 in 1975 and would've been the 1976 Series MVP if only for the fact that the other team's catcher happened to hit .533.

When Sparky Anderson was asked after the Reds' clincher how he would compare Munson to Bench, he snapped, "Don't embarrass nobody by comparing them to Johnny Bench."

Munson would have gotten wind of the comments eventually but just happened to be entering the interview room as Anderson spoke, and the gruff but sensitive catcher chafed.

It didn't help that Bench attempted to console him.

"I told Thurman that all comparisons are futile," Bench said. "Somebody will always come along who's greater than either of us. What you have to do is play for the moment. That's what I've learned: grab all the moments you can."

Still, it would not get any easier for Munson as the Yankees were about to accommodate one more ego in their already crowded clubhouse.

* * *

Catfish Hunter had been the Yankees' first official free agent the year before, but he was allowed to leave the A's on something of a technicality when A's owner Charlie Finley failed to make a payment on his insurance coverage.

But after Curt Flood's legal battle in opposition of baseball's reserve clause and Andy Messersmith and Dave McNally were declared free agents by the courts after playing without contracts, it cleared the way for a new reserve clause to be written and true free agency to exist after the 1976 season.

With no farm system to speak of and the mentality of winning at all costs, diving into free agency was a natural for Steinbrenner. And Reggie Jackson was a natural for New York.

Piniella had the same initial opinion of Jackson that his teammates did, calling him "a hot dog" in his 1986 book.

But Piniella also made it clear that he felt sorry for Jackson, whose talent he respected immensely, and the isolation Jackson must have felt when he first joined the club, despite the fact that he brought on most of it himself.

Jackson swooped in declaring himself the team savior. Most notable was the famous *Sport Magazine* interview in which Jackson declared himself, "the straw that stirs the drink" and dismissed Munson, the team captain, as unable to put "the meat in the seats" and do for a club what Jackson could.

Jackson later backed off a bit, saying he thought the conversation was off the record. But the damage was already done. And if it wasn't, Reggie kept the pressure on himself with outlandish statements about his abilities on a regular basis.

Piniella tried to get along with Jackson from the start, but it quickly became clear to him that doing so and maintaining his other relationships was not always going to be easy.

"Pretty soon, there was an obvious division in the clubhouse," Piniella wrote. "Almost every player could be categorized as in Billy's camp or Reggie's camp or Thurman's camp. It got so if I was talking to Reggie, I might get a cold shoulder from Graig or Thurman. It seemed there was no way to get along with everybody, but I tried desperately to maintain some sort of neutrality."

Hunter knew Jackson from their days in Oakland together and did not take his bluster seriously, said Moss Klein, Yankees beat writer for the *Newark Star-Ledger* for 17 years. "The first day Reggie showed up at spring training, it was very awkward," Klein recalled. "This was a team that was just in the World Series, and he was going to make them better. He used the expression 'the magnitude of me.' All the players were offended.

"But the first day in the clubhouse, Catfish crossed over to his side of the room and went out of his way to shake hands. Lou followed along with him. Lou was honest with Reggie, and Reggie seemed to appreciate it."

One example Klein offered was a game in Milwaukee before the 1978 All-Star break, in Jackson's second year with the club.

"Most of the players were on the field for batting practice but we were all talking to Reggie, and Reggie was going on and on like he always did, gesturing and talking," recalled Klein. "And right in the middle of it, Piniella, who was always very courteous to writers, walked by and said, 'Reggie, you've gotta tell me, why are they talking to you? You haven't played the game yet. Why are you always talking?' Reggie shrugged at him. Lou just said what he felt."

Murray Chass, the beat writer for the *New York Times*, said he remembers Piniella staying above board when it came to all matters of clubhouse politics.

"Lou was his own man," said Chass. "He did what he thought was right, and he wasn't going to worry too much about what others thought. Thurman let his teammates intimidate him when his friends thought he was talking to reporters too much. He didn't want to risk that. But Lou didn't do that. Lou was above it. His personality, his stature, he was just above it."

Meanwhile, as the Yankee soap opera chugged along, each day a new story featuring the latest digs by and toward any combination of Martin, Steinbrenner, Jackson, and Munson, the club hovered in third place behind Boston and Baltimore. What was once humorous, even inside the clubhouse, was no longer very funny.

And even the usual bus banter turned cold and awkward when Jackson would try to chime in as he did once when, stuck in traffic next to a semi-trailer, he yelled out to Rivers, "Hey Mickey, that's you in 10 years, driving a truck."

"Yeah," Rivers replied, "but at least I'll be happy driving a truck."

All of that seemed minor, however, compared to the afternoon of June 18, when the rest of the country observed firsthand the animosity festering within the Yankees.

It was a nationally televised game between the Yankees and Red Sox at Fenway Park, when a seemingly routine fly ball dropped into right-center field, out of the reach of Jackson. Jim Rice raced to second as Jackson seemingly took his time getting to it.

In a rage, Martin sent Paul Blair to replace Jackson.

In many of the players' views, including Piniella's, Jackson had been sulking out there and loafed on the fly ball. He had recently been moved down to sixth in the batting order from his customary cleanup spot amid remarks by Martin that he never really wanted him on the team in the first place and that Jackson upset the chemistry of a talented 1976 club.

When Jackson got to the dugout, a national audience saw player and manager go at it verbally, and they were eventually separated physically by coaches. Pitcher Mike Torrez called to Jackson in Spanish to go inside the clubhouse and calm down.

When the inning ended, Piniella was met at the top step of the dugout and told that Reggie wanted to see him in the clubhouse.

"Lou, what should I do?" Piniella wrote of their conversation that day. "This guy doesn't like me. He wants to embarrass me. He wants to fight me. Should I stay here after the game and fight him here in the clubhouse?"

Piniella talked him into showering, dressing, and going back to the hotel. "No good will come out of anything for you, for Billy, or for the ballclub, if you two guys have a fistfight here," Piniella told him.

Jackson asked him how he could let Martin get away with humiliating him on national TV.

"You can't win when you fight with the manager," Piniella said. "He has to make the decisions. That's the way it has got to be, and that's the way it will always be as long as there is baseball." And so Jackson went back to the hotel. And Steinbrenner considered firing Martin.

As Bill Madden, the beat writer from the *New York Daily News*, remembered it, it was only the combination of Jackson, as well as Piniella and Munson talking Steinbrenner out of it, that prevented Martin from getting fired.

Jackson didn't want to be the cause of Martin's firing and promised to no longer discuss the incident. And Martin promised not to rip Reggie in the press. But Jackson made thinly veiled accusations of racism by the Yankees manager just a few days later.

Years later, a few beat writers say they did hear Martin make racist remarks toward Jackson. In his autobiography, Piniella said Martin treated all players, except for Jackson, alike, but that it had nothing to do with race.

"They simply could not get along," he wrote. "It happens sometimes. It happens on ballclubs. It happens in offices. It might even happen in your family."

And in that regard, Piniella acted as the even-tempered middle brother with common sense.

"Lou was really the one that saved the day," said Maury Allen, who partnered with Piniella on his 1986 autobiography. "If he would have punched out his manager, he would have been finished. Lou saved him, and it was all done in Spanish."

As tensions and tempers continued to boil, Piniella would talk with Reggie, often times in Spanish. Jackson's father was Puerto Rican, and both grew up speaking the language. Piniella enjoyed their conversations because he didn't get much of a chance to speak the language, and he was able to practice.

But as the Yankees remained in third place within a couple games of Boston and Baltimore shortly before the All-Star break, Martin's fate still in the balance, Reggie still batting sixth, and Steinbrenner joining the club on the road, Piniella and Munson hatched a plan.

It actually wasn't much of a plan at all but merely an idea reached after a few drinks in a Milwaukee bar after a loss to the Brewers. The discussion in Steinbrenner's hotel room that night between the Boss, Munson, and Piniella—and eventually with a drunken Martin—has been well-documented.

After midnight and with Steinbrenner in his silk pajamas, Munson and Piniella told the Boss they wanted him to know how they viewed a situation they felt had become nearly intolerable. They told Steinbrenner that he should stop ripping Billy in the papers and that if he wasn't going to fire Martin, he should be allowed to continue to manage the team in peace. Oh yes, and that Reggie should be moved back to cleanup.

But just when they were making progress on those fronts, Martin returned from a night out, overheard their voices in the room next to his, and pushed past Steinbrenner to find Piniella and Munson cowering in the bathroom.

"Two traitors," he called them.

Eventually, they calmed Martin down, and he actually came around to the idea of Jackson batting fourth. The Yankees and Jackson went on a tear and ended up winning the pennant. And Piniella formed a bond with Steinbrenner after that night that would change their relationship from then on.

Steinbrenner respected his opinion and asked for it on occasion. And Piniella could tease Steinbrenner, even in public, without fear of retribution.

"Lou was looked at as George's boy, but it didn't bother anybody," said Bill Madden. "He was George's boy in the way he could talk to George. Guys liked that. But Lou never got any special favors from George."

A favorite theme in Steinbrenner's stories centered around how tough he had to be in the shipping business. Once he gave a clubhouse speech about dealing with some shady characters down on the Cleveland waterfront. After the meeting, Piniella cracked, "George, the only time you were on the Cleveland waterfront was when you drove your father's seventy-foot yacht to the dock and said to the guy at the gas pump, 'Fill 'er up.'"

The room howled, and Steinbrenner smiled. And Piniella realized he could not have gotten away with that a year earlier.

"Lou had a whole different kind of relationship with George Steinbrenner from anybody I saw while I was there," said Fred Stanley. "Lou had a way of getting on George, could say stuff, embarrass George and George could be angry with him, but he was the only person who ever did that to George. And George respected Lou, respected him for having the balls enough to say it to him. And you had to have a set of those to get in his face and kid with him in the clubhouse."

With every controversial comment by Steinbrenner in the papers, Piniella would disarm the Boss and lessen the tension by teasing Steinbrenner about it. And, as it was with Hunter, nothing was off-limits.

"People were writing everything every day, so Lou had a thousand things to get on him about," said Stanley. "Lou wouldn't ever tell George just 'Go to hell' in his face. I could never see that. But he would take something George would say and turn it into 'Are you kidding me?' He'd get on him about the docks or about his football career or what lacked of his football career.

"One day, the flu was going around, and George was in the trainer's room getting a B-12 shot. There were a bunch of people in there, and Lou walked in and said to [trainer] Gene Monahan, 'Hey Gene, you could put on a blindfold and throw that dart anywhere in the room and hit George in the ass.' Boy, did he get angry. But it was hilarious."

* * *

On August 23, 1977, the Yankees moved into first place for the first time since July 9. And stayed there.

On September 3, the news that Piniella had agreed to a new two-year contract for the 1978 and '79 seasons was announced in the press box 15 minutes after his home run increased a 3–2 Yankees lead over the Twins to 5–2.

Piniella and Steinbrenner had actually discussed his contract two days earlier, but the sixth inning apparently seemed as good a time as any to make it public.

At 34 and hitting .343 as a part-time outfielder and the team's main designated hitter, Piniella told reporters he was happy with his raise from $80,000 to a guaranteed $110,000 and $125,000—all done without an agent and after the team's first offer.

"I don't think I'm a star," he said. "I think I'm a good ballplayer. I'm probably the only guy who could be a free agent without an agent. I never once considered what I was worth on the market. Their first offer was a fair raise and I took it. If they had asked me what I wanted, I don't know what I would have told them. I don't care what others are making."

Piniella even went so far as to say that his .343 was misleading in his relatively limited role and shouldn't be compared to the league's top hitters like Rod Carew.

All that good faith was tested, of course, when Piniella was informed by the league several weeks later that the language of the contract was ambiguous and that only the first year was actually guaranteed by the Yankees.

However, Piniella was focused solely on the team and the American League Championship Series.

Down 2–1 in the series against their old rivals, the Royals, the Yankees faced elimination in Kansas City. But after the 6–2 loss to Dennis Leonard in Game 3, a mini-Yankees pep rally ensued over drinks at Trader Vic's in the Crown Center.

Piniella, Munson, and Nettles decided there was simply no way they were going to lose the next day to the smaller, less powerful, and less formidable Kansas City Royals. But when they returned to the hotel that night, they were told to leave their bags in the lobby the next morning in the event the team lost and had to return to New York.

Piniella did not take this particularly well. He called the Yankees' traveling secretary, Bill Kane, who was just following the orders of general manager Gabe Paul. "You're suggesting we might not win," Piniella told Kane.

When Kane relayed what Piniella had said back to Steinbrenner, the Boss agreed with his player. The Yankees didn't pack their bags. And they won the next two games—6–4 behind five strong innings by Sparky Lyle, and 5–3 on a three-run ninth inning Yankees rally—to advance to the World Series.

Martin had started Blair ahead of Jackson in Game 5 in a purely instinctive move and it paid off, with both players making key late-game offensive contributions. And Piniella, who finished the season with a .330 average, was hitting .333 in the playoffs heading into the World Series against the Los Angeles Dodgers.

"Boy, I loved him at the plate with two outs, man on second," said Michael. "Nobody could do it better. I can only think of a handful—Thurman, George Brett, Hal McRae—who could do it like Lou. During our rivalry with Kansas City, Lou was in his prime as a hitter and, along with Reggie, one of the toughest outs around. Lou hit it just about as hard as anybody."

Blair singled home the winning run in the 12th inning of Game 1 at Yankee Stadium. The Dodgers evened the series by pounding

Hunter, who was nursing a sore shoulder, and gave up three home runs in the first three innings en route to a 6–1 loss.

Back in Los Angeles, Mike Torrez won Game 3 for the Yankees, going the complete game with nine strikeouts while New York hitters roughed up Tommy John with three runs in the first inning of the 5–3 victory.

Ron Guidry threw a four-hit, complete-game 4–2 victory in Game 4, putting the Yankees within one victory of the world championship, a game in which Piniella drove in a run and made a leaping grab in left to rob Ron Cey of a home run in the fourth that would have tied the game at three.

The Dodgers routed the Yankees 10–4 in Game 5 to send the series back to New York. And in Game 6, Jackson homered three times (combined with his last at-bat in Game 5, four home runs on four swings of the bat, each off a different Dodgers pitcher) to seal the 8–4 win and the World Series. Jackson hit five in the Series, forever cementing his nickname of "Mr. October."

The team everyone outside of the Bronx hated, the one they called the best that money could buy, had prevailed. And in the elation and exhaustion of the winning clubhouse, Piniella reflected how weary they had become of it all—both physically and emotionally.

"I don't think this club could take another week of this," he said. "Not another season like this. If it's not going to be tranquil, this team is not going to win. This team can't stand this anymore. They can sign all the free agents they want and they won't win. It doesn't have to be a big happy family, but you have to have enough concentration to play the games. It surprises me that we were able to win."

Piniella's teammates did not disagree, but Stanley says there was almost no other way out.

"There was not a whole lot going on in New York back then in any other sport," Stanley said. "We were the center of attention and there was so much turmoil between Reggie and Thurman, Reggie and the press; there was always something going on, somebody taking a shot.

"But I'll be honest, with the group of guys we had, I don't think they spent a whole lot of waking hours thinking how bad it was. You kind of get hardened to it, expect it. We'd have a clubhouse meeting and Billy would tell us, 'Be very careful what you say and how you say it because it will come back to bite you.' He wanted us to be careful, because nothing tears up a clubhouse more than when players get on players. You lose a lot of energy because you're fighting two battles.

"And after all of that, we did it again, in even more dramatic fashion the next season. So I guess it tells you the character we had on the ballclub. That, and a lot of talent."

* * *

The rich got richer and more controversial that off-season as the Yankees added Rich "Goose" Gossage, arguably baseball's best right-handed relief pitcher, to a bullpen that already included Cy Young award–winning left-handed reliever Sparky Lyle.

They also named Al Rosen, a star of the Cleveland Indians in the 1950s and hero to a young George Steinbrenner, as executive vice president replacing Gabe Paul.

If there was any question as to whether Piniella's wish would come true and the Yankees would settle down out of self-preservation, that dream was quickly vanquished.

Reggie Jackson showed up late to spring training, and the zoo began anew. Piniella would rant about how tired he was of it all, how he should just quit, but no one seemed to be listening. Even his wife Anita would shut him up by remarking, "Lou, the kids need new shoes."

Actually, Piniella threatened to quit several times as a player, but no one ever took him seriously. Moss Klein recalled one time when the Yankees were wrapping up a long West Coast swing in Oakland in the early 1980s.

"I had to make a flight back home, Lou had a bad game, the game went long, I'm rushing to get out of there, and as I'm about to leave the lockerroom, Lou motions me over," Klein said. "He said, 'Moose, I just wanted to let you know this is it for me. I can't hit anymore. I've lost it. I'm going to quit and I just wanted you to know.' I said, 'Lou, you know you don't mean this,' and he said, 'No, I do.' Of course, the next day he was fine and laughed about it."

The laughs, however, were few and far between as the 1978 season got underway. The arrival of Goose Gossage meant the slow demise of Sparky Lyle. The Jackson-Martin sparks continued to fly. And by late June, the Yankees were already eight games behind the Red Sox, who hovered around a ridiculous 20 games above .500.

In his book *The Bronx Zoo*, Sparky Lyle's entry on Friday, June 23 reads:

"Piniella was complaining to reporters about how bad the atmosphere in the clubhouse is, that there are people who don't want to be there. That's true. I'm one of those guys. You could probably find out the same thing from almost everyone on this club. They wouldn't give a damn if they were traded or not. We know we have a good ballclub, but when you're eleven and a half games behind and you're losing and things are happening to you like what's been going on this year, you don't bother looking for the bright side. You don't even think about it. Every little thing that goes wrong is intensified.

"Lou says guys are unhappy and want to go. Hell, Lou's one of those guys, too. He's always pissing and moaning. He's always saying, 'Ah crap, I wish Billy and George would leave me alone to do my job.' And just about everybody on the club is guilty of that except maybe the new guys.... [Outfielder Gary Thomasson] wants to play baseball, and maybe if we could get that attitude back, we'd go out and play better. But George is pissing everyone off with all this crap between him and Billy, and Billy's pissing the players off, and those things alone are enough to destroy a ballclub."

* * *

Just before the Fourth of July, Steinbrenner and Martin got together to film a Miller Lite commercial in which they engaged in the long-running debate, "tastes great vs. less filling." The commercial ended with Steinbrenner telling Martin, "You're fired."

"Oh, not again," replied Martin as both giggle.

In an interview with the *New York Times* in 2003, Marty Blackman, who brought the two to the advertising agency that produced the commercial, said Steinbrenner had one reservation about filming the ad.

Steinbrenner asked if they could wait a week to do the filming because he would be making a decision on Martin's future. The running joke at the agency until the commercial aired was whether Steinbrenner would be saying "you're fired" or "you're hired."

In real life, however, nobody was laughing. Steinbrenner was telling reporters the Yankees had no chance of catching the Red Sox, and the infighting had become untenable.

"The lineup card has become a confrontation of egos between George and Billy," said 15-year Yankee veteran Roy White. "You can't get a clear explanation of why you're playing or why you're benched.

"You're either George's boy or Billy's boy [White was one of Billy's]. I'm convinced I was benched because I was playing too well and showing up George. We'd laugh about it...kid each other about how George has got [Lou] Piniella playing and me benched, or how Billy has benched Reggie to show his defiance.

"We're just guessing about this...that's the sad part. But it seems like they trade off—Billy gets to play so many of his favorites if George gets his way on other positions.

"It'd be funny if it wasn't so sick."

And it just kept getting worse. During a Monday night game in New York against Kansas City on July 17, Martin ordered Jackson to lay down a bunt with a man on, one out, and the score tied in the tenth. With Al Hrabosky, the Mad Hungarian, on the mound, the infield pulled in and Martin switched the sign to have Jackson swing away. Jackson attempted to bunt on a fastball and missed.

With Martin losing it in the dugout, third-base coach Dick Howser walked down the line and told Jackson the bunt sign was off. But again Jackson tried to bunt. Jackson tried to bunt a third time and struck out, the Royals eventually winning the game in the eleventh.

Jackson was suspended for the insubordination for five games, all of which the Yankees won as the Red Sox's lead was down to 10 games. But Martin was still hot. Jackson made some sarcastic remarks to the press when he returned, and then Martin heard from Bill Veeck that Steinbrenner had suggested a managerial swap earlier in the season—Billy for White Sox coach Bob Lemon.

With a few drinks under his belt, Martin walked through O'Hare Airport with reporters, talking about Reggie and George before blurting out, "One's a born liar and the other is convicted."

After the team arrived in Kansas City, Martin tearfully "resigned." And Steinbrenner got his wish. Lemon, who had been fired by Veeck the week before, was named the new Yankees manager on July 25.

It wasn't that Lemon did anything remarkably brilliant. But the instant calm made a huge difference. "You walked in the clubhouse," pitcher Ron Guidry told *Newsday*'s Steve Jacobson of those days under Martin, "and there was something in the air that could explode at any minute."

Days later, on Yankees Old Timers' Day, it was announced that Martin would be the Yankees manager in 1980, at which time Lemon would become vice president and general manager. The distraction by now was minimal. The Yankees were still focused on 1978.

Twenty years later, Piniella still referred to those days and that team as his favorite, a team that was 14 games behind Boston on July 19.

It was about that time that Piniella stood up in the clubhouse and told his teammates matter-of-factly, "Play like we know we can and we'll catch the Red Sox or be awfully close."

It was so simple, so sincere, that it resonated throughout the room.

"If he hadn't said it, would we have done it?" said Lyle. "I don't know. When we heard it come out, everybody looked up and thought, 'He's right.'"

On August 15, the Yankees had trimmed the Red Sox lead to seven games. The Yankees dropped two in a row to Seattle. Piniella looked ahead on the schedule and saw a four-game series with Boston beginning September 7, thus violating a sacred sports code that no one usually admits to but everyone does.

"If we get to Boston with those four games only four games out, we will win it," Piniella said, obviously not caring much about the code.

On September 1, the Yankees were 6½ back. On September 10, they completed a four-game sweep of the Sox at Fenway, no less, and tied it up.

"In my time," said Piniella, "no team ever inflicted such a pounding on another club as we did to the Red Sox those four games."

The Yankees won the first two games by a combined 28–5. They won the second two by a combined 14–4. It was the first Yankee sweep in Fenway since 1943. The Yankees had erased 14 games in 53 days.

Within the week, the Yankees were three and a half games ahead. Hunter had won 10-of-12 games. Guidry was on his way to a Yankee-best 25–3 with a 1.74 ERA.

Then, with eight games to play, the Red Sox came back to life, winning all eight. The Yankees lost three of their last nine, all to the Cleveland Indians. And the Yankees and Red Sox were tied.

Despite the inherent stressfulness of the situation, however, Piniella described the team as relaxed and loose as they left Yankee Stadium for the bus ride to the airport and the trip to Boston for the one-game playoff. Piniella needled the Boss, who had lost the coin toss for home-field advantage a couple weeks earlier.

"George, if you hadn't lost that flip, we would at least be playing in the stadium," he told Steinbrenner. "You didn't do your part. Let's see if we can do our part and win."

He continued teasing him on the bus.

"Remember in Milwaukee, just before the All-Star break," Piniella reminded Steinbrenner, "you told the press we were too far back to win it. You gave up on us. You have to be the luckiest guy in the world. We are going to win this thing tomorrow, and you'll make all that money. Don't give up on us so soon."

Steinbrenner laughed.

Around the batting cage the next day, Piniella observed the Red Sox and thought they were even more relaxed than the Yankees. The crowd, however, was not. And the tension in the air was palpable until Carl Yastrzemski hit a solo homer in the second inning that unleashed a roar so loud that Piniella admitted he had to "retain my concentration and not jump around with those cheers."

History will forever show that the dramatic, game-winning blast in that game came with the Red Sox leading 2–0 in the seventh, off the bat of Yankees shortstop Bucky Dent, who stroked an inside slider by Mike Torrez just over the Green Monster in left for a three-run homer. Munson doubled home another run, and a Jackson home run in the eighth made it 5–2, enough to hold off a two-run rally by the Red Sox in the bottom half of the inning.

But ask most any player, coach, reporter or astute fan who was there that day or watching on television which play really won it for the Yankees, and they will all point to Piniella. The "sun game" at Fenway is really all you have to say and they will all concur.

It bothered outfielders from the sixth inning on, but now, as the bottom of the ninth began with the Yankees holding onto a one-run lead, the sun hung just over the roof and right directly into the eyes of Piniella manning right.

"Just let the ball stay away from right field, I prayed," Piniella wrote in his autobiography.

But as fate would have it, Gossage walked Rick Burleson with one out, and the left-handed Jerry Remy followed with a line drive right at Piniella.

"I saw the ball leave the bat and that was the last time I saw it," wrote Piniella. "I knew if the ball got by me, the runner would go to third or maybe score the tying run. I couldn't allow Burleson to see that I had lost it in the sun. I kept my composure as I searched for the ball, I kept backtracking as hard as I could. I wanted to give myself more room to find it. Out of the corner of my eye, I saw that damn ball landing a few feet to my left on the grass."

As he awaited the ball, Piniella slapped his glove like he had it all the way. Once it bounced, he lunged at it and fired a direct strike, knee-high, to Nettles at third, freezing Burleson at second and ensuring he would not go to third.

The next batter, Jim Rice, hit a towering fly to right that Piniella was able to catch. If Burleson had been on third, he would have scored for sure. Carl Yastrzemski popped out to Nettles behind third for the last out.

"It was one of the all-time great plays," said Al Rosen of Piniella's decoy and throw. "Without that play, the game is over. It was just an unbelievably adept play. You could see he fought the sun all the way. I played in that park, and a lot of balls were misplayed. The whole thing happened so rapidly, but it was only because of Lou's character and determination that he made that play."

Interestingly, Piniella pointed to his play in the sixth inning that rivaled the sun play, and it was a move that, in all probability, not a soul at Fenway even noticed. With Boston leading 2–0, Fred Lynn came to the plate with runners on first and second and two outs. When Lynn worked the count to 3–2, Piniella, on his own, moved roughly 15 feet to his left.

"I figured that Guidry didn't have his good stuff, that when the count went 3–2, he'd throw Lynn a fastball and Lynn was a dead fastball hitter," Piniella recounted to the *Seattle Post-Intelligencer* upon his hiring in 1992.

"I called over to Mickey [Rivers] in center and pulled him over, too. We shifted the whole outfield on our own. Why? Just a feeling, instinct, whatever you call it."

On the next pitch, Lynn hit the ball deep into the right-field corner, and there was Piniella perfectly positioned—but not where anyone would have put him with Lynn hitting off the lefty Guidry—to end the inning.

The Yankees would defeat the Royals for the second year in a row 3–1 to capture the American League pennant and then came back from two games down to win the World Series against the Los Angeles Dodgers.

They were world champs again. And things would never be the same.

The Piniellas welcomed their third child, Derek, on Opening Day 1979, and the season marked the arrivals of Tommy John and Luis Tiant, two more high-priced free agents, along with the return of old teammate and buddy Bobby Murcer to the Yankees.

But two weeks into the season, Yankees DH Cliff Johnson got into a silly locker room fight with Goose Gossage, who injured a thumb in the brawl and was lost for three months of the season.

In anger, Steinbrenner ordered the trade of Gossage's replacement, Dick Tidrow, when he couldn't be Gossage, and on June 18, Steinbrenner fired Lemon and brought back Billy Martin a year earlier than promised.

For Rosen, it was too much. Lemon had lost his youngest son in a car accident the previous fall, and for Rosen, it meant firing a heartbroken friend. He resigned a month later. As Piniella later described it, the rest of the country got what it had been wishing for with the fall of the great Yankees, who would finish 89–71, in fourth place, and 13½ games behind first-place Baltimore in the division.

"The Yankees of 1979 were a very tired team," Piniella wrote. "We had finally been worn down. The magic was gone. The desire seemed gone. The other teams lay for us with their best pitching. Except for the Yankees of 1936–39 and the Casey Stengel Yankees of 1949–53, no team had ever won four pennants in a row. We weren't about to do it, either."

In late October, Martin punched out a marshmallow salesman in a hotel lobby, lied to Steinbrenner about what happened, and was gone again, replaced by Dick Howser.

But the Yankees had lost far more than their manager and their aura.

The year before, Thurman Munson began pursuing in earnest his interest in airplanes, and in the spring of 1979, he got his pilot's license and bought a small prop plane.

Piniella flew with Munson a few times, once even flying with Munson back to New York with Reggie Jackson, whom Munson had made a real effort to warm up to. Not long after, Munson told Piniella and Murcer that he planned to buy a jet for $1 million. After a game in Chicago on July 31, Lou and Anita Piniella and Munson spent the night at the Arlington Heights home Murcer still had from his days with the White Sox, and talk of the plane continued. Murcer, in particular, thought Munson had made a mistake purchasing such an expensive and powerful machine.

"It's strange how many things I still remember about that," Murcer told *Chicago Tribune* columnist Mike Downey in a 2006 interview. "I remember all of us being up late [after] a day game. It was pretty late when I went to bed. But I couldn't sleep because I kept hearing these two guys, Lou and Thurman, arguing about which one was going to be the best pinch-hitter.

"Why they were talking about pinch-hitting, I have no idea. But they were going at it. Thurman was one of a kind, the same way Lou is."

Munson had his new plane at a local airport and invited Piniella and Murcer to see it the next day and go for a ride, which they both later turned down after seeing the plane and becoming nervous at its size and power.

Munson flew the plane back home to Canton from Chicago that night and the next day, decided to take it back up for a test spin. With two friends and licensed pilots next to him, Munson crash-landed a thousand feet short of the runway. His friends escaped with injuries. Munson, 32, who suffered smoke inhalation and a broken neck on impact, died in the crash.

All of New York, it seemed, was heartbroken. The Yankees lost their next two games before Munson's funeral, where both Murcer and Piniella eulogized their friend, Piniella quoting Scripture and Murcer bringing the vast crowd to tears as he spoke the words, "He lived, he led, he loved."

That night following the service, the Yankees were trailing 4–0 to Baltimore when Murcer drove in five runs, including a two-run single in the bottom of the ninth, for the 5–4 victory.

"That was the happiest I ever saw Bobby at the stadium, to get that big home run to win the ballgame up in the upper deck," Piniella said in July 2008, shortly after Murcer's death from complications related to brain cancer at age 62. "It was a special evening and he was so happy and so proud. I remember him crying. Bobby was emotional, and he was caring. He was a loving person."

Munson's locker was left with his uniform hanging, a shrine to the Yankees' catcher and to Piniella, much more.

"The locker was also a constant reminder of how fickle life was," Piniella wrote. "We were young athletes, healthy, strong and vibrant, seemingly immune to disease and death, and then this tragedy hit us. It was a lesson none of us who were on that 1979 Yankee team could ever forget. You might be on top one day, and the next day gone.

"In a way, athletes die twice. We die the day our careers end; we are usually young men when that happens. Then we die again, finally, completely. Thurman's death left a lasting scar on all of us."

The Yankees returned to the American League Championship in 1980 after winning 103 games during the regular season but lost to the Royals as Piniella had just five at-bats in two games. New York won the pennant again in '81, beating Billy Martin's A's before losing to the Dodgers in the Series as Piniella batted .438 in 16 at-bats.

Piniella batted .300 in postseason play with three home runs and 18 RBIs, which amounted to 10 postseason series and 140 at-bats as the Yankees went 7–3 with two World Series titles during his playing career.

The Yankees had signed Dave Winfield after the 1980 season. Major League Baseball went on strike for 50 days in '81, the same year Reggie Jackson played out his final season in a Yankee uniform before going to California. The team traded for Ken Griffey in '82. And from the winter of '79 to the winter of '83, the Yankees went through a few more managerial changes—from Martin to Howser to Gene Michael, back to Bob Lemon, back to Michael, to Clyde King, back to Martin, to Yogi Berra.

Like the rest of his teammates, Piniella rolled with what had become common practice. In the winter of 1982, Steinbrenner rewarded him with a three-year contract (he had asked for two) for $350,000, $375,000 and $400,000. Anita Piniella called and thanked Steinbrenner, a gesture that touched him to the point that he would mention it often afterward. But he was not so touched that it prevented him from inserting a clause into the contract requiring Piniella to report at 200 pounds or be fined $1,000 a day.

In the 1990 book *Damned Yankees* by Bill Madden and Moss Klein, they called the "Great Piniella Weight War," the "most vocal and volatile" conflict between favorite son Piniella and Steinbrenner.

They told the story of that winter of 1982, when Piniella was asleep in Tampa one morning in early January, when Anita came into the bedroom and told him that Howard "Hopalong" Cassady was at the door. Cassady, the former Heisman Trophy–winning running back from Ohio State (1955), had been hired by Steinbrenner as a part-time fitness instructor for the Yankees.

He told Piniella that George had sent him to work him out three days a week because he was concerned about Piniella's weight, seeing as he was getting into his late thirties.

Piniella was not pleased.

The two went to a nearby health club where Cassady laid out an obstacle course of sorts, complete with tires, rings, and chin-up bars, plus all the Nautilus equipment. Piniella tried the course the first day, worked out briefly on the Nautilus, and then said to himself, "This is crazy. I'll be so worn out by the time spring training comes I won't be able to lift a bat."

So he hatched a plan.

"What's the standard time I'm supposed to do this course in, Hoppy?" he asked.

Cassady told him if he could get it down to 12 minutes, he could quit.

"What's that favorite brand of yours again, Hoppy?" Piniella asked.

"Why, Carlos Primero," Cassady said, "it's expensive as hell, why?"

"Well," said Piniella, "I'll bet you a bottle of that you can't do this course in 12 minutes."

Cassady jumped on it and while he began stretching, Piniella went over to the refreshment stand and bought himself a glass of orange juice. Then he took Cassady's stopwatch, sat down in the grandstand, found a newspaper, and said, 'Okay, Hoppy, any time you're ready.'"

As Cassady took off, Piniella sipped the juice and read the paper.

"Great show, Hoppy, 14 minutes," Piniella yelled down as Cassady panted across the finish line. "That's pretty damn good!"

The routine was repeated two days later, Piniella with his O.J. and paper, Cassady huffing and puffing as he became determined to finish the course in 12 minutes, brandy be damned.

"You're getting better, Hoppy," said Piniella. "This one's just a little under 13!"

When they went over to the Nautilus, Piniella told Cassady he had never worked with weights before and soon, Cassady was demonstrating.

"Watch," said Cassady, "I can do even more."

"Damn," said Piniella, "you're really in great shape, Hoppy."

Both laughed at the private joke. And that spring training, Piniella came in at 215 pounds.

On February 22, Piniella was down to 207, and he received notice from Steinbrenner that he would be fined $7,000 and $1,000 more each day until he met weight and would be in breach of contract by March 1, one week later, if he did not.

The war of wills played itself out in every New York paper until Piniella blew up after a B game against the Rangers in Fort Lauderdale on March 16. The game went 11 innings, all of which Piniella took part in, and after he stepped out of the shower, he was told he had to get over to Pompano Beach for the A game.

Piniella refused, even after Steinbrenner called and ordered him to get to Pompano and fined him another $1,000.

Piniella was livid. "I'm sick and tired of this," he said. I was invited here early and I end up getting fined $1,000 a day. I'm not happy with the damn fines. I'm like Smith Barney. I've worked hard for my money. To be suddenly treated like Little Orphan Annie is ridiculous."

Steinbrenner gladly fed the publicity machine.

"Sometimes, Lou has to be treated like a 19-year-old," he told reporters. "Everybody in Tampa will tell you that. I've got it in black and white. He knew about the weight clause. He knew what he was signing. If I'm a man and my employer was paying me $350,000 a year, which is more than the president of the United States is making, and there are 10 million unemployed people out there earning nothing in this country, I'd sure as hell take seven pounds off to honor my contract.

"Someday Lou Piniella will be out of baseball and in business. Boy, he'd last five days in business."

Eventually, the latest drama became old, Bob Lemon was fired 14 games into the season, and Steinbrenner never collected the fines as far as anyone knew.

Piniella's "real" retirement as a player was announced in early June 1984. Though he had been considering it for a while, the plan started to take shape in his last spring training, when it was decided that if young outfielder Brian Dayett had a good spring, hit well, and showed he was ready, Piniella would quit.

Unfortunately, Dayett didn't hit.

While Berra played his old war horse Piniella that spring, he did not start him. Piniella would be trotted out to replace Dave Winfield or Steve Kemp or Ken Griffey in the late innings, nod as the fans yelled "Looooou," but it wasn't how he wanted it to be.

His body ached and he was annoyed at arriving at that place in his career, as inevitable as it was.

"It really hurt me," he wrote. "It was annoying. I had had a good career, not a great one, but a consistent, solid, big-league career and I was picking up other veteran outfielders. I would rather have played 15 innings in a B game than be used like that."

The retirement announcement leaked in Boston of all places, on June 14, where the news was flashed on the scoreboard the same day he made the decision. The Fenway Park crowd gave him a standing ovation.

"Those people all stood up for him," said Yankees pitcher Dave Righetti. "That was respect. That tells you something."

Piniella went 3-for-3 in a 12–11 Yankees victory and joked afterward that maybe he should reconsider.

His last game would be that Saturday, two days later, at Yankee Stadium against Baltimore, the team abiding his wish that he stay active for one last home game, one last game in the pinstripes. In his first at-bat in the second inning, the crowd of 37,583 gave him a minute-long standing ovation.

He went 0-for-5 on the day, hitting into a double play in his final at-bat but driving in the game-winning run with a third-inning fielder's choice in the 8–3 victory. He also nailed Ken Singleton at second when Singleton tried to stretch a hit into a double.

"I hope the guys didn't watch me today because I'd set them back years," said Piniella, overly humble after retiring with a .219 batting average and .319 in 22 World Series games. "I couldn't wait for a good pitch. I was very anxious out there, overanxious."

In the top of the ninth, Berra sent a replacement to left so that Piniella could come off the field to another round of cheers. Anita stood behind the dugout, weeping.

"Believe me, this was a day I'll remember the rest of my life," he said. "I had goose bumps the whole day."

On August 5, the Yankees honored him on Lou Piniella Day. Piniella's wife Anita and their three children, Louis Jr., Derek, and Kristi were there, along with his father Louis and his mother Margaret.

He was presented with an array of lavish gifts including two cars, two trips to Hawaii, one to Acapulco, and another to Japan. Also a bashed-in watercooler and two replacement fluorescent light tubes to symbolize the many more he broke on his way from dugout to clubhouse.

The crowd chanted "Looooou," and Piniella, standing before a microphone at home plate, thought of Lou Gehrig standing on that same spot as he prepared to address the crowd, tears streaming down his face.

He was truly lucky, he thought. He was able to feel the gratitude and affection from the crowd for a long, productive career, and he could optimistically look forward to many years of reflecting back on all of it.

"For the past 10 years, every time I came up to home plate, you people supported me with chants of 'Lou, Lou, Lou,' and I can only tell you how the adrenaline flowed when I heard that, and the desire welled up in my body to do well for you," he told the crowd. "I am forever grateful for that. I thank you for all your warmth, all your kindness, all your support. I love you all. The way I feel today, this is not a farewell, this is only a hello."

* * *

It was the first job interview of his life. And Lou Piniella was nervous.

This was still the Yankees, regardless of the fact that he had already been in the pinstripes for 12 years as a player and coach. Regardless of the fact that Steinbrenner had christened him as the manager-in-waiting in spring training under Yogi Berra and again while on Billy Martin's staff.

Piniella hated all that talk. It was 1985, and while he was ready to start thinking of becoming a manager, he knew he still had a lot of learning to do. But he had been working with Yankee hitters for two years now, before his retirement as a player. Maybe he should have seen this coming.

The first time Steinbrenner had mentioned anything about moving into management was actually August 1982, a full two years before Lou's retirement, when he told Piniella he wanted him to work with the young hitters the following season.

"Does this mean I won't be playing anymore?" Piniella asked.

"You're still an important player," Steinbrenner told him, "but this will start you in another direction down the road."

Piniella felt great. He had begun to see the end of his career coming and he was ready. His body was aching, he was grumpy when Steinbrenner had threatened to fine him over a weight clause in his contract, and he bristled under Bob Lemon's riding. This was nice. This was good.

Over the next two seasons, as he contemplated retirement, he attended meetings with management and actually felt as if he was being heard. Though he was a bit uncomfortable with the dual role, concerned that he maintain his integrity both as a teammate and as a coach, he was learning and maybe even maturing at nearly 40 years old.

Steinbrenner pointed out that he was no longer kicking over watercoolers.

"That's because I found out how much a watercooler cost the ballclub," Piniella wrote in his 1986 autobiography.

He started making critical observations during the 1984 season. And he noticed how Berra, now the manager having replaced Martin, seemed to agree with everything Steinbrenner said in the meetings before really asserting himself later in the season, perhaps when the constant talk of being fired had simply worn him down.

"It was a lesson I took to heart," Piniella wrote. "You can't manage scared. Sooner or later, you'll be fired—every manager knows that—but while you have the job, you must do it your own way."

Of course, he was blissfully unaware of how the pressure under Steinbrenner could bear down on anyone.

February 1985 marked the start of Piniella's first full season as a Yankee coach, but he could hardly enjoy that spring training. Now Steinbrenner was actually telling the press that Piniella would "probably be the next Yankees manager."

The year before, the young players especially had observed in Piniella a genuinely dedicated teacher of hitting. Pitcher Dave Righetti remembered that Charley Lau, Piniella's hitting mentor, was one of the first hands-on batting coaches, a luxury position then for most ballclubs.

"And when they did have them, they were not as hands-on," recalled Righetti. "When Lou took over, he'd be in front of that mirror with the guys, and nobody really had seen that before. And he'd do it anywhere with a guy. The shower, anywhere. He was just really passionate about it."

That year, Piniella took special interest in Don Mattingly, who was coming off his first All-Star selection the season before and had won the American League batting title. Mattingly had hit 23 home runs in 1984 and Piniella saw more potential there.

"For me, Lou was the guy who really had me starting to hit with power," Mattingly said. "As much as anything, he just kind of showed me how the swing worked, which really helped me for teaching too [first as a coach with the Yankees, then with the Dodgers]. He taught me the mechanics, the chain reaction—when you do this, it causes this. I just learned so much about how the swing works.

"Lou would come back to you and say, 'You know, I was in your stance last night and I see right here, you've got to do this' and it always made sense to me. I was always able to take it and use it. He would do it himself and knew exactly what move I was making, what I was doing right and wrong, and he could make a small change and make a big difference. He had me shifting my weight, taught me how to stay back, from Charlie Lau, to use your bottom hand more because that's what creates all the power. I had been using my top hand."

Mattingly hit 35 home runs that season and was named the American League MVP.

But that spring of '85, Piniella was easily distracted after the speculation Steinbrenner had generated by anointing him the next manager.

Piniella sensed some of the players were being a little standoffish and he was embarrassed that Yogi seemed hurt by all the talk. He even went to Berra offering to quit if it would help lessen the pressure but Yogi assured him it would be okay.

Piniella had been anxious to start learning more from the other coaches, infield play from Gene Michael, and pitching from Jeff Torborg and Mark Connor, but the distractions were proving too much to accomplish much of that.

Berra was fired after the 16th game of the season. And Martin, in his fourth go-around as Yankees skipper, lasted only for the remainder of the 1985 season after his second bar brawl and more public feuds with Steinbrenner over the team and his salary.

And there was Piniella. Ready or not. And a little stunned that night in late October 1985, when he received a call summoning him to a meeting with Yankees general manager Clyde King and assistant general manager Woody Woodward during Game 5 of the World Series between his old team, the Kansas City Royals, and the St. Louis Cardinals.

By 6:30 the next evening, sitting in the Steinbrenner's office, Piniella was offered the position of manager of the New York Yankees. A one-year contract for $150,000.

"I think I'd like a two-year contract at $200,000 a year," Piniella recalled saying. After all, he reasoned, he had been making almost that much as a coach.

King told him he'd have to check with Steinbrenner, and Piniella was off to the racetrack, where one of the horses he owned won its race that night. The next day, Piniella was out on a family hike and missed two phone calls by King, who said he would call back but didn't as Piniella impatiently watched Game 6 of the Series.

He should have expected what he would awake to the next morning.

"Lou! Lou! Lou! Piniella To Get Yankee Job," the New York headlines screamed. If only he was so sure of it himself.

By the time he reached the Yankees' offices that Sunday afternoon, he had decided he would concede the length of contract if necessary. He wanted the job, and he was fairly confident that he would be asked back for a second year if he performed up to his expectations.

Sure enough, the Yankees offered one year, but at the $200,000 he wanted, and Piniella jumped at it.

"My heart leaped," Piniella wrote. "I tried to keep my voice even. 'Okay, that's fine. We have a deal.'"

King congratulated him and called him "Skipper," and Piniella became shaky. *Skipper.* Wow. That was what they called Billy Martin, what Piniella had called so many of his former managers—those he liked, those he despised, those with far more experience than he had. He had never been a manager before, let alone a big-league manager, let alone the New York Yankees' manager.

Well, check that. He had taken over for Martin for a series in Cleveland the previous season and it was not exactly a positive experience. So bad was it, in fact, that Piniella went briefly AWOL for a game after, and word spread through the clubhouse that he had quit as the team's hitting coach.

Piniella preferred not to even think about it. But it was an experience that would help define him, traumatic as it was.

He was just starting to get comfortable in the coach's role when the Yankees hit a skid in late July 1985, losing five of six games to drop seven back of first place in the division. Martin was hurting. He had back spasms and while getting an injection for the pain while the team was in Texas, the doctor accidentally punctured a lung and he had to be hospitalized.

Steinbrenner called and informed Piniella that he was to take over while Martin was sidelined and immediately, Piniella saw the red flags. It wasn't Billy who had asked him to take over but Steinbrenner. How would Billy respond? As it turned out, not particularly well since, as Piniella found out, Martin was informed of the switch by Bill Kane, the team's traveling secretary.

Piniella hadn't talked to Billy. Billy hadn't talked to the team. And as the team flew into Cleveland, Piniella was uneasy. The next day, he didn't even know if he was supposed to make out the lineup card, a question that was soon answered when he was told by one of the coaches that Billy would be doing it.

Martin called from his hospital bed to give Piniella the lineup, informing him in no uncertain terms that he was still the manager, still in control of the club and worse, would be in "constant contact" with him.

Anticipating trouble, Piniella agreed that injured catcher Butch Wynegar would answer the dugout phone when Martin called and relay his comments and orders to Piniella or through bench coach Jeff Torborg. Next, Piniella had to practice giving signals, something he had never done before. He had never even learned them because he was afraid, he later explained, that he would then watch Martin and wonder if he would have made the same moves, and he didn't think that would be particularly productive.

Gene Michael, former Yankees manager and now third-base coach, helped him with signals that would be easy enough for him pick up right away, and Piniella stood in front of a mirror in the clubhouse before the game to practice flashing them.

Sure enough, Martin called in each of the first three innings to see what was happening and to check on things like who was getting up and ready in the bullpen. He even called a pitchout and positioned his outfielders based on Wynegar's play-by-play.

Trouble was, no one was very sure Martin was of sound mind. "By the end of the thing, Billy was making no sense," recalled Torborg. "At one point, I think he had a few drinks. I can remember Butch saying one time, 'But Billy, I do like you.'"

All reporters saw was Wynegar talking on the phone, then running to Piniella, and the next day the headlines reflected it.

"Billy Manages Yankees To Victory From Hospital Bed," they read.

The next day, the phone in the dugout never stopped ringing. "This is George Steinbrenner," one caller said. Next it was Billy, ordering someone to pinch-hit or calling a pitching change. Only it wasn't the real Steinbrenner or the real Martin but Indians fans who read that day's paper and made the prank calls that were sailing through the stadium switchboard suspiciously easily. When Martin really did call, he was fuming over all the busy signals.

Now the players saw what was happening and were giggling over the silliness. To Piniella, two days into his managerial career, interim though it was, he had already lost control of his ballclub.

The Yankees won their first two under their temporary skipper, all Martin's doing, of course. Over the next three games, all of which the Yankees lost, one player showered, dressed, and told Piniella he had to attend to a matter at home. Piniella turned him down and referred him to Clyde King.

Another player refused to go into the game as a pinch runner. And another, after Don Mattingly hit into a game-ending double play, openly questioned Piniella's decision in not having him steal second.

Torborg recalled Piniella having him tell a player to enter the game and the player refused. "I was representing Lou and the guy blew me off," said Torborg. "It was very uncomfortable and it made Lou even madder when he saw I was going at it with this particular player."

Recalled Moss Klein, "Each game something went wrong and Willie Randolph was critical of something Lou did. Randolph later felt bad, it wasn't fair to put Lou on the spot. But it was just a very awkward situation."

The prank phone calls to the dugout continued. Piniella himself second-guessed every decision he made, wondering if that was how Billy would have done it, and stewed over his lack of authority. On one trip to the mound, a fan screamed at him, "Is that your decision or is it coming from a hospital bed in Texas?"

"My job," he wrote in his autobiography, "had become a mockery."

After his first game in Cleveland, a victory, Piniella recalled that the trainer, Gene Monahan, had given him a ball inscribed with his name, the date, and the score to commemorate his first official managerial victory.

After the last game in Cleveland, Piniella also recalled that he took the ball and threw it into the urinal in the manager's office.

Piniella told Klein he was quitting, a pronouncement Klein had heard a couple times before when Piniella was still playing.

"I was on the team flight coming back, we get to the Newark airport at 2:00 AM and I'm standing at the luggage carousel with Lou," Klein said. "He tells me, 'This is it, I'm not coming back.'

"I said, 'What do you mean?'

"He said, 'Look, I've been hanging in as a coach. I want to manage, but after going through what I did the last few days, I know I don't want to manage, so what's the point?'

"The next night, the Yankees are playing the White Sox but Lou says, 'I'm not going to show up.'

"I said, 'Come on, Lou, you'll go home, you'll think about it,' but he said, 'No, this time I'm serious. There's no future, so what's the point. I'll do something else. I'm not going to be at the ballpark.'"

Klein had a day off the next day after the long trip, but knew he had to go to the ballpark to see if Piniella showed up. He tried not to elicit any suspicion from the other beat writers.

"A couple guys were surprised to see but I just said I was working on a feature," Klein said. "Then I looked around and sure enough, no Lou. But Billy was back, capturing all the attention. At one point, Billy motioned me over, closed his office door and said, 'I know he talked to you. Anita is on the phone and she wants to talk to you.'

"I didn't want to get involved. I knew if Lou didn't show up, I'd have to write the story. In Billy's office, I get on the phone with Anita and she said, 'I know Lou is down, but he's going to come back tomorrow. Can you just not write the story tonight? If he comes back tomorrow, he doesn't want to deal with this.' I said fine."

Klein's memory is astounding. He recalls the days of the week for every story. He also recalls that this was the night that Dale Berra and Bobby Meacham were thrown out at home plate on the same play. And he remembers his own personal adventure intermingled with Piniella's "retirement."

"So I figure, I'm safe, everyone's busy with that and I can get out of there," Klein said. "At 1:00 that morning, the phone rings and it's Marty Noble [who covered the Yankees for rival *Newsday*]. He said, 'Why were you here tonight?' I said, 'I was working on a feature.' And he said, 'Did it have something to do with Piniella not here tonight?'"

Noble, like the others, might not have even noticed except that White Sox manager Tony La Russa had gone looking for Piniella to say hello and found out from the other coaches that he wasn't there. La Russa mentioned it to his catcher Carlton Fisk, who was friends with Noble. Fisk asked Noble after the game why Lou wasn't there and Noble, knowing Klein was friendly with Lou, assumed he must have been checking on him.

"I said, 'Look, we can't write the story tonight. Tomorrow, if he's not back, I'll tell you and we can both have the story,'" said Klein. "Sure enough, the next day Lou came back. I talked to him; Marty did too. He said, 'I just overreacted.' But he did have a one-day retirement."

Jeff Torborg recalled meeting with coaches in Martin's office the day before, trying to figure out how they were going to talk Piniella into coming back.

"I knew he was furious," Torborg said. "It was a first for him and being the type of competitor he was and the fact that he was such an emotional guy with a short fuse, then to have that nonsense going on. It was a circus. And he was not going to be embarrassed. Lou didn't need that."

Piniella spoke to Martin and Steinbrenner, both of whom sympathized and coaxed him back. He was uncomfortable being the manager-in-waiting, Piniella told them. He was a coach and maybe one day he would be the manager. But until then, he did not care to be put in that position again.

Steinbrenner told reporters that the episode had made Piniella stronger. Billy Martin, meanwhile, ended the 1985 season with an ugly fistfight with Yankees pitcher Ed Whitson that resulted in a broken arm and ribs for Martin, and the Yankees ended it with 97 victories but two games out of first in the AL East.

Typically, Martin exacerbated his situation with salary demands in the press, reasoning that if Earl Weaver and Sparky Anderson were making the big bucks with their teams out of the playoffs, then he ought to make $500,000.

Steinbrenner disagreed.

On October 27, 1985, Piniella was named the new manager of the New York Yankees, the 14th manager in Steinbrenner's 13 years as team owner.

"I know it's a tough job," Piniella said in a conference call with reporters. "But my God, it wasn't easy playing here. I've been here a long time and I've seen different changes in the manager's position.

I'm no fool; I'm coming in here with my eyes open. I know I could be replaced. I just plan on doing a good job."

Would that even matter? Dick Howser, after all, was the last manager the Yankees hired with no professional managing experience, and he led the team to 103 victories in 1980 and was still fired. And the Yankees were not exactly proving to anyone that they were stable. As reporters wrote their postmortems on another Martin "era," no one could prove anyone from the Yankees even officially told Martin that he was out. All the team would say was that Steinbrenner allowed King and Woodward to make the decision.

Of course, no one bought it.

"We felt it was in the best interests of the Yankees to make a change," said Clyde King in making the official announcement. "I don't care to go into details."

Both King and Woodward contend now that it was their decision to make. "I remember Woody and I went back to the stadium on a Saturday, and we had to make our decision real quick," said King. "Woody was very helpful and I said, 'My pick is Lou Piniella,' and he agreed right away. There was no discussion.

"Lou had done everything he needed to do. There was enough fire in him, the knowledge from having played for several good managers and that helped. Lou had it all."

Berra said in a 2008 interview that Piniella was ready, fittingly slipping in a famous Yogi-ism.

"You don't know anybody can be a manager that fast but he was intelligent," Berra said. "He sat on the bench when he wasn't playing and he observed a lot by watching. That's what you do if you want to become manager sometime."

But Berra also knew from experience that it wouldn't be easy for Piniella.

"That's the thing," he said of the fact that Steinbrenner made it tough on every manager he had. "And he always held these meetings. You just couldn't take it much longer with George."

King said Piniella's ability to walk the line as a player between the sort of leader Steinbrenner would confide in and the sort of teammate other players would follow, was what got the Yankees' front office believing he was managerial material.

"Lou fought for his team, he would run into walls, he would dive for balls," said King. "I'll never forget the play he made at Fenway with the sun in his eyes, being smart enough [to bluff that he was going to make the catch], making that throw [to third to hold Rick Burleson at second and Jerry Remy to a single in the Yankees–Red Sox one-game playoff in 1978].

"Lou did whatever it took to win. He always put the team first. Lou never looked at his average. If there was a man on second with nobody out, Lou would be the one to hit to the other side, and when you see a player like that, you know one day they're going to be a leader."

King said he suggested that Piniella spend a season managing in winter ball. "I asked him, 'Lou, the winter league is going to go soon. I can get you a job for three months,' and he said, 'Clyde, I really don't think I need it,' and as it turned out, he really didn't," King recalled. "He said, 'I've learned from some good managers.'"

Woodward, also in a 2008 interview, said that the odds were against Piniella succeeding. "I have to admit, if someone asked me today, 'What avenue should you take to be a major-league manager?' you would say, 'You manage in the minor leagues for a period of time just so you're running a team by yourself, or you go to winter ball and manage a team.' Many good managers have taken that approach. But I also must admit in this case I wasn't even worried. Everything was just right, he could handle New York, the fans liked Lou. It still remained to be seen how he handled things in the dugout, but he had good training."

Piniella told reporters that he had been offered jobs in Puerto Rico and Venezuela but that he had kids in school and other commitments to his family.

"I just didn't feel it was that important to manage in the winter leagues as a prerequisite to managing in the major leagues," he said in the conference call.

Piniella also revealed the length of his contract and said he was okay with it.

"We talked about a two-year [deal]," he said, "but quite frankly, I'm a new manager and the organization felt better about one year. I played a lot of years with a one-year contract and it made me prove myself every year. If I do a good job, I won't have to worry. If I don't, well, it remains to be seen."

In an interview with Ira Berkow of the *New York Times* in November, Piniella made it clear he wasn't exactly sure himself how it all went down.

"I guess I was sort of hand-picked," he said, "but George called me and said he was surprised. He thought they'd choose somebody else."

Piniella originally asked Berra to be his bench coach, admiring, among other things, how the former manager "nurtured" pitchers, something he admitted he knew little about.

Admitting that he was similar in his "aggressiveness" to Martin, Piniella said he aspired to have the tolerance of Berra. "He showed me that patience is an art," he said of Berra, who ended up turning down his offer. "Just because you have a certain position of responsibility, it doesn't mean you have to be uncivil."

Al Rosen, president of the Yankees in 1978 and '79, had heard that some compare Piniella's managing style to that of Martin's but disagreed.

"I like to see guys with fire in their bellies but there are different ways to express it, and I don't see similarities between Lou and Billy," Rosen said. "Lou, while fiery and demanding, doesn't evoke antagonism and doesn't hold grudges. I doubt that Lou, other than getting in the face of a player, ever tried to purposely embarrass a player in public."

Michael was not inclined to make many comparisons either.

"Lou was very cooperative, and that's what let him get along with everybody," he said. "He didn't have a big head of hatred for Billy, but he didn't necessarily like him. He did respect him as a manager because he copied him a lot when he started managing. I knew then that he respected him."

In preparation for his first managerial job, Piniella said he planned to be a stickler for being on time and would treat every player equally when it came to team rules. He felt that was something too easy to compromise on when dealing with veterans, and that was the last thing he wanted to do.

As for Billy, he felt badly for him. He had been his manager and his mentor in many ways and here he was taking his job. He had to convince himself it was not his fault; it was not his decision. And to make himself feel better, Piniella remembered a conversation he had with Martin at the end of the season at a dinner with the coaching staff.

"You will manage this club next year," Piniella recalled Martin saying.

"No, Billy, you'll be back," he told him.

"You'll manage this club next year and you can call me anytime you want and I'll give you any advice you need," Martin had said.

It still made Piniella sad.

The next day in the New York papers, the Royals' victory in the World Series seemed very small indeed compared to the giant headlines announcing Piniella as the new Yankees manager. In his autobiography, Piniella described a transformation that occurred inside him that night, the realization of the immense responsibility that was now his.

Just 14 months after he had stood in Yankee Stadium being honored upon his retirement on Lou Piniella Day, he was in charge. And if he forgot, there was George to remind him.

"Remember, you're in charge," Steinbrenner told him after the first staff meeting with Piniella as manager. "You make the rules but be sure you enforce them."

Years later, managing the Cubs, Piniella still remembered the conversation. "He said, 'I'm going to be tough on you, but you're capable. Go down and win me a championship.' That, I didn't do. I tried my darndest, but I learned a lot there in the few years I was managing the team."

In the winter of 1985, Piniella reflected that whatever happened in the year to come, it was going to be all right.

"I realize what a lucky guy I am," he wrote. "I have a beautiful family and a nice home. I have more money now than I could ever have imagined when I was a kid in Tampa. I have wonderful friends. I am a contented man, and success or failure as a Yankee manager cannot change that."

* * *

Lou Piniella looked forward to his first spring training as Yankee manager. But as it got underway in the late winter of 1986, he soon learned that especially in New York, or even in Fort Lauderdale, no one was going to give him a coronation.

Could he handle one of the toughest jobs in all of sports with no experience behind him? Could he motivate players who were former teammates? Could he handle a pitching staff? And most important, was he capable of leading the Yankees back to the World Series?

Reporters interviewed other former first-timers like Pete Rose, second in the voting for Manager of the Year the season before as player-manager with the Reds, and Jim Frey, who won the American League pennant with Kansas City in his first year with the Royals. Piniella's former manager and longtime nemesis Earl Weaver even chimed in.

"I don't care who you are, you're going to have some flare-ups with your personnel, so that's where going through it a time or two before could be advantageous to you," Weaver was quoted as saying. "You don't want to be a hothead and paint yourself into a corner in any one situation. There are many ways to handle any one situation, and the more you handle those situations, the better off you're going to be at it."

Gee, thanks Earl.

Piniella found himself constantly defending himself.

"Managing is a people business," he said. "You're dealing with individuals. If you can get along with people, if you have knowledge of the game, if you're willing to listen and learn, there's no reason why [prior experience] is a prerequisite for the job. If the Yankees felt that way, I wouldn't have the job."

Piniella said he wouldn't be afraid to ask for help from his coaches and brought in veteran Joe Altobelli, who led the Orioles to the world championship in his first year succeeding Weaver. Piniella said he would also count on his familiarity with players to help him know his team that much better.

As for his famous temper, Piniella promised that people would see a different side of him.

"Look, I don't want to lose what got me here," he told the *New York Times*. "What kept me in the major leagues was my dedication to the game and my temperament. It brought out the best in me. I can't lose that aspect. But I'm not going to be out on that field to show anybody up or make a fool of myself. There has to be a valid reason. I plan to be as level-headed as I possibly can. I've got that Spanish temperament, that blood, whatever it is, and I get a little excited. There's nothing wrong with that."

The Yankees would finish 17–11 in the spring of 1986, and a winning record in the spring was always very important to Steinbrenner. Win games in the spring, he preached, and you'll sell tickets in the summer.

Piniella tried to be optimistic. He knew Steinbrenner considered him to be like another son. He figured maybe he'd be immune to all the second-guessing and meddling Steinbrenner had made a habit with Billy and every other manager he'd had.

"Maybe I'm going to be the guy to break the mold and stay here for a number of years," Piniella said.

But he wasn't deluding himself. Among the few adornments in his new office in Yankee Stadium was a cartoon that had two bums sitting on a park bench, looking at a newspaper.

"Here's a part-time job," the first bum said. "It's outdoors and lasts for just a few weeks this summer."

"What is it?" the other asked. "Yard work or construction?"

"No," the first bum said. "Managing the Yankees."

He tried to make light of it. At the first sign of Steinbrenner's tactics—second-guessing his lineup in a spring training game—Piniella joked that The Boss could trade places with him. Be the manager for the day. Make out the lineup. Flash signs for stealing and bunting and the hit-and-run to third-base coach Gene Michael, who would relay them to the players.

In Phil Pepe's *The Ballad of Billy and George*, he described how Steinbrenner first agreed and then tried to back out.

"Oh, no you don't," he told Piniella. "You're not going to trick me that easy. You're the manager. You do the managing. I'm the owner. I'll do the second-guessing. That's the way it's supposed to be."

Despite some tension over the waiving of 47-year-old future Hall of Famer Phil Niekro—George for, Lou against, George wins—at the end of spring training, everyone was optimistic as the new season dawned.

Opening Day was glorious. A capacity crowd of 55,000. Yanks vs. Royals with Piniella's old buddy, Dick Howser, the Kansas City manager. Piniella estimated he must have smoked two packs of cigarettes before giving the umps his lineup card, and he was puffing on another cigarette in his office surrounded by reporters when he took Steinbrenner's call on the infamous red phone after the game, a 4–2 New York victory.

"I was really feeling high," Piniella wrote in an afterword to his autobiography. "I thought to myself how nice managing the Yankees was going to be. Then reality set in. George isn't too quick with his compliments.

"It was the last time he congratulated me all year."

Piniella would only get ejected from three games in his first season as manager, which was 27 short of the prediction from his old friend and former Yankees coach Mike Ferraro. He would play Dave Winfield despite the Boss' suggestion that he not. And the Yankees would win 90 games, though missing the playoffs.

"When he was first hired, he was not a good manager," said Michael. "He didn't have a good idea how to manage, he didn't know how to handle pitchers yet, he didn't know how to handle the base running part.

"In a lot of ways, he was a lot like Billy in that he was quick to judge. Lou didn't like that about Billy but Lou was like that. And like Billy, he didn't have a lot of patience.

"He'd lose some confidence in players and was too critical at times. I knew it was one of those things he had to get over. I used to point it out to him when he was first managing, 'Lou, you're a little too volatile in the dugout towards players and too critical. You can't show that in the dugout. You have to keep it to yourself.' He eventually got over it."

But of all the things that would begin to distinguish Lou Piniella as a manager in his first year on the job, there were moments that will only be remembered by a few intimately involved. One of those was Dave Righetti, who said he will never forget Piniella for the sacrifice he made for him during that 1986 season.

"The time Lou came was perfect for me," Righetti recalled. "There was a lot of turmoil. There was a ton of it over what to do with me. Should we start him? Should we keep him in relief?"

Three summers before, Righetti, at the tender age of 24, had fired a no-hitter for the Yankees but the next season, because of a surplus of starters, he was moved to the bullpen to replace Goose Gossage as the team's closer. A former Rookie of the Year, Righetti would prove effective at each, following up a season in which he won 14 games with a season in which he would save 31. In 1985, he had another strong year with 29 saves, but he struggled under the public debate and internal team criticism of where he should stay.

And to make things harder, just as he began building confidence as a reliever, Berra waffled on the subject.

Before Piniella was named manager, Righetti panicked. "I thought, 'Oh my God, who's going to be here to make the decision? And is he going to be around to make sure it happens?'"

Piniella, said Righetti, made sure. And he was sure. Particularly when Righetti needed him most during what he called "easily the worst episode of my career."

It was the last weekend before the 1986 All-Star break and Righetti, on his way to breaking the major-league save record of 45 held by Dan Quisenberry and Bruce Sutter, was about to be named to the American League All-Star team. But he had been struggling of late, and when the second-place Yankees arrived in Toronto to play the Blue Jays on June 19, Righetti was greeted by damning quotes from The Boss.

"The late-inning guys were doing a lot more pitching then and I had blown a few games, not all in the ninth, sometimes in the seventh or eighth," Righetti recalled. "We were winning some of those games too, but you start to feel guilty. And then I open up the *Globe and Mail* [Toronto's paper] and it's not a real big sports section and it was like George did it on purpose or something.

"It was on the front page. I was crushed. I'm like, 'Jesus, is he trying to motivate me?'"

In an interview with the paper, Steinbrenner, fuming over a four-game slide, most recently to the division-leading Red Sox, lambasted a number of players, including favorite target Dave Winfield, Ron Guidry, Ken Griffey, and Piniella, who he said was a "young manager and he's made some young man's mistakes. Let's leave it at that."

But, of course, Steinbrenner did not leave it at that regarding other players.

Of Winfield: "He's clutch on defense but not on offense. People make the mistake of comparing him to Reggie Jackson."

Of Guidry: "He's supposed to be our ace but he's been absolutely terrible. If Guidry can't handle it, he won't be in the starting rotation. I'm concerned about the way he looks. He's got nothing on the ball."

By comparison, what he said about Righetti was almost tame: "I expected a lot from him but he's been disappointing," said Steinbrenner. "He's single-handedly blown four or five games."

Steinbrenner's latest comments only made matters worse. That night, Righetti was the losing pitcher as the Jays won 10–9 in 10 innings and handed the Yankees their fifth straight loss.

Afterward, Righetti agreed with reporters that the Yankees' deficit in the divisional race was getting bigger. "But we're not panicking like the guy upstairs," he said.

Righetti then walked to the other end of the clubhouse and yelled, "He's never played a game in his life for this team."

The next night made that night seem downright pleasant, however, as Righetti came in with an 8–2 lead in the ninth and gave up a game-tying grand slam to George Bell.

"Doug Drabek got in a little trouble in the ninth," said Righetti. "He was a rookie going for his first win, there were two guys on, and by the time the third guy came up to the plate, I was on the mound. I think I threw one pitch to warm up."

Righetti, summoned in with the Yanks leading 8–2, struck out pinch-hitter Buck Martinez before Damaso Garcia, who had delivered the game-winning double off of him the night before, lined a single to drive in a run. Tony Fernandez followed with another single to make it 8–4, and Righetti then walked Garth Iorg to load the bases.

"I struck out [Lloyd Moseby] for two outs," Righetti recounted 22 years later. Then on my [second] pitch to George Bell, he hits this high fly ball and I'm going, 'That looks like it might go out of here. Please don't.' But it does for a grand slam to tie the game and the place goes nuts."

Righetti stood on the mound as Bell circled the bases, looking toward Don Denkinger for the new ball and steaming.

"The unwritten rule is that umpires who had any respect for you, when they know you just gave up a big homer, they won't throw you the new ball right away," said Righetti. "They'll kind of wait a little, then slip you the ball quietly. But Denkinger was just standing there and I kept saying, 'Give me the ball. Give me the ball,' and he wouldn't do it.

"I must have said, 'Give me the damn ball,' and he wasn't going to do it. I should've realized that. But now everyone is done high-fiving and he says, 'Here's the ball,' and I said, 'No, here's your ball,' and I turned and threw it over the right-field fence. It went from pandemonium to where you could hear a pin drop. I could actually hear Phil Rizutto up there, 'Well, there's nothing wrong with his arm.'"

After the game, which the Yankees came back to win 10–8 in the tenth, Righetti declined to speak to reporters. But Piniella offered only support.

"Seeing Rags throw the ball over the wall reminded me of myself," Piniella said. "When I struck out, I'd go out to right field and try to heave the ball out of the stadium if I could. I was proud to see him do it. It got the frustration out of him. He'll be back in there tomorrow."

The next day, talk back in New York, this time from Steinbrenner and his son Hank, now in the front office, as well as up in the booth, where Billy Martin was a commentator and "special consultant" to the club, centered on returning Righetti to the starting rotation.

"He's killed us," said the Boss. "I'm not going to baby my players. He's earning a half-million dollars a year, and he's got to be able to take the pressure. We don't need Righetti like he's been. We need him like he should be."

But Piniella stood behind his pitcher and was adamant about keeping Righetti in the bullpen, where he had saved 76 games in barely two and a half seasons.

"As long as I'm the manager, he's our reliever," said Piniella after Righetti had lost another lead to the Jays in another 10-inning game the Yankees won, 4–2. "He's saved 16 games and you can add another 16 or 17 by the time the season is over. He's human. Hitters fall into slumps and so do pitchers. We need him in the bullpen. That's where he belongs."

That was all Righetti needed to hear. He would break Quisenberry and Sutter's record by one save that season with 46, the clincher coming in a game in which Piniella would give him the ball to pitch the last out in the ninth. "It was the first time I ever got a save that way," said Righetti.

"Now, it's no big deal. Then, people thought it cheapened it. But Lou said, 'No, he deserves it, he earned it.' In a funny way, I didn't know how to act but obviously, I appreciated he did it."

And twenty-two years later, he still appreciates what Piniella did for him.

"Lou came out and said, 'I don't care what anybody says, he's my guy.' He put all his eggs in my basket. In a sense, he put his career as a rookie manager on the line for me. There was somebody fired every year almost and for Lou to do that, it showed how confident he was in himself and what he thought was right. And I'll never forget it as long as I live."

The good news for Piniella in 1986 is that he survived the season. And the next, becoming the first Yankees manager since Martin in 1976–77 to manage the team for two consecutive full seasons. The Yankees would draw 50,000 more fans than the previous season, always important to the Boss. And despite finishing second again to the Red Sox, Piniella would even get a two-year contract extension and a raise to $250,000 for 1988 and $300,000 for 1989.

What he could not have envisioned was that he would spend part of the '88 season and '89 as the team's general manager.

Spring training of 1987 was, as are most major-league spring training camps, brimming with optimism. But once again, the questions centered on Steinbrenner, Piniella's job, and how long he figured he would have it.

Piniella told reporters he promised himself he would not worry about it.

"You can't play scared," he said. "You can't manage scared."

He appeared calm at least.

"I'm certainly going to be more relaxed," he said. "I know my job better. Last year, I didn't just have to prove to the organization and the players that I could manage, but also to myself. Now that barrier is out of the way, I'm confident. I've got a two-year contract. I know my personnel, and I feel secure in my position."

Piniella believed he had greater depth that season. In his first season as manager, his team won 90 games with only one pitcher having won more than 10 games. But the Yankees had traded for Rick Rhoden, signed Gary Ward to a free-agent contract, and re-signed Willie Randolph. Still, there was criticism over the club's failure to sign baseball's best pitcher, Jack Morris, or their own Ron Guidry over a difference of $50,000.

On the day before the Yankees broke camp in Fort Lauderdale, Steinbrenner was asked if Piniella would still be around in May if he had a bad April. It would appear a ridiculous question unless you considered that Yogi Berra was launched just 16 games into the '85 season.

For the record, Steinbrenner said, "Yes."

On June 10, Piniella was ejected from a one-sided Yankees loss to Toronto. The Yankees and Blue Jays had the best records in the American League, but Piniella was not happy, and not just because of a borderline call on a Blue Jays steal.

Toronto had just swept the three-game series with the Yankees batting a collective .161. The Yankees had lost five of their last seven games against AL East opponents and had 19 more to go in a row. Rickey Henderson and Don Mattingly were out with injuries.

On July 22, the Yankees lost 3–1 to the Twins in Minneapolis, the fourth loss in their last five games, and Steinbrenner said he intended to fly back from his home in Tampa to attend the Yankees' game against the last-place White Sox.

"If this continues, then you'll hear from me," Steinbrenner said of the Yankees' slump.

Things were about to get worse.

In early August, with the Yankees leading the American League East by one-half game with a 66–45 record, Steinbrenner issued a scathing public critique of his manager while the team was in Detroit.

The two had been at odds since Piniella had complained about the club's unwillingness to call up catcher Joel Skinner from their Columbus farm club. Steinbrenner was enraged two days later when he tried to contact Piniella in his Cleveland hotel room to discuss the matter, and Piniella was not there to answer his call and did not return two messages.

The Yankees' irascible owner made thinly veiled threats that he was going to fire Piniella for his insubordination and had Joe Altobelli and Clyde King join the team on the road, a move many viewed as Steinbrenner sending the two to spy on Piniella.

Then, while the team was in Detroit, Steinbrenner revealed private comments in a statement to reporters that had supposedly been made by Piniella, including that Piniella had asked to have Rickey Henderson traded. He also implied that Piniella had called Mark Salas, one of the Yankees' catchers, "a bum."

Steinbrenner later told reporters that Piniella never said that. "That was my statement of how can a guy be great one minute and a bum the next?" he said.

Yankees players read the statement in the trainer's room after the game in Detroit, and in a spirited show of unity and support of Piniella, lit the paper on fire afterward.

Still, the damage had been done. Piniella and Steinbrenner did not talk to one another for 26 days, and the team ended up 23–28 the rest of the way, finishing the season in fourth place, nine games in back of the first-place Tigers.

Three years later, as manager of the Cincinnati Reds, the episode was still eating at Piniella.

"The biggest mistake I made was not answering George back," Piniella told reporters on the eve of the National League Championship Series. "I was being loyal because I was getting paid. I should have come out and blasted him. I should have made my point. For a young manager with no experience to take over a team like that, managing players you played with and still winning 90 and 89 games, that wasn't a bad job."

There were extenuating circumstances that 1987 season, to be sure. Piniella went 101 games without Rickey Henderson, Don Mattingly, or Willie Randolph in the lineup. But even as Piniella moved into second place behind Billy Martin for most games managed under Steinbrenner, a somewhat oxymoronic distinction, there was little question that the season had taken a toll on everyone.

"It's been hard since Detroit," Piniella conceded in an interview at the end of the season. "It just took a lot out of me. It toughens you. It hardens you. I'm sure [the players] noticed the change."

"He became a lot more subdued after that thing with George," second baseman and team captain Willie Randolph told the *New York Times*. "I think it would have worn down most managers. You give your all, you're living and dying with the team, it's got to weigh on you emotionally. Any time you manage a ballclub all season, it has got to take a little out of you. If you're an emotional type like Lou, it takes a little more."

"Other people it kills," said third baseman Mike Pagliarulo. "With Lou, maybe it will help him down the line."

With speculation about Piniella's impending firing hovering over the last months of the season like the suffocating summer heat, Steinbrenner allowed Piniella to hang, issuing cryptic remarks about the future and some not so cryptic.

"If I made a mistake [in hiring Piniella], it was in not demanding that he manage in the minors," Steinbrenner told the *New York Times* on August 13, 1987, during their 26-day estrangement. "I may have done him a great disservice because of that, and maybe it's my fault. But if you're going to be boss of a team, you cannot be one of the boys. You've got to do what needs to be done to win."

The Times cited multiple team sources as saying that Steinbrenner sent Piniella a letter saying that he was waiting for an apology and an explanation for him not returning the call in Cleveland, where Piniella's fate seemed to be sealed.

"I haven't heard so much as a peep," said Steinbrenner. "I am more disappointed than angry. He says he's hurt. Well, I'm more hurt."

Not so hurt, however, to completely banish one of the favorite sons from the organization. On Monday, October 19, 1987, the Yankees announced that Billy Martin would be replacing Piniella as manager and, in typical Steinbrenner fashion, Piniella would become general manager, replacing Woody Woodward, who said that he asked to leave four weeks earlier.

It would be the fifth and final time Billy Martin was hired as the Yankees' manager.

Of course, Steinbrenner's announcement came right in the middle of the Cardinals-Twins World Series. And Piniella's mind was on other things. Moss Klein, the longtime Yankees beat writer from the *Newark Star-Ledger*, called Lou at home and Anita told him he was at his restaurant. When Klein called there, Piniella was on the phone with Steinbrenner. On his other line was his stockbroker.

October 19, 1987, would later be called "Black Monday," the largest one-day percentage decline in stock market history worldwide at the time. "Lou said later, 'I couldn't wait to get George off the phone and get rid of my IBM stock before it went out of business,'" Klein recalled.

Some Yankees players were stunned at Piniella's firing/promotion, some annoyed, and some, who had been there for a while, treated it as just another day at the circus.

"I feel like Lou didn't have to be fired, unless it had to do with something he and George went through," said Randolph, a former Piniella teammate. "But if it was done strictly based on what he did on the field, I don't think he warranted being fired. I thought he did a decent job."

For Piniella, his dream job had been taken from him. And maybe a bit of his spirit along with it.

"It could be fun," he said. "Or it *should* be."

Nobody ever said that the general manager's job was supposed to be fun, however. And as New York digested Piniella's change in jobs and the fifth incarnation of Billy Martin, Dave Anderson pointed out one of the many ironies of the situation in the *New York Times*.

"As the Yankees fell to fourth place in the final weeks of the [1987 season]," Anderson wrote, "Steinbrenner acknowledged having made a mistake in not having Piniella manage in the minors before taking over the Yankees for the 1986 season. But typical of Steinbrenner's strange logic, he has now knighted Piniella as a general manager with no front-office experience."

Woodward said he thought it was a mistake from the beginning.

"My contract was for two or three more years," said Woodward, "and I said, 'George, I'm going to leave,' but he wouldn't let me go. I don't know where he came up with the idea [of naming Piniella GM] but I thought putting Lou in the front office was taking a very good big-league manager and putting him in an area that wasn't right for him. You could see this fella had ability in the clubhouse to control his team, utilize talent, and you were sending him upstairs and putting him behind a desk? It didn't make sense.

"Personally? I was tickled to death because I was able to leave. But I didn't think it was a good move for Lou, I really didn't."

Still, as Piniella got to work on his new job that winter, his boss praised his work ethic.

"The only time I haven't let a general manager get involved in things is if he hasn't done his homework," Steinbrenner said. "This guy is doing his homework. I'm throwing things in his lap, and I defy anybody to come in and shoot holes through what he's done so far."

Piniella countered by saying that he felt Steinbrenner trusted him.

"I can make the moves that need to be made," he told the *New York Times*. "The man has faith in my ability to know talent and make viable trades."

Righetti admitted it was strange. First Piniella was their teammate, then their manager. "And now he's really my boss," Righetti said of Piniella's move to GM. "My contract was up, I was a free agent for the first time, and now it kind of gets personal because he's going to deal with my agent and everything's on a different level now. He was just yelling at me for hanging an 0–2 pitch or something. Now he's got to do this contract with me. It was uncomfortable, without a doubt."

On the surface, it appeared that Piniella was comfortable as the middle of a George and Billy sandwich. In the papers, however, the story went that Martin spent most of the season "backstabbing" Piniella to Steinbrenner and others around the league, both in regard to Piniella's field managing and general managing. Piniella also had to endure Martin sitting in the owner's box his first months on the job. Martin was under contract as a special consultant and often critical of Piniella from many accounts.

But Piniella defended their friendship and Martin's critiques during his broadcast work for the Yankee telecasts, saying he had a right to his opinion and that he "loved" Martin.

Conversely, Piniella was probably the best friend that Martin had in the organization, someone who could be the perfect buffer between him and Steinbrenner. But clearly Martin resented Piniella serving in a role that he always felt he could and should handle from the field. And Martin had some leverage.

Again and again, Steinbrenner's comment from August 1987 would come to haunt Piniella. After Piniella had said he wanted more input as manager into player moves, Steinbrenner told reporters that he considered Piniella to be "the worst judge of talent in the organization."

Steinbrenner had been bickering at the time with Piniella, and so it could be argued that George was just being George. It was also put forth that perhaps Piniella was only placed in the GM role as a pawn, so that Steinbrenner had another available threat for Martin. "You mess up? I can have Lou back in the dugout tomorrow."

The whole thing was embarrassing to Piniella at a time when he was trying to establish credibility as a general manager. And in May 1988, he had had enough, resigning after seven months as GM, saying he would remain with the Yankees in a scouting and player-evaluation capacity.

Piniella cited the daily grind of the job, which he disliked intensely, rather than any problems with Steinbrenner or Martin, despite reported friction between the two.

"After 25 years in uniform," Piniella said, "I wasn't used to the office aspects of it, the confinement. I enjoy the baseball part of it very much. When I talked to other general managers about talent, I enjoyed that aspect.... As GM, you're close to the action but also far away. Now I have a chance to go out and watch other people play."

"The whole production was a dog and pony show," said Klein. "Steinbrenner wanted Lou and Billy to go around together, and Lou didn't like that at all. On one hand, he wanted to see what being an executive was like, but in his heart, he liked being on the field."

Bill Madden agreed.

"Lou would've been a great general manager if George would've let him," he said. "He's actually a pretty good judge of talent. George gave him the job and then told him he couldn't do it."

Meanwhile, typical chaos reigned as Bob Quinn, former vice president for baseball administration, was set to become Steinbrenner's 11th general manager in 16 years, but Steinbrenner would not finalize anything.

So what should a general manager from another club do if he wanted to discuss a potential trade with the Yankees, Quinn was asked by the *New York Times*? "Call Lou Piniella," Quinn said.

Asked the same question, Piniella said, "I would say he's got to talk to Bob Quinn."

One day after Piniella announced his resignation as GM, Dave Anderson, columnist for the *New York Times*, wrote in his lead, "Now that Lou Piniella is no longer the Yankees' general manager, he's the obvious choice to be recycled sooner or later as the next Yankees manager."

It was an obvious assumption. After all, this was the way Steinbrenner did things.

Piniella did say, "I'd like to manage again. And there's a very good chance I'll be a manager again."

Still under contract to Steinbrenner with the last contract extension he had signed as manager, Piniella could technically be ordered back to manage by Steinbrenner, if and when he fired Martin for the fifth time.

"A lot of the contracts with the Yankees were personal services contracts back then," Woodward explained. "You didn't necessarily sign a contract saying you were GM or this or that, so the Boss could move you from one position to the other and you had no choice, at least the way we thought. I don't think anybody ever tried to challenge it. We thought he could do it, you kept making money, and they paid very well."

That said, Woodward laughed, "I really didn't think Lou would go back after the first time [he was fired], so I was a little surprised he came back for a second tenure."

Everyone knew that was an eventuality, and sure enough, on June 23, 1988, a month after he had resigned as general manager, Piniella began his second tenure as Yankees manager replacing Martin. Piniella signed a three-year, $1.2 million deal, only $50,000 more than he was making per year, but it was his longest contract this time.

The Martin firing was preceded by a road trip in which the Yankees lost seven of nine games and fell into second place. But as always the case with Martin, there was considerably more involved.

On a May road trip to Texas, Martin was ejected from a game for arguing with the umpire. What followed was a brawl in a topless bar that resulted in 40 stitches near his ear and reportedly, Steinbrenner's first suspicions that Martin had a drinking problem.

Martin was ejected from another game, throwing handfuls of dirt at umpire Dale Scott and receiving a three-game suspension.

But problems were also traced back to Piniella, who many believed resigned his post as general manager because of his conflicts with Martin over personnel. Of course, there was also the story that what really pushed Piniella to quit was the day he was listening to the radio in his car and heard of a player move by the Yankees that as GM he knew nothing about.

But on the day Martin was fired, Piniella appeared confident he would be back in the Yankee uniform to stay—at least for a while.

"I am not an interim manager, that I can tell you," he told reporters. "I wouldn't come back on an interim basis."

Piniella was the Yankees' 16th manager in 16 seasons, the fourth manager to come back for at least a second regime since Steinbrenner had become the principal owner of the team in 1973. And he would make his presence known immediately.

In his first game, he moved right fielder Dave Winfield back up to the third spot in the batting order from fifth and sixth, where Martin had him. He also said he would return Dave Righetti to the bullpen as his stopper.

The Yankees were 40–28 and in second place, two and one-half games out of first in their division when Martin was fired. They would go 45–48 the rest of the way under Piniella but slipped to fifth place the last two days of the season and finished three and one-half games out as New York failed to reach the playoffs for the seventh consecutive season.

That was all Steinbrenner needed.

On October 7, 1988, for the second time in 355 days, Piniella was fired as Yankees manager, this time being replaced by Dallas Green—this time for the last time.

"When George hired Lou as manager, he wasn't ready," Gene Michael said. "When he let him go, Lou was a really good manager. That's the ironic part about it."

Now Piniella was truly a hot commodity with speculation immediately surfacing that he could go to Houston, the Angels, the White Sox, or Seattle, where Woody Woodward was now the Mariners general manager.

In almost three seasons, Piniella's clubs had a record of 224–193 for a .537 winning percentage.

Steinbrenner praised Piniella and pointed to injuries and pitchers' problems hurting the team but was not very specific about why he was firing him again.

"The bottom line with Mr. Steinbrenner is winning," Green offered. "Apparently he wasn't satisfied with the way Lou went about it or the results."

Piniella spent a good part of the next month fishing, swimming, and walking on the beach in Florida. He was still under a three-year personal services contract with the Yankees and had the option to come back in broadcasting or scouting, but he wasn't interested. His heart was still in managing.

Just not in New York.

"If the situation were right, yes, I'd be interested," he said. "But I don't want to go through what I went through here."

Steinbrenner felt it difficult to let go of the fatherly pull he had on Piniella. At one point, Stan Williams, a longtime friend, coach, and scout for the Yankees, recalled the Blue Jays wanted Piniella to come to Toronto to talk about their managerial opening.

"Steinbrenner said, 'You can go, but I'm not going to give permission for the club to sign you,'" Williams said. "Lou said, 'Why the hell should I go then?' George said, 'It'll be a good experience for you to learn how these things go.'"

All in all, Piniella was relieved. He had known Steinbrenner was going to make a change for the last several weeks of the season. And now it looked as if his 15 years with the New York Yankees were really over.

"Things didn't work out, and I'm very happy, extremely happy, to be in the position I'm in," Piniella said.

Still, observed Madden, "There was always that pull in him that he never accomplished what he believed he could've accomplished in New York, and I think he would've wanted to do it one more time."

CHAPTER 5

Good-bye George, Hello Marge

L ou Piniella may have considered Billy Martin to be a mentor, but he was not about to follow him down the road of serial managing where the Yankees and George Steinbrenner were concerned. Two times was bad enough. Piniella was not interested in going for the trifecta.

After the Yankees, he briefly considered going to the Blue Jays. "They stay with people and give you a chance," he said of Toronto at the time. "That's something I'd like to see them do [in New York]."

If Piniella needed any reminders of why he did not want to climb back onto the Steinbrenner merry-go-round, Dallas Green had just been fired in the late summer of 1989 and the Boss had given Piniella all of a half hour to decide if he wanted to manage the Yankees again after offering the job over the phone.

On top of that, Piniella was actually enjoying his new endeavor as a baseball color analyst for the Yankees, especially the free time it afforded him for his family, golf, the track, and other business involvements. Most of all, he appreciated the noticeable absence of stress.

Although he still had two years remaining on a personal services contract with the Yankees and remained loyal to the organization after 16 years, Piniella had not exactly moved past the fact that he had been fired twice as manager.

"I'm bitter about that," he told Steve Jacobson of *Newsday.*

However, as is so often the case among those in coaching and managing on any level, it's not that easy to walk away. The next job is always gnawing at you, the next challenge, however unappealing, is still enticing.

At 46 years old, "It isn't entirely out of my system," Piniella admitted to Jacobson. But Piniella was looking for continuity, for a place where he could settle in for a few years and develop a relationship with his coaching staff, his scouts. A place where he could be a real authority figure to players who did not tune him out because as much as they may like him, they know he'll be gone before they are.

Whether consciously at the time or not, Piniella was looking for a place where he was free to actually make decisions that managers make regarding their ballclub without the owner barking demands and constantly interfering.

Marge Schott would not necessarily appear to be the dream boss. But to Piniella, Schott and Cincinnati seemed like paradise.

So much so, that on November 3, 1989, Piniella took a $50,000-per year pay cut from his Yankees contract in signing a three-year deal for a reported $350,000 annually to manage the Reds. He replaced Tommy Helms, who had taken over on an interim basis after Pete Rose was banned from baseball the previous August for allegedly gambling on baseball.

Still, Piniella would later wonder why he bypassed five managing jobs because he was not ready to return, only to then go to the Reds.

"I had a nice job with little pressure and little aggravation," he said. "It was better-paying. That, plus the fact that if I did come back and failed, people would say George was right in the first place."

For former Yankees executive and now Reds general manager Bob Quinn, hiring Piniella was a no-brainer. For the Reds, coming off a fifth-place finish in the National League West with a 75–87 record and still smarting over the Rose scandal, it symbolized a fresh start for a proud and wounded organization that needed to move on from its hero.

Piniella's charm helped ease the transition.

"I was in Cincinnati once for the 1976 World Series and that was for three days," he said at his introductory news conference, referring to the Reds' four-game sweep of the Yankees. "I'll be here longer this time, I hope."

Just 17 months earlier, Piniella had surrendered his Yankees general manager position to Quinn, when he returned to the dugout to replace Billy Martin. Now Quinn, hired three weeks before Piniella, said it was his familiarity with and respect for Piniella that led to his hiring.

Quinn and Piniella were soulmates of sorts having bonded under the sometimes comical, often unbearable pressure Steinbrenner brought to bear on all of his underlings. When Quinn was GM, Piniella served under him as manager. When Piniella was GM, Quinn was officially his assistant. It was the way the Yankees worked, interchanging positions at every whim and mood swing of the Boss.

"We had no choice but to bond," said Quinn with a laugh. "But it was a great move. It sort of helped us stave off George. We helped George out but it took two of us to do it. We had a wonderful business relationship, per se."

Quinn was the third generation of his family to run a major-league ballclub. His father, John Quinn, assembled the Milwaukee Braves clubs that won the 1957 World Series and the '58 National League pennant. Bob "Grandpa Quinn," ran the Browns, Red Sox, Dodgers, and Braves, once hiring Casey Stengel as a manager. In 2008, Quinn's son Bob was the executive vice president of finance and administration and CFO of the Milwaukee Brewers.

In other words, Bob Quinn knows baseball. He resigned from the Yankees September 1, 1989, for a variety of reasons. "I told George I had worn out my welcome and I needed a change of scenery," he said.

Among the indignities Quinn had to suffer at the hands of Steinbrenner was being sent to spring training without a secretary as punishment for a perceived transgression. Another time, after being given permission to attend his son's graduation from Ohio State, Steinbrenner tried to call him back to New York after he was halfway there. When Quinn refused, he was bad-mouthed around the office. Another time he was told by Steinbrenner that since he "messed up" on a previous order, he was to pay his own way on a business trip to Tampa.

"He taught me how to work; I'll say that," said Quinn. "There was no such thing as hours. I would get a call every night. But usually between the two of us, Lou and I, we were able to keep George at arm's length 90 percent of time."

Noteworthy among the other 10 percent was the time Piniella, then Yanks GM, went golfing with the team's VP of marketing during the off-season.

"George had an in-house guy take roll every day to see who was at their desk at 8:30 and again at 4:30," Quinn recalled. "We had a plan that if George called, our secretary Mary would say Lou had a dentist appointment. Well, all day George's office called and at 4:40, George himself called [from Tampa] and [yelled] 'Mary, where has he been all day?' When Mary said 'the dentist,' George said, 'You have the number of the dentist, don't you?'

"When Mary said she did not, George told her, 'Well Mary, you just cost yourself a day's pay. And none of you can leave the office until I hear from Lou.'"

Quinn got a hold of Piniella and informed him of the urgency that he call the Boss. When Piniella called, Steinbrenner asked where he was. "Why, I'm at the dentist George, they told you."

"Okay Lou," Steinbrenner responded, "Put him on."

On another occasion, this time on a golf outing with Piniella and Quinn during winter meetings, they were trying to finagle a shortstop from Atlanta GM John Mullen and his manager Bobby Cox in a proposed trade. Sure enough, when they got off the course there was a stack of messages waiting for them to call Steinbrenner.

"Lou takes one look at me," said Quinn, "and says, 'I'll take care of George if you pay for the golf.'"

Quinn laughed as he told the story in a 2008 interview. He hadn't spoken to Lou in while, "but he remains very dear to me," he said.

In Cincinnati 18 years earlier, Quinn felt the same way and was prepared to do anything he could to persuade Piniella to join forces again. Through Anita Piniella, Quinn found him on a trip to Las Vegas with a friend and told him the Reds job was "tailor-made" for him. The joke was that Schott always took credit for hiring him.

"Marge Schott thought Piniella was a rum-punch drink you picked up in Puerto Rico," Quinn chuckled again. "She didn't know Piniella from a bale of hay. But Lou comes over, meets Marge, and they hit it off."

In Piniella's press conference, both Schott and Piniella "thanked" Steinbrenner for letting Piniella go. After Steinbrenner reportedly had demanded compensation for Piniella when the Blue Jays were interested in hiring him the previous spring, he let Piniella go to the National League Reds for nothing in return.

"One is usually enough; two was certainly enough," Piniella said of the Yankees' managing carousel. "It was time for me to go on the field somewhere else. I thought I did a good job managing in New York. The owner got a little impatient at times, but that's his prerogative."

Stan Williams, who would become his pitching coach in Cincinnati, agreed it had to be a relief for Piniella to get out from under Steinbrenner's hold. "When you become one of George's chess pieces, he owns you or at least he wants to," Williams said. "George was on him all the time."

For Reds fans still mourning the departure of Rose and often leery of outsiders, the hiring of Piniella was met with open minds by many.

"The way Pete exited, it didn't leave that much pressure on Lou," said Andy Furman, at the time a sports talk show host for WLW, the flagship station of the Reds. "If Pete was fired or quit, that might have been harder but because Pete was banished, they had no choice. So the attitude was, 'Let's see what this guy is like.'"

Just the same, there was a segment, said Furman, who was slow to welcome him.

"Looking back now, it had to be a very difficult decision for Lou because he was in a sense, a no-name here and he was still replacing a god, a guy who could walk across the Ohio River," Furman said. "Those were the same people who said Lou won with Pete's guys, which was ridiculous. Pete didn't have a bad run, but he finished second four times."

He also finished in fifth place in 1989, marking the end of a disappointing baseball decade for the city after the Reds dominated the 1970s with the Big Red Machine winning five division titles, four National League pennants, and two World Series titles in a span of seven seasons. The Reds were the only team in the NL West to fail to win a divisional title in the 1980s.

One day before the season started, Piniella inadvertently ran into Rose on the golf course. He had seen pitcher Tom Browning, who he had yet to officially meet, and as he walked over to the eighth tee, he noticed Rose standing there.

"If I could have been anywhere else in the world at that moment, I wanted to be there. It was just so awkward and weird," said Browning.

Browning said he wasn't even sure if he should introduce the two.

"After all, Lou was here pretty much to take over Pete's team, one that Pete spent four seasons putting together and quickly turning into a winner," Browning wrote in his book, *Tales from the Reds Dugout*. "Then, it had been taken away when Pete was kicked out of baseball. And now it was handed over to this new guy."

Browning needn't have worried.

"Pete, I'm Lou Piniella and it's a pleasure to meet you," Piniella said, offering a handshake. "If you wouldn't mind some time, I'd really like to sit down and talk to you about your team."

"How he handled that," said Browning, "how he diffused the tension was incredible. I thought it was so cool, because I'm sure he was as uncomfortable as I was. But he handled it with as much grace and compassion as he could and immediately put everybody at ease.

"I knew right then we had something special in Lou."

Reds president and CEO Marge Schott announced Piniella's hiring by saying, "This cleans the slate. We can move onto the 1990s. I think we've got the right man, the best man. I like this guy…. When he has to be tough, he will be tough."

Piniella assembled a coaching staff with National League experience by retaining Tony Perez and adding Jackie Moore and Sam Perlozzo to go along with pitching coach Stan Williams and bullpen coach Larry Rothschild.

"He came to the National League basically as a virgin," said the Reds' radio voice Marty Brennaman of Piniella's lack of National League experience. "But the thing that impressed me is that he came to Cincinnati, surrounded himself with coaches who had vast National League experience, and listened to them until he reached the point early in the '90 season that he understood the way the NL game is played.

"He never gave the impression that he had all the answers. He was very, very comfortable relying on Sammy Perlozzo and Jackie Moore and Stan Williams. He had zero ego and in turn, he had the most loyal coaching staff that has ever been associated with Reds baseball. No one there was trying to get his job, undermining him in subtle ways. Everyone had his back."

Among Piniella's first moves was to change jersey numbers from 14 [also Rose's number] to 41. It was not all he planned to change.

"It's a new start," said Piniella and indeed it was as he had never played or coached in the National League. "The most important thing is to go to spring training and instill a positive attitude in the players…I don't think we'll have an attitude problem."

No, but they did have another even more serious problem at hand.

The seventh work stoppage in baseball history began on February 15, 1990, when owners, afraid of a midseason strike—which had halted the 1981 and 1985 seasons—locked the gates to major-league training camps. The lockout would last 32 days.

No one was happy, of course, least of all Piniella, who never even got a chance to meet most of his new team.

"We're going into uncharted waters here," he said when the lockout ended. "I've been in professional baseball since 1962, and there has never been such a short spring training. Naturally, you'd like more time. But there will be equal time for everybody. The disadvantage is that we won't be able to take a good look at everybody."

Catcher Joe Oliver, a second-round draft pick of the Reds in 1983, had just made his big-league debut in July 1989 and remembered the initial impression Piniella had on the club.

"His first meeting in spring training impressed everybody because he threw the hammer down, creating the mentality right away of having pride in the organization, respect for the game, working hard," Oliver recalled. "Not that Pete didn't have that, but we had a black eye there and Lou was coming in and laying down the new law. We had to be accountable. That was the tone from the first day.

"I remember guys walking away just really excited."

Schott, ever with her eye on the bottom line, was consumed by the fact that her season was not starting on time, with the traditional National League opener at Riverfront Stadium. Instead of April 2, the Reds would have to wait until April 17 for their home opener, eight days after they started the season on the road.

"If we don't have our opening day, a lot of people couldn't care if we ever open up," Schott said. "It's a primo thing here."

The only primo thing Piniella cared about was winning and doing so right away. And he had chosen his new job carefully.

"This is a good ballclub I'm coming to," he said in his news conference, though most had picked the Reds for no better than a third-place finish in their division. "It's not like I'm going into a rebuilding process. This is a ballclub that can win next year."

Browning remembers Piniella's first address to the club as short, powerful and to the point, echoing those same sentiments.

"Look, you guys are way too talented not to win," Piniella told his new team. "You're here to win and I'm here to win. And I don't give a damn if you don't like me."

"He got our respect right away because of his demeanor, how he came across, how professional he was," said Browning. "But he also mingled with the players in spring training, got to know who we were on a personal basis."

One person not on board was the man passed over for the job. Tommy Helms said he had no hard feelings against Quinn or Piniella but said he had been "kicked around" by Schott and that he could not see returning to the Reds in any capacity as long as Schott was still the owner.

"I think Lou Piniella has got to be the luckiest man in the world," said Helms, under whom the team went 5–14 to finish the season. "I just wish that I had someone pushing me like he did. I know Lou, I like him, he was a great player. He can't lose. If the club is healthy, they can't lose."

Though the team was young, Piniella knew he had speed on the basepaths in Barry Larkin, Chris Sabo, Eric Davis, and Mariano Duncan and intended to give them the green light to steal. He had Billy Hatcher in left and Paul O'Neill in right. And he was enthusiastic about two Yankee products—first baseman Hal Morris and left-handed pitcher Tim Birtsas—and former Yankee Jose Rijo, who at age 18 with the Yankees in 1984, was the youngest player in the majors.

The Reds traded closer John Franco for reliever Randy Myers in 1990, to join Norm Charlton and Rob Dibble. Dibble was like a school kid when he had first heard that Piniella was taking over as manager.

"I was an Oakland A's fan as a kid, one brother was a Red Sox fan and the other a Yankees fan," said Dibble, who was born in Bridgeport, Connecticut. "I was kind of a hot dog in Babe Ruth League and high school, I wore my socks up high and I had a leg kick like Dennis Eckersley. But when I saw Lou, with his long hair, hard-nosed attitude, kicking over watercoolers, mad all the time, he was kind of a mirror image of how I saw myself as an everyday player until I got to the minor leagues and pitched full time."

That said, Dibble said he liked the fact that Piniella was bringing a new definition of discipline to the club.

"I thought he brought the Yankee tradition and class to the Reds," he said. "He wanted you in a suit and tie. He stressed that. We had to keep our hair short and no facial hair. I loved the fact that we were very uniform and structured, and I stayed right in line in the early days, to a point."

Piniella had planned to push fundamentals hard in spring training with an eye on manufacturing runs with the hit-and-run, delayed steals, and the occasional suicide squeeze. Due to the strike, that would have to be done after the season started. But he pushed his point immediately as O'Neill laid down a sacrifice bunt in the second game of the year, his first in 1,094 career at-bats.

"He was very tough on young players, no doubt about that," said Oliver. "He's trying to see what kind of mental makeup you have. If you can't handle your manager getting on you, how are you going to react to the seventh, eighth, and ninth innings with the game on the line? I got it a lot because I was a catcher running the game and an extension of the pitching staff.

"But he's offensive minded, always a hitter, so he hammered home that you can't ever give into the pitcher."

Piniella told his team that there was no reason they should not dominate the competition, and that is precisely what the Reds did, winning their first nine games to start the season.

Recognizing early in the season the firepower and depth he had with his bullpen, Piniella capitalized. While the opposition was still getting its starters into regular-season shape, Piniella brought in his relievers early, saving his starters and overpowering hitters.

The Reds were 33–12 by early June, at one point 26 games over .500 at 59–33.

Although no one had predicted great things for the Reds that season, "after the first month of the season, we knew we were going to win because Lou instilled that in us," said Billy Hatcher, who went on to coach under Piniella at Tampa. He just told us, "If we can get off to a good start, play 100 percent, don't beat ourselves and make teams beat us, we're going to have a chance to win."

"I remember Lou telling us one time, we have 162 games—we're going to win 50 for sure. We're going to lose 50 for sure. I want you guys ready for the other 62. When they're going to be, I don't know, but that's what I want you ready for, to bust our behinds for those other 62."

It was a wonderful time for Piniella. Aside from missing Anita and the kids, who stayed behind in Allendale, New Jersey, until school ended in late June, he quickly grew fond of the small-town feel to Cincinnati, calling it a "bigger Tampa." He shared a three-bedroom townhouse with pitching coach Stan Williams in picturesque Hyde Park, a neighborhood of Cincinnati.

The coaches worked hard, hashing over the game with Piniella for hours afterward, maybe watching a little ESPN, and then back at it the next day, except when they decided they needed a little break.

"We'd go to the track and bet three or four races, have a nice lunch, and then go to the ballpark," said Williams. "It was great relaxation for Lou, a nice diversion."

Piniella got out among the people, often strolling downtown to his favorite cigar shop.

"Everything in New York seems like it's an hour, hour and a half away. Here, you're 15 minutes away from everything," he told local reporters. "It's much nicer."

He also seemed to enjoy the more relaxed press corps, often calling out, in typical Piniella fashion, "Hey Wolfman, how're you doing?" to popular FM disc jockey Wildman Walker.

Rob Parker, then a beat reporter covering the Reds for the *Cincinnati Enquirer*, recalls one instance in particular when he saw

Piniella in a different light. Like all hard-working beat guys, Parker was not always on Piniella's good side depending on the day and the last story he wrote.

"But one day we came into his office for our usual routine and I guess it was all over my face," Parker recalled. "My father had died and I was living alone in Cincinnati and the funeral was days away and Lou saw me and said, 'You look terrible, what happened?' He came from around the desk and gave me a big hug. That's what kind of guy he is."

Other beat writers also remembered that day 18 years later, and recounted the story. "I'll always remember that," said Jerry Crasnick, the beat writer for the *Cincinnati Post*.

But they also recall the Piniella who never took losing well.

"He was really, really bad after losses," Crasnick chuckled. "Once, Ron Oester had four hits in a game and the next day he wasn't in the lineup [and the Reds lost]. I was diplomatic but I said, 'Oester had four hits and he's not playing,' and Lou said, 'You know so much, you make out the fucking lineup and threw the lineup card at me.'

"But I just remember on a personal level, one thing I always liked, love him or hate him, he was very genuine, just unvarnished emotion. If he was in a surly mood, he didn't try to fake it to get through it. He could be very entertaining and what he did, throwing his arms [around Parker], you could see he really cared about the guy. A lot of managers wouldn't do that. And it was a neat thing."

He was even a good sport with the eccentric Mrs. Schott and her various idiosyncracies. When she gave him her St. Bernard Schottzie's dog hairs for good luck, he dutifully put them into his back pocket, once going as far as to rub them on his bare chest at her behest.

"He'd just go with it," Williams recalled. "She used to come and kiss him all the time. I said, 'Lou, I don't know what you're making but whatever it is, it's not enough.'"

His patience with Schott would be severely tested over the years with her heartless displays of penny-pinching. And this was also years before Schott's racially insensitive comments got her banned from baseball. But by all accounts, Piniella was never anything less than respectful to his boss and even patient as long as the Schottzie discussions came after victories.

"Lou is a passionate, family-oriented guy, not two-faced," said Furman. "A lot of people who worked for Marge kow-towed to her, then ripped her to shreds behind her back. But he made her feel good about winning and gave her the last of the great years of Cincinnati baseball. It was a magical year."

"Of course," said Joe Oliver, "you tolerate a lot more when you're winning. But that's how I remember it, that he was very respectful and understanding that while it was his team on the field, it was her organization. She would call some unorthodox meetings form time to time, but he had respect for her knowing she wanted some type of input."

It was a season, however, in which Piniella was allowed to thoroughly flex his coaching muscle for the first time, and he focused significant attention on hitting with his own unique approach.

"I would see him trying to figure out what guys liked to do in their spare time," said Oliver. "Paul O'Neill was a tennis player so he would start incorporating hitting techniques with Paul based on that. Chris Sabo loved golf, and he would do the same thing.

"He would watch all of our swings, then start plugging it in, pick your brain, your approach, your thought process. You would see him in the dugout mimicking what each guy did and then try to plug it in and try to put it on your level. Lou was one of the best hitting coaches I ever had and he was a manager."

His pitching coach agreed.

"I told him, 'You're probably the best hitting coach I know,'" Williams recalled. "He took offense to it, thinking I meant he wasn't a good manager. I told him, 'No, it means you're a great hitting coach.'"

At times, Piniella seemed impetuous, at others, inspired.

He also thought nothing of shifting Eric Davis from center to left in August. He yanked Todd Benzinger, the team's leading RBI man through 67 games after he injured his hand, moved the rookie Morris to first, and Benzinger never really resurfaced.

Once again, though he had had somehow acquired a questionable reputation for handling pitchers, he worked magic through a rash of injuries—in the 1990 season to Danny Jackson, Tom Browning, Jack Armstrong, and Rick Mahler. That, while keeping his "Nasty Boys" Dibble and Myers fresh.

Piniella communicated with his players and he knew how to have fun with them on occasion.

"We were on a flight one time and we'd do certain things to stop a losing streak like shaving our heads or whatever as a show of unity," said Dibble. "Well, this one time we decided that anyone who didn't have a 100 percent silk tie, we'd cut it at the knot and hang them in the middle of the plane. When we got to the coaches, Lou said, 'I don't have a tie, just take my shirt.' So Eric Davis literally rips the shirt off his back.

"Lou was always one of us and I'll always love him for that."

His arguments with umpires also tended to have a unifying effect. In August, as the Reds' lead was shrinking, Piniella reacted to a questionable call by Dutch Rennert at first base by pulling it out of the ground and heaving it into right field. Seemingly dissatisfied with the first throw, he then retrieved the base and threw it even further.

"To me at the time, that was about losing his mind over a call he thought was wrong, the best show we'd seen all year," said Marty Brennaman. "But that was wrong. It was all about fighting for his players and they had tremendous respect for him for that. There are players who get screwed on calls and their manager never leaves the dugout."

The Reds were in an offensive malaise at the time and had lost five straight going into that game. They would win that game and then five of the next six.

Another time during the considerably rockier second half of the season in which the Reds finished a game below .500, Piniella tried to keep his team loose by picking his lineup out of a hat.

Before the Rennert game, after the Reds had lost their fifth in a row, Piniella called a team meeting and as players braced for the worst, he broke the tension by telling them the tale of the tortoise and the hare.

"Or we'd lose a few games," said Hatcher, "and he'd bring out those World Series rings and put them on. He messes with your head. He shows you—'You want that grand prize, this is what you have to do. To be a champion, you have to sacrifice your goals for team goals.' And he'd get you to do those things."

The Reds did it well enough to go wire-to-wire, becoming the first National League team in history to ever occupy first place the entire length of the regular season.

They finished with 91 victories to win the Western Division title, the second team in the league to win a division title with only one 15-game winner (Browning). They also did it without a hitter in the top 10 in average, home runs, or runs batted in (Davis finished with 86 but played only 127 games due to injury).

They would "back in" when a Dodgers loss clinched the division for the Reds during a rain delay. The next day, tired and hungover, the Reds dropped their third straight to the Padres in a seemingly meaningless game with three games left to play in the regular season. Well, meaningless to everyone but their manager.

After the game, Browning recalled Piniella "storming into the clubhouse."

"Listen to me right now," an emotional Piniella told his team, "I will not let this team go into the playoffs in a losing posture. I will not!"

"Believe me," said Browning, "it was a tearjerker moment. He actually had tears in his eyes. We were playing cruddy, just playing out the season, getting a little lackadaisical and he was like, 'I love you guys and I will not let you go into the playoffs in a losing posture.' A losing posture. That's a phrase I will not forget for the rest of my life. He was looking out for us even when we weren't."

As he looked toward the playoffs, Piniella reflected on his first season post-Yankees with a sense of gratitude at simply having his voice heard.

"Most of the managers who are highly successful and stay in it for any period of time work for an organization that lets them do their jobs," he told the *Cincinnati Post's* Jerry Crasnick. "That's why this has been the best learning experience for me, because I've been able to do my job.

"Nobody has told me who to play, when to pull a pitcher, when to steal a base, or how to handle my clubhouse. In New York, I had to go through the lineup [with Steinbrenner] before the ballgame, then explain why I did things during the game—and the reasons were never good enough.

"Here, I have input in trades and on who I want in my clubhouse. Nobody gets sent out of here if I don't want them out of here. In New York, I'd come in after a game and there'd be a bag packed. I didn't know."

Still, with all that said, Piniella called his firing in New York the "only reason" he was celebrating a division title in Cincinnati.

"I thought I did a good job [in New York] and could be better," he said. "I really don't need to be a major-league manager to be happy. There was something missing that I wanted to get accomplished."

That mission would have to wait a game after the Reds dropped their first postseason game in 11 years, a 4–3 loss to the Pittsburgh Pirates in Game 1 of the National League Championship Series.

Diminutive Billy Bates, pinch-running for Ron Oester, was cut down attempting to steal second on his own in the ninth inning when Davis, running on his own, made it to third. Davis also made an uncharacteristic misplay that helped the Pirates score the game-winning run.

The Reds tied the series with Paul O'Neill driving in both Cincinnati runs in a 2–1 victory and making a great throw to nail Andy Van Slyke at third base.

O'Neill, a Columbus, Ohio, product who grew up dreaming of one day playing for the Reds, continually tested Piniella's patience. Much like Piniella in his penchant for flinging helmets, he had more natural ability, a talent for sulking, and thus confounded Piniella and his coaching staff in Cincinnati.

"O'Neill's a great kid," Piniella was quoted as saying, "But from my perspective I see so much talent there that I expect him to knock the cover off the ball at times."

Quinn felt badly about O'Neill's time in Cincinnati.

"That was one guy I wish I could've helped and I felt helpless," Quinn said. "Paul would hang his head and Lou doesn't like head hangers. They were a lot alike in that Lou was a hothead too as a player. If he didn't get a base hit, he would throw stuff and so would O'Neill.

"But Lou was not a head hanger. He was a fire eater."

O'Neill, traded in November 1992 to the Yankees for Roberto Kelly, went on to win the American League batting title and become a four-time All-Star with the Yankees, though he never did hit 30 home runs in a season, which Piniella and Tony Perez thought he was capable of doing. But ironically, he became an all-time favorite with New York fans for his heart, in much the same way Piniella did.

During the 1990 season, O'Neill broke his thumb and also was platooned with Glenn Braggs. But for the NLCS, the Reds would need O'Neill's left-handed bat.

With the series shifting to Pittsburgh for the next three games, it was Mariano Duncan in Game 3, whose three-run home run was the deciding factor in a 6–3 Reds victory. In Game 4, O'Neill and Chris Sabo homered, Jose Rijo turned in seven effective innings, and Randy Myers and Rob Dibble shut the Pirates down after that for a 5–3 Reds victory and 3–1 lead in the series.

As Piniella had preached since the first day of the lockout-shortened spring training, the Reds were going to win with fundamentals, defense, and with all 25 players contributing. Indeed, they would advance to the World Series with limited offensive contributions from their stars, Davis and Sabo. But Davis made a dazzling defensive play in the eighth inning, perfectly playing Bonilla's ricochet off the center-field wall and nailing Bonilla at third.

"It's over," said Rijo, with one game still remaining. "Unless they make a great comeback, which I doubt, we've been putting together great games when we've needed them all year long. I don't think we're going to let it get away now."

Rijo spoke a little too soon as the Pirates took Game 5, 3–2, behind pitcher Doug Drabek, and Piniella was red-faced as he was second-guessed afterward for his substitutions in the eighth inning.

On the CBS telecast, Tim McCarver saw the scenario unfolding and pointed it out in earnest to the viewers, warning that Piniella's moves could backfire, which they did when catcher Jeff Reed was forced to face lefthander Bob Patterson with the bases loaded and one out in the ninth. Reed, who had to bat because Piniella had lifted his starting catcher Joe Oliver for pinch-hitter Ron Oester, grounded into a double play to end the game, which McCarver had warily predicted with a graphic between innings.

Eighteen years later, McCarver remembered it clearly.

"It was the most detailed, most complicated point I've ever spoken about on the air," said McCarver. "Lou had to make two changes in the top of the eighth—one was to pinch hit for his catcher and the other to pinch hit for his pitcher—the seven and nine holes.

"I said normally if you replace two guys and pitcher is one of those guys, you're going to protect your pitcher. But in this situation, because you only have two catchers, you're going to have to protect your catcher and bat your catcher ninth where you were going to pinch-hit him in the seven hole."

With the lefty Patterson in the Pirates' bullpen, McCarver quickly called his producer and had him use as a graphic the Reds' lineup in the ninth, which had O'Neill, Davis, Hal Morris, Sabo, and the guy in the seventh hole, Reed, as the first five hitters.

"In the top of the eighth," said McCarver. "I said, 'This could be a moot point, but what could happen in the ninth—if you have Reed batting fifth in a one-run ballgame—you could have him batting with bases loaded; whereas if you have [pitcher Scott] Scudder in the seven hole and Reed in the nine hole, then you can pinch hit for Scudder. If you get to Reed, the game is going to be tied.'"

With the Reds' lineup on the screen, McCarver went over the scenario, highlighting the seven and nine hole, then showing the way it should've been in his opinion—the pitcher batting in the seven hole and Reed in the ninth. When Reed hit into the double play to end the game, McCarver was satisfied, if not a little surprised with himself, that he had seen it in advance. He also had a feeling Piniella would not be happy.

Indeed, when Piniella was asked about each of his moves in the postgame press conference, he threw up his arms. "What it boils down to is you [reporters] are going to second-guess any [expletive] thing I do anyway, so it doesn't make any difference."

The next day, the *Cincinnati Post* reported that Piniella and McCarver "talked out the issue" before the next game.

"Piniella characterized the discussion as amicable," the story said. While he didn't appear to agree with McCarver's comments, he defended McCarver's right to make them.

"As long as it's his opinion, it's fine with me," Piniella was quoted as saying. "But one thing is for certain, I think I'm more qualified to talk about my personnel than Tim McCarver is.

"I had a nice conversation with him. I don't have any problems with him. I've got to manage how I feel is best and that's all I can do. When you're an analyst like he is, you have to give your opinions. I respect that right. I think he does his job well. I think I do mine well, too."

In reality, Piniella did not take it quite so well. McCarver had armed himself, he said, with some stats from a friend at the Elias Sports Bureau. Reed, he was told, had been with the team the whole year and was 9-of-26 versus lefties that season.

"But the fact that he had only 26 at-bats meant that those were lefthanders brought in the sixth and seventh innings of a 9–1 game and Jeff got a hanging curve ball and whack," said McCarver. "But never in a tight situation was Jeff Reed called upon to hit against a lefthander in 26 at-bats."

Piniella did not want to hear it. He had explained the night before that he pinch hit for Oliver (leaving no other catchers on the bench and forcing Reed to stay in the game) because the Reds were two runs down and, "If Oliver gets on in that at-bat, we're going to have to pinch-run for him anyway [since Oliver, which McCarver did not know, had twisted a knee and ankle the night before]. That's why I pinch hit for him."

Piniella also had Morris bunt, thus allowing the Pirates to dictate that Reed was the man who would have to beat them.

Piniella pointed out that Reed had hit left-handed pitching all year. If the Reds were two runs down, he wouldn't have Morris bunt. But one run down, the pressure is on the defense and there are many ways to score from third base.

But Piniella was not in the mood to explain himself to McCarver when he confronted the former catcher, who was standing with broadcast partner Jack Buck and McCarver's friend from Elias.

"He aired me out," McCarver laughed. "Jack and Steve had their heads down and I had to take it. Lou was going 'Jesus, you kept going on and on and on.' I said 'Lou, it was a very sophisticated point, my job was to go on and on and on. The fans listening don't have a clue what I'm talking about. We had to show it, we had to talk about it again. I said it might be a moot point. And I have to tell you, if I had to do it over again, I'd do the same thing. I just want you to know.'

"Lou was like, 'I must have had 50 fucking people call me.'" McCarver told him he understood and offered to bring him a tape so he could listen to it himself. That night, he watched it again himself and determined he had been fair.

Asked if Lou was still angry today, McCarver laughed again as he had the entire time he retold the story. "This is the beauty of Lou," he said. "I've had run-ins with Leyland, with La Russa, Willie Randolph, Jeff Torborg when I was with the Mets, Davey Johnson and have had adversarial relationships.

"The next time I saw Lou after that was in spring training of '91. Cincinnati traveled to Port St. Lucie for a Mets game. And he could not have been chummier or nicer.

"Then we're at the White House in 2006 with 14 people for a cocktail party with President and Laura Bush," said McCarver. "We had never talked about [the argument] since, never in the booth [when the duo did Fox broadcasts together] and never at dinner or drinks afterward. It just never came up.

"But we're with the president and he said, 'You guys have known each other a long time.' And I said, 'Mr. President, we had a verbal knockdown a couple years ago' and I told the story and Lou said, 'No, I don't remember that.' I said, 'You don't remember that? You undressed me in front of Jack Buck.' The president loved it.

"Lou is just one of God's great people. But I'll tell you, it was not fun being aired out by Lou Piniella."

The thing is, Piniella did not forget. Not right away anyway. He told Steve Jacobson that he spent the rest of that night and the off-day rethinking his rejection of the double-switch. "Over and over and over until I was half nuts," he said. And he concluded that he had not made a mistake.

In Game 6, Pittsburgh manager Jim Leyland tried the ultimate double cross by starting his set-up man, righty Ted Power, in an obvious attempt to get Piniella to platoon with a lineup of lefties only to then bring in his original left-handed starter Zane Smith.

But Piniella was no rookie. He had seen Billy Martin attempt the same ploy, recognized it, and made only one switch—Braggs for O'Neill—while having Benzinger switch-hit. Every move Piniella made worked, including bringing the left-handed Charlton in to face the right-handed Carmelo Martinez in the seventh because he wanted Leyland to leave Martinez in to bunt. Charlton got him to pop out.

In the eighth, Piniella double-switched, putting Randy Myers in the third hole and Glenn Braggs in the seventh spot and in right field.

The Reds' dramatic 2–1 victory was sealed when Braggs climbed the outfield fence, robbing Martinez of what would have been a two-run home run and sending the Reds to the World Series for the first time in 14 years.

It was certainly appropriate for a Reds team that committed just two errors in six games against the Pirates and led the National League in defense during the regular season. Reds pitchers also held the Pirates, with their "Killer B's," to 15 runs and a .194 batting average.

Piniella went with a classic matchup move with the score 1–1 in the seventh, when he pinch-hit righty Luis Quinones for the lefty O'Neill (who was 8-for-17 in the series and had singled the previous time up) and Quinones drove home the winning run with a single.

Norm Charlton and Randy Myers combined with Danny Jackson on a one-hitter. Myers and Dibble were named co-MVPs of the NLCS.

If anyone wondered whether Piniella still harbored insecurities from his days of constant judgment by George Steinbrenner, the victorious Reds manager reinforced that thought after the victory.

"I've got one thing to say," Piniella said. "George, I can manage."

His team was equally as confident, despite the fact that they were about to face the heavily favored Oakland A's, the defending world champs, two-time defending AL champs, and a team fresh off a sweep of Boston in the ALCS.

"Everybody talked about the A's that year but Pittsburgh had the best team in baseball," said Hatcher. "They had Barry Bonds, Bobby Bonilla, Andy Van Slyke, Sid Bream. We knew they had a good team. And when we beat them, there was no doubt in our minds we were going to beat the A's. No doubt in our minds."

No doubt in Piniella's mind either, apparently.

"After we beat the Pirates," said Quinn, "Lou said, 'We're going to beat the A's.' I hadn't had a drink in 27 years but I said, 'Give me a drink of whatever you're having.' The A's were so heavily favored and while we had good starting and relief pitching, I had trouble accepting his confidence."

It was Reds versus A's. The Nasty Boys versus three former AL Rookie of the Year Award winners, Jose Canseco, Mark McGwire, and Walt Weiss. It was also a petri dish for *Chicago Tribune* columnist Mike Royko's Ex-Cubs Factor, Royko's theory that the A's had no chance because they had more ex-Cubs than the Reds. But no one else felt that way, including the mighty A's, who watched as the two teams' practices overlapped before the Series started and giggled among themselves as they watched the Reds players running the stairs in the stadium.

It was also Lou Piniella and Tony La Russa, Tampa natives and boyhood pals who grew up three miles apart, teammates on the Colt League World Series runners-up and on American Legion Post 248, that proudly made up "West Tampa" T-shirts for Louis Piniella Jr. to wear and pass out during the World Series.

Tampa boys.

When *Tampa Tribune* columnist Tom McEwen and his younger colleague Joe Henderson traveled to Cincinnati for the Series, Henderson remembered McEwen asking him to come along as he walked down to the clubhouse. "I'm going to go see Lou," McEwen told him.

Media are not allowed into major-league clubhouses before postseason games, much less the World Series, but McEwen was sure this would not be a problem.

"Tell Lou that Tom and Joe are here from Tampa," he told the cop at the door and "three seconds later," to Henderson's amazement, they were escorted into Piniella's office.

"Tom says, 'You ask the baseball stuff,' but Lou is gregarious and laughing and not worried about a thing," Henderson said. "We sat there for at least 20 minutes and then Lou called over to the visitors' clubhouse, got La Russa on the phone and said, 'Hey Tony, it's Lou. I'm sending Tom McEwen and Joe Henderson over.'

"Then he hung up and said, 'Go on over, Tony's waiting for you.' Only Lou would do that."

In his 2007 interview with Frank Deford for HBO's *Real Sports with Bryant Gumbel*, Piniella admitted that it wasn't always easy to be compared to the "cerebral" La Russa.

"I get envious a little.... When they describe Tony, [it's] 'pensive, studious,'" said Piniella. "When they describe me, [it's] 'fiery,' you know?"

Piniella and La Russa, however, played down any personal rivalry and in a 2008 interview, La Russa said he did not feel the two were competing against one another in 1990.

"The most competitive we've ever been was when Lou played for Tampa Jesuit, the Catholic high school, and I played for the public school, Tampa Jefferson, because that's when we really were competing," La Russa said. "Lou was really a great player, I was less than mediocre. He was the player; I was not.

"Managing, when he was at Seattle and I was at Oakland, it's never easy to manage against a friend because if you win, your friend is unhappy. I think it would be tougher if we were in the same league and met in the division playoffs or NLCS. But we both got to the World Series and at that point, it's the team who plays the best that wins.

"I was disappointed we competed so poorly. It didn't have anything to do with Lou being the manager. It wasn't any extra disappointment or aggravation because of that. I felt Lou had gotten his team to compete better than I did the A's."

Piniella had wanted to move Eric Davis from cleanup to leadoff in Game 1 of the Series, but he wanted to make sure Davis was okay with it first. Davis, who was 4-of-23 in the NLCS and had a sore left shoulder, was not.

"When I have things in mind, I always discuss them with my players," Piniella said. "Your players have to feel comfortable with what you ask them to do. It's a very important consideration."

Davis may have appreciated the communication but he was not thrilled about the suggestion, which nonetheless produced the desired effect as Davis remained in the cleanup spot. On the first pitch of his first World Series at-bat, he hit a two-run home run off Dave Stewart as the Reds shut out the A's 7–0 to take a 1–0 lead in the Series.

The headline in the *Cincinnati Post* the next morning read "Davis Stuns Goliath."

In Game 2, Oakland was leading 4–3 in the seventh inning when Debbie Browning, Tom's very pregnant wife, was watching in the stands at Riverfront Stadium when she went into labor. As this was her third child, she knew when she had to rush to the hospital.

The clubhouse manager had come to the dugout to inform Browning what had happened and he took off in a panic.

"I had no idea that doctors can slow these things down, she didn't tell me any of that," Browning laughed. "So I ran out in my uniform, my turf shoes, I didn't even stop in the clubhouse, I ran right through the clubhouse."

On the bench, Reds coach Stan Williams was in deep concentration, studying his pitcher's every move.

"Steamer," said Piniella, calling to Williams. "You'd better tell Tommy to put his spikes on. We may have to use him late in this game."

Browning had been scheduled to start Game 3, but if the game went into extra innings, Piniella wanted everyone ready.

"I went down the bench to get him," said Williams, "but he wasn't there. I grabbed the assistant trainer and said, 'Go to the clubhouse and tell him to get his spikes on, grab his glove, and get his butt up here. Then I went to tell Lou."

Piniella spun on Williams when informed that Browning was not there.

"Where in the hell is he?" he snapped. "How in hell could you let this happen? You can't just let guys leave."

Williams couldn't let it pass.

"I usually just took stuff because I didn't want to snap back at him and challenge his leadership and position, but I snapped this time because it was so ridiculous," said Williams. "How in the hell am I supposed to know a guy left our club?" he shouted at Piniella. "I'm watching my pitcher."

At the hospital, Debbie was being prepped for a C-section while Browning wandered into the doctors' lounge to watch the game. "We put an APB out for him," Williams said.

On the radio, Marty Brennaman beseeched Browning to come back. And in the CBS television booth, Tim McCarver heard and was about to get back on Piniella's good side. "Tom, if you're out there and listening," he said as Browning sat in front of the TV in stunned silence, "Lou Piniella needs you to come back to the stadium to pitch."

While Browning tried to figure out if he was coming or going, Joe Oliver hit a bouncer that skipped over third base in the tenth inning to drive in Billy Bates with the winning run.

"As soon as Billy Bates touched home plate, the door to the doctors' lounge flew open, they said she's ready and we went and had a baby," said Browning.

The next day, Browning met the team for its flight to Oakland, and Piniella pulled him aside to congratulate him. "And damn it," said Piniella, "if you ever have to take off like that again, just tell someone." Two nights later, Browning was the winning pitcher for the Reds as Chris Sabo's back-to-back home runs paced the 8–3 victory and put the Reds within one game of clinching.

In Game 4, the A's scored a single run in the first inning of a Jose Rijo gem and then not again as the Reds shocked the baseball world by completing their dream season with a sweep of the A's to win their first World Series title since 1976.

Hatcher set a World Series record with seven consecutive hits. Chris Sabo had five at one point, including his two homers. Billy Hatcher's .750 batting average (9-for-12) broke Babe Ruth's record for a four-game World Series. Jose Rijo, the winning pitcher in Games 1 and 4 who retired the final 20 batters he faced, was named the Series MVP.

Back in August, unhappy with Rijo's laid-back demeanor, Piniella had pitching coach Stan Williams inform the Reds' starting pitching staff that they were going to go to a four-man rotation down the stretch.

All agreed, including Rijo.

"I'm glad to hear that, Jose," said Williams, "because you're the one we're going to bump from the rotation."

Rijo went 6–2 in his final eight regular-season starts and turned in one of the most dominating World Series in years allowing one earned run in 15.1 innings on nine hits, striking out 14 and walking five for an earned-run average of 0.59 in his two victories.

"A refusal to be a happy loser," said Stan Williams, lauding the job Piniella had done. "That's what he brought. He harped on it, beat on it, insisted up on it."

Piniella had lifted a city from a state of baseball depression, people who once reeled as they watched their hero shipped off to federal prison now proud and defiant. "Piniella brought baseball back," wrote the *Post*'s Paul Daugherty. "He offered the ultimate catharsis for a punch-drunk town and its sad baseball team. He wouldn't take losing for an answer."

Piniella had out-managed La Russa, who had the image of the computer genius to Piniella's impulsive intensity. And he had upstaged Steinbrenner, who had fired him twice.

And when it was over, the juxtaposition was too good to be true—Piniella, with a cigar in one hand and a beer in the other in the ecstasy of a victorious locker room, while on television at that very minute was Steinbrenner hosting *Saturday Night Live*. Piniella hoisting the World Series trophy, George in a clownish skit dropping his pants.

"I have an announcement to make," Steinbrenner said in his monologue, airing at 11:30 PM Eastern time. "At 11:15, I bought the Cincinnati Reds."

Piniella would have had to laugh if he cared at that point. Besides, even he had to know that there is no such thing as a last laugh in baseball. The next two seasons would prove that.

Heck, even the next two hours would prove that as Schott became furious when she learned that the Reds' sweep meant the owners did not profit off of the Series. Through the first four games, 60 percent of the gate receipts went toward the players' share of the Series money with the remaining 40 percent split equally between the two clubs and the commissioner's office.

After the fourth game, the gate receipts are divided equally among the two teams and the commissioner's office. This is to safeguard against players throwing games in order to extend the Series and put more money in their pockets.

Enraged, Schott refused to host a celebration party at the Reds' hotel and when the team got together on its own, with the club's other limited partners offering to foot the bill, she insisted there would be no food. The Reds' players celebrated winning the 1990 World Series by going on a burger run to a nearby fast-food place. Piniella ate dinner later that night at a Carl's Jr.

Two weeks short of two years later, Piniella said he would not be returning as Reds manager, saying he wanted to make a change.

Injuries ravaged the Reds in 1991 as they finished 74–88, and despite putting 14 players on the disabled list the next season, Piniella guided his team to a 90–72 record in 1992, as they finished second to Atlanta in the NL West.

"The Braves were starting to come into their own," said Browning of the '91 and '92 seasons, "and Lou had a Triple A shuttle going back and forth and still won 90 games [in '92]. He probably did his best managing job that year. But a lot of things just accumulated."

The Reds would go through a span of 14 losses in 16 games. After the 14th loss, Chris Sabo, who was named to the National League All-Star team for the second year in a row, tangled with a fan outside Busch Stadium, though no charges were filed on either side.

That same day, Piniella talked to Dibble about what would turn out to be the pitcher's third suspension of the year—this time for throwing at a Cubs player running to first. After that meeting, Dibble apologized to teammates for saying on a radio show that they did not support him in that incident.

Dibble had already sat out three games for throwing behind the head of a Houston player in April and was also suspended for throwing the ball in the stands in Cincinnati later that month and striking a 27-year-old first-grade teacher, also in April. Later in the season, Dibble would be involved in a brawl with Houston shortstop Eric Yelding.

If that wasn't enough, Pete Rose criticized Piniella for chastising players in the press after Piniella and Myers traded comments in the paper. And Marge Schott made Bob Quinn pay his own way to the All-Star Game as punishment for misreading a technicality and having to trade a top prospect rather than lose him to free agency.

In August, Piniella, angry after umpire Gary Darling overruled a home run by Cincinnati's Bill Doran by calling it a foul ball, accused Darling of being biased against his club. Darling and the Major League Umpires Association filed a $5 million defamation suit against Piniella, and the case was settled out of court with Piniella apologizing and retracting his original comments.

Schott and the Reds did not support him publicly or financially in the case, and though National League president Bill White eventually got the Reds to pay 50 percent of his attorney's fees, Piniella never forgot it.

The next season was punctuated by Piniella's wrestling match in September with Dibble.

But in the end, Schott simply did not tell Piniella what he wanted to hear, which was simply that she wanted him to return.

When the two did meet after the 1992 season, Schott reportedly wanted to cut the team's $37 million payroll, and there were rumors she also wanted to cut Piniella's $625,000 salary, though her final offer would've kept him at the same figure. But it didn't matter by then.

"I was never approached once," he said. "When it got to a situation where the newspapers and radio stations were taking polls...hey, an organization shouldn't let it get to that.

"If we would have turned over like a beached whale, it would have been one thing," he said. "But this club continued to play hard. I take a lot of pride in what we did."

And later, it was apparent that Piniella never really got over the lack of support in the lawsuit.

"The big reason that I left there was when I got sued by the umpires, I was left alone," Piniella said in *Marge Schott: Unleashed*, the 1993 book by then–*Cincinnati Post* reporter Mike Bass on the life and times of the controversial Schott. "I was one of her key employees and the posture I got was, 'You handle it yourself.' What I said was wrong and I realize it, but I said it in the heat of battle and I said it for the good of the ballclub, not myself. And, hell, I never got any backing.

"When you work for people and you pour your heart and soul into a job, you expect more. I've got a ball team to concern myself with, and it's hard doing two things at once. The ballclub had liability insurance and lawyers working for it, but what I got was, 'Well, our insurance rates would go up.' What the hell do they have insurance for?"

Quinn's contract was also coming up, and ever the whipping boy for Schott's outrageous behavior, he was virtually ignored.

"[Schott] listened to everyone from the local grocer to people in her car dealership to her neighbor, the tire guy, and she lacked the necessary baseball acumen," said Quinn. "If she had just reached out, particularly to Lou, I would've been hopeful [he would have stayed]. She wanted Lou back, but she wasn't sure she wanted Lou back. And by then, he had made up his mind."

In five full seasons as a major-league manager, Piniella's teams had finished with 90 or more victories three times. The 1987 Yankees had 89 wins.

Quinn, voted Executive of the Year by his peers in 1990, was fired two days after Piniella said he was not coming back, resulting in an outraged show of support from the Reds' division rivals.

"I think Bob Quinn did the best job of any GM in baseball last winter," Atlanta general manager John Schuerholz was quoted as saying.

Quinn had acquired Tim Belcher, Greg Swindell, Scott Ruskin, and outfielders Bip Roberts and Dave Martinez that previous winter and lost only outfielder Eric Davis and pitcher Randy Myers, whom he acquired for John Franco, off his roster. But the Reds' farm system was bare after mining it over the years for players like Larkin, Sabo, Oliver, O'Neill, and Browning.

"It's always tough to repeat unless you have unlimited resources," said Quinn. "I did what I could but I always felt Lou didn't feel I did enough, though Marge sat down and said, 'This is the budget, we have to stay within it.' That 1990 payroll was $32 million and $37 million in '91."

Quinn still has the telegram George Steinbrenner sent to him and Piniella in 1990, along with a case of champagne, after the Reds won the World Series. It read, "Atta boy, Bob, I knew you could do it."

Schuerholz agreed.

"He worked with the skills of a surgeon in identifying and directly strengthening the needs of that club," he said of Quinn. "I think it's tragic he wasn't retained."

Braves manager Bobby Cox said nothing surprised him but added a caveat.

"I think most owners are a little more humane than Mrs. Schott," Cox said. "That's brutal."

When Schott died on March 2, 2004, Joe Henderson, the columnist for the *Tampa Tribune* who has known Piniella since the earliest days of his pro career, reminisced with him about the time Marge left Schottzie's ashes in Kyoto, Japan, during a Reds postseason tour when Piniella was manager.

"There were the monks, and they had this green tea that's supposed to ward off evil. It was all to give homage to Schottzie and ensure, I guess, that Schottzie went to doggie heaven," Piniella said.

He laughed a bit, then softened as always.

"You know, I really liked Marge. I really did," he said.

Anita Piniella did as well. She got to know Schott beyond the idiosyncrasies and worse. She had even gone to visit and stayed with Schott in her Cincinnati home the previous summer.

"She was living by herself," Anita told Henderson. "Her dogs had died, and she was all alone, except for someone who came by to check on her. She couldn't get up and down the stairs, so she had to live in a room by her kitchen. It was kind of sad. We just talked about the good times and Lou. She loved Lou."

Lou recalled the rubbing of Schottzie's fur on his chest and the telegrams he would get from the dog during the season: "You played a dog-gone good game last night. Love, Schottzie."

But he also remembered her generosity with kids and animal causes. And apparently, forgot the other stuff.

"Look," he said to Henderson, "don't say nothin' bad about Marge, okay?"

CHAPTER
6

The Wizard of the Emerald City

So he could now add World Series–winning manager to his resume, but Lou Piniella was not particularly interested in sending out any resumes for the time being. And if he was, he would not have sent one to the Seattle Mariners.

Who would have? Baseball's graveyard, Seattle was a place where managers went to disappear, where careers died, and Piniella had some other matters he had to resolve after leaving the Reds.

An active businessman throughout his baseball career, Piniella had dabbled in everything from the stock market to landscaping to real estate. He had owned restaurants, car dealerships, and thoroughbred horses. He had sold municipal bonds and played company pitchman.

After retiring from the Yankees in 1984, he invested with a group of nine others in a variety of businesses in New York and Connecticut, including restaurants, a used car business, and residential real estate. But by the early '90s, the recession had dug its teeth into the investments and his partners declared bankruptcy.

Piniella, however, would not. In large part because of the other partners' legal entanglements, it took nearly 10 years to resolve debts that amounted to nearly $350,000 with a portion of some of his

149

Mariners paychecks (approximately $8,000 per month, according to documents obtained by the *Tampa Tribune*) garnished by court order to pay off a New York brokerage company.

"Many times I got up in the middle of the night and hit my head against the wall," Piniella told Art Thiel, columnist for the *Seattle Post-Intelligencer* and author of *Out of Left Field, How the Mariners Made Baseball Fly in Seattle*.

"I don't know how many times I said, 'How can you be so stupid?'"

His longtime friend and attorney Tony Gonzalez, who advised Piniella at the time along with attorney Larry Solomon, said Pniella's associates were not friends but "guys who hung around him and encouraged him to get involved in deals that couldn't miss."

"As a businessman, Lou is very, very bright and motivated but at the time, he was distracted by the obligations of being a baseball player and you can't be playing for the Yankees and own three restaurants in Kansas City or a car dealership in New York.

"The one with the deep pockets was Lou, so when things got rough, they all abandoned ship and Lou had to face the music because he would not go bankrupt, he's an honorable person and he wanted to make sure everyone came out whole."

When asked after that, Piniella said he always advised young players to be careful with their money. "I tell them I got burned," he said. "Be conservative, because you'll make enough over your career to not need anything else."

But none of this was on his mind in October 1992, when Woody Woodward approached him about the managerial opening in Seattle.

Woodward had tried to hire Piniella in 1988 to replace the fired GM Dick Balderson. Piniella had been the first choice of Woodward, a friend and the man who preceded him as GM of the Yankees in October 1987. But recently fired for the second time as Yankees manager, Piniella was seemingly trapped by one of Steinbrenner's famous personal services contracts.

Toronto was also interested in Piniella at that time, but Woodward said he knew there was no way he'd end up with the Blue Jays.

"George would not let him go to Toronto because they were in the AL East," Woodward said. "I think the Boss was very smart there. He wasn't going to let that happen while he was able to control it. He wasn't going to let someone of Piniella's talent take a team in the East and end up beating him. It was a smart move."

Steinbrenner eventually surprised Toronto GM Pat Gillick by demanding starting pitcher Todd Stottlemyre in return for Piniella, but Gillick turned him down.

Woodward had hopes he might work around Steinbrenner's contract and lure his friend to Seattle and as a favor to Woodward, Piniella flew out to talk to him, then-owner George Argyros, and team president Chuck Armstrong. But in the end, worried about the shaky financial ground the club was on at the time, Piniella passed without trying to find a way out of his Yankees deal and entered the broadcast booth.

Woodward was discouraged. Since their inception in 1977 as a by-product of a lawsuit, the Mariners had yet to have a winning season and were generally ignored by their fans.

"When I first went to Seattle [in August 1988], I went to George Argyros and said, 'There's only one man to bring out here to help me get this turned around,' and I told him it was Lou," Woodward said. "But it just wasn't the right time for Lou."

A year later, Argyros put the Mariners up for sale and Steinbrenner would relent in allowing Piniella out of the final year of his contract to take the Reds' job. And after Piniella left Cincinnati, Woodward was waiting for him again.

"I was into the third ownership group at that point [in less than five years]," said Woodward, "and I went to [then-chairman] John Ellis and said, 'You need to meet Lou. He's the guy I'd like to get.' By that time, we had started to win some games and my thinking was that if I could get Lou in there, that would be the piece we really needed to teach these guys how to win."

Initially, Piniella was still not interested in Woodward's pitch. He needed to resolve his business problems and on top of that, anyone with any sense was advising him to stay away from Seattle.

"Back in those days, the so-called experts, most from back East, were saying that baseball would never work in the Northwest," said Woodward. "I had a different read on it because I had been there a while and had seen things begin to take shape and said, 'Lou, if we can just get a team playing in September to where it really means something, baseball will take off. It has always been big in football and it will in baseball too.'"

Woodward was resolute. He told Piniella that he would like the new owners, that the resources and commitment were there, and once again, as a favor, Piniella agreed to fly out and talk, though he told them he did not anticipate taking the job.

Ellis, the American face of a Japanese ownership group who also owned Nintendo, did not consider himself a baseball expert. "I was just kind of roped into the job of trying to save a team for a community," he said.

"So there we are," continued Ellis. "I had heard about Lou Piniella but just vaguely, and all of a sudden here was this guy who was bigger than life."

Over cocktails and dinner, Piniella met with Woodward, Ellis, and several others in the ownership group, successful young Microsoft computer and McCaw Cellular hotshots who were new to baseball and apparently eager to play hardball with the famous manager.

They challenged Piniella, asking why they should even be interested in hiring him after he was "let go" by Cincinnati. Both Woodward and Ellis were mortified.

"They were numbers guys and technical supermen interested in statistics," said Ellis, "and I thought, 'My gosh, they're going to turn this guy off,' and he might have turned the other way. I know I might have been turned off, though in retrospect, it represented a piece of the challenge [to Lou]."

Still, Ellis ended the "interview."

"John and I were concerned where the questions were going and John put a stop to it at that point," said Woodward. "I had no doubt. I knew going in that Lou was the guy I wanted and John Ellis picked that up right away and agreed, so he didn't want it to get way off base. But when Lou and I were leaving, I don't remember any major concerns by him other than, 'This is a different type of ownership.'

"I said, 'Lou, you're exactly right.'"

Piniella was unfazed, but there was still the question of whether he would take the job and if he did, whether he would stick around long enough to see the task through.

Ellis and Woodward were not sure. And apparently neither was Anita Piniella.

"No, no, no, no, no," Piniella told Thiel in recalling his wife's words on the plane ride back home to New Jersey. "She said, 'You're not going to Seattle. Just get that totally out of your mind.'"

Her objections were certainly reasonable. Seattle was, well, far away. The Piniellas had three children, the oldest of whom, Louis, 23, was working on Wall Street, while Kristi, 21, and Derek, 13, were still in school and in need of their father. And the rest of their family and winter home was still in Florida, while the Mariners' spring training home was in Arizona.

Ellis was worried as well.

"More than anything else, I wanted somebody who could come in and bring in the flavor of Major League Baseball to Seattle," Ellis said. "And when I first met this guy, I said to myself, 'My gosh, if ever there was somebody who epitomizes an old-time ballplayer, here he is.' I was basically sold on Piniella from the minute I met him.

"What I wasn't sold on was that this wasn't a job he would take for a while until along comes a better one. Here was guy from Florida, by way of New York. Could he come live in the Northwest and bring a club back to life that was almost dormant?"

Before Piniella flew back home, Ellis had a few words for him.

"I said, 'Lou, what I'm really concerned about is whether you really care about this job. I want to restore baseball in Seattle and I want to begin to create a tradition here, and if your idea is to just come here for a year or two and depart for other places, then I don't think I really want you.'

"As I heard later from Woody and Lou, this really made Lou mad because when he went home, he was saying to himself, 'Who the heck is this guy Ellis who is questioning if I'm serious?'"

Piniella told Thiel he recalled three questions of Ellis in particular:

"Are you scared of the situation?"

"Are you afraid you can't make it happen?"

"You don't think you're good enough to get this thing going?"

"He challenged me," Piniella said. "And I love challenges."

He promised Anita that if she could see her way clear to supporting his decision, he would move the family back to their hometown of Tampa, where their families still lived, and that he would build them a house on the beach. The Mariners agreed to an unlimited travel budget to fly Anita and the kids to Seattle for visits. He found a beautiful waterfront home. And he got a three-year deal paying him $800,000 annually, which would help with those business troubles.

Ellis called it "a whole-hearted acceptance."

Piniella had beaten out Davey Johnson, Tom Trebelhorn, and Doug Rader for the job. He had convinced his wife it was the right thing to do to take a position as far away from Florida that he could possibly go and still be in the continental United States.

Now all he had to do was figure out how to turn around a team that had the worst record in the American League (64–98) the previous season under Bill Plummer.

"There is a great nucleus of young players to build with and we're not too far away from putting a viable product on the field," Piniella said at his introductory press conference on November 9, 1992.

He promised to instill confidence and aggressiveness.

On paper, his new team looked darned promising with American League batting champion Edgar Martinez at third base, Ken Griffey Jr. in center field, Jay Buhner in right, Omar Vizquel at short, and Tino Martinez at first. Early on, Piniella recommended trading the often-injured Kevin Mitchell and got reliever Norm Charlton from Cincinnati in return.

"This club lost 98 games, but it's not a club that should lose 98 games or come close to losing 98 games," he said.

Of course, Piniella also inherited a pitching staff with the second-worst ERA in the American League. But first, Piniella would have to change a culture of losing, and he was tested immediately.

Schooled early under the often unreasonable expectations of George Steinbrenner, who wanted to see results immediately in spring training to boost regular-season ticket sales, Piniella carried some of that with him.

In their first spring training under their new manager, the Mariners played all 28 exhibition games as the visiting team while their new complex in Peoria, a suburb of Phoenix, was being completed. It was a beautiful place and the team could train there, but the stadium wasn't ready. That made for a rocky road, both figuratively and literally as they spent most of those days on a bus.

The situation was not helped by the fact that the Mariners lost their first six exhibition games and nine of their first 10.

"Every game was a 45-minute to an hour bus ride and as the losses built up, Lou spoke louder on the bus and most times, it wasn't good," said Rick Griffin, who had been the team trainer since 1983 and would spend 10 years under Piniella.

On one particular occasion, Griffin and many players recalled, the Mariners led the Cubs 8–2 "and I thought we might finally win and we'd get a nice bus ride back to Peoria," Griffin said. "But the lead melted and in the ninth inning the Cubs hit a grand slam and we ended up losing 8–7 for our ninth loss."

As they pulled out for the ride home, Piniella noticed a little park across from the complex with some 10-year-olds playing catch and yelled out for the driver to "stop the fucking bus."

When it stopped, Piniella stood up and snarled at his team: "Why don't some of you pitchers get off and see if you can get some of these kids out, because you sure as hell can't get big-leaguers out."

"The bus was pretty quiet the rest of the way back," Griffin said. "And by the end of spring training, everyone knew what was expected."

If they didn't, Piniella locked the snack room in Peoria for a week to send a message about sacrifice and discipline. "He's like 'Apple Jacks? Cheerios? Sandwiches with freaking toothpicks? Flavored coffees? What the hell are we running here? This ain't no freaking country club.' And he locked it up," recalled pitcher Chris Bosio, who would later become a minor league hitting instructor and scout for Seattle before serving as Piniella's pitching coach his first season in Tampa.

In time, players would get used to scenes involving food in the clubhouse.

"If there had been a bunch of mental mistakes in a game, guys picked off, oh yeah," said Jay Buhner, "I saw the carpet catch on fire many a time from Lou kicking over the food table and the Sterno cans landing on the floor and guys trying to put it out with milk."

"The funniest part," said Bosio, "is that the carpet is smoldering, smoke is rising, we're laughing and Lou glances back like 'Oh,' tells us to 'shut up,' and keeps right on talking. It smelled like dead cats in there after that."

The Mariners went 15–5 the remainder of that first spring and Piniella definitely made an impression. One player who learned quickly what Lou Piniella and the big leagues were all about was Bret Boone.

Boone had made his major-league debut the previous August for the Mariners, but he was about to take his first at-bat under the new Seattle manager and wanted nothing more than to impress him.

"We were facing the Angels and he had me hitting second," Boone recalled. "Chuck Finley was a lefthander who threw a split finger and in the minors, we didn't see that very often. Vizquel had led off with a double and Lou says, 'Okay son, get him over. Get him over.'

"I was a kid, I was scared to death, and I was going to show everybody. So I go up there, I take my first swing and I hit a foul ball over the first-base dugout. That's my get-it-over swing. Then he throws a split, I get fooled, and I hit a bullet to third. Gary Gaetti dove for it and doubled us up.

"I walk away thinking, 'Wow, I hit the crap out of that ball.' And I go to the bench, everyone's giving me high-fives, 'Way to swing it.' I look over at Lou and he says, 'Yeah, you hit the crap out of it son, now go get your running in and when I tell you to get the runner over, you get the runner over.' That's how it started with Lou."

Boone was the third generation of a major-league family that had produced his grandfather Ray, his father Bob, and his younger brother Aaron, who would go on to heroics with the Yankees in 2003 when his 11th inning, game-winning home run in Game 7 of the American League Championship Series sent New York to the World Series.

"Sure I was around the big leagues my whole life," Boone said, "but I was around it as a kid and now all of a sudden it was my job and like every other rookie, I wanted to prove I belonged there. And all I could think of was, 'I'm swinging hard and just trying to make it and this guy keeps getting on me every day. What does he want from me?'

"I was walking on eggshells all the time. I was back and forth to the bigs three times before I came up and stuck at mid-season. It was a big learning experience for me and he ended up being my all-time favorite manager that I ever played for."

One of the first calls Piniella made after being named the Mariners' new skipper was to call the team trainer. Piniella liked talking to trainers—felt that the information they held was as valuable as anyone else's in the organization, and his first conversation with Griffin lasted three hours.

"We talked about every single player, we talked about every conceivable thing," Griffin recalled. "Lou talked about winning and the effort he expected to be put forth by everybody. There was an entirely different level of expectation. Before he came, the focus was always to get the team to .500, but that wasn't Lou's focus.

"He told me that night, 'Within three years we will be in playoffs. This team has a lot of talent and once we get things straightened out, we'll be in the playoffs in three years.'"

By "straightened out," he meant finding out who was *not* going to be on the Piniella program.

"That was his first year to me," said Griffin. "A weeding out. And it wasn't only the players, it was everybody—the coaches, the trainers, everybody involved in the organization had to pick it up to a higher level and do things differently and to a level perceived by Lou to be putting forth every effort they had."

Buhner, a mainstay on the Mariners in his fifth full season with the club, watched the new boss in action and loved it.

"I thought, 'Thank God we finally got someone in here with a spine and a backbone.' That's what needed to be done," Buhner said. "Maybe he was a little too extreme, but Lou knew how to command respect and get you to respect yourself and the uniform you're wearing. He found out who the veteran guys were, the leaders, and he let the rest take care of itself. And right out of the gate, he stuck his foot in a few people's asses."

As Boone and the others soon learned, the players who won the most respect from Piniella were the ones who showed no fear. The others got a foot in the ass.

"I always told the players, 'You need to go into his office, stand up to him, and you need to talk to him like a man if you want to get his respect, because if he doesn't respect you, he'll never accept you. It's important not to be afraid, to voice your opinion, to speak one-on-one.' Some guys couldn't do it and many, many players didn't weather the storm."

One player who did was a young pitcher named Ken Cloude, who had been called up from Double A in 1997 and who had a couple of injuries.

"Lou didn't like pitchers and he particularly didn't like young pitchers," Griffin said. "He was pitching against Baltimore and he had only given up one or two hits through seven innings. Lou went to the mound to take him out in the seventh after he walked the first guy and Cloude says, 'Go sit your ass down because I'm going to get this guy out and I'm going to get out of this inning.'

"Lou came back to the bench and goes, 'I like this guy. I'm going to sit my ass down.' The guy had a couple good years and Lou respected him. He liked guys who had fire in their bellies. And if you had fire in your belly and backed it up, he loved you."

One player who did not click with Piniella was Jeff Cirillo. Cirillo, who had been a .313 hitter for the Colorado Rockies the season before he was traded to the Mariners in 2002, never bought into the idea that he was supposed to get in his manager's face to win his respect.

"I grew up to respect authority in front of you, whether it's the president of the company you work for or your teacher or your high school baseball coach," Cirillo said. "I don't think any of them want you to get in their face."

The idea put forth with the drill sergeant approach is that if you can't take it from them, you surely won't be able to take it in battle or in a crucial situation in the ninth inning, and better to know that as soon as possible if you're the drill sargeant.

"But see, that has nothing to do with anything, no bearing," said Cirillo. "Tom Kelly had that approach, that he embarrasses you in spring training to see who he can count on in the seventh game of the World Series and who will fold. But it's two different scenarios."

It was an adjustment for everyone in the organization, including Griffin.

"Lou didn't like people getting hurt," Griffin said bluntly. "Most times when a guy gets hurt, you tell him and the doctor tells him. But Lou didn't necessarily accept that. It didn't matter the explanation. He made it be known he didn't like guys being hurt, he didn't like sitting around.

"But what it did was it spilled over into everyone working harder to get back quicker, pushing harder in rehab. If the doctor said two weeks, Lou want them back in one week. Lou had a way of talking to you where there was no uncertainty."

Occasionally, Piniella would back down, like when Griffin, after "an extremely spirited conversation" literally showed him how Edgar Martinez could not run with a severely pulled hamstring.

"One of the trademarks of the teams I have managed," Piniella told the press when hired, "is they will play hard, get dirty, and have fun."

The fun part might not have been immediately evident. Before it was over, the '93 Seattle Mariners would revive baseball, or at least lay the foundation, in a city that had all but given up waiting.

During that season, Chris Bosio pitched a no-hitter, Ken Griffey Jr. tied a major-league record with eight home runs in eight straight games, Jay Buhner hit for the cycle, and Randy Johnson won 19 games and struck out 300.

The Mariners also took part in an epic brawl in June with the Baltimore Orioles that seemed to signal they were through being pushed around. If they were not buying into what Piniella was selling, they were sure doing a pretty good impression of it.

"Before [Piniella] got to Seattle, our big goal was to finish above .500," said Buhner. "Well, screw getting above .500. When I was traded from the Yankees [where he played under Piniella in 1987–88 before being shipped to Seattle in an infamous uneven trade for Ken Phelps], we were winning on every level. It was an organization where the mentality was imprinted on you that it's not *how* you would win but that you *will* win, period. If you didn't, we just ran out of outs today. Lou brought that mentality in. And after a while, you're damn right people buy into it."

Seattle would finish that first season in 1993 at 82–80, only the second winning team in Mariners history. In the first game of a four-game set against the White Sox in the Mariners' second-to-last series of the season, Bo Jackson launched a three-run homer to carry the Sox to a 4–2 victory and clinch the AL West title.

Afterward, with the roar of the Comiskey Park crowd still audible, Piniella sat his team down in the visitor's clubhouse and with emotion choking his voice, told them, "Everyone listen to that. That is what you play the game for, to celebrate and win and go to the playoffs. When you work out this winter, every time you run, every time you throw the ball, every time you lift a weight, remember that celebration because that's going to be us."

And then he walked the length of the clubhouse to his office, tears running down his face.

"And that was that," recalled Ken Griffey Jr. "Short, sweet, and to the point."

"A lot of us teared up," said Bosio. "That was Lou. No parties at our expense. Absolutely not."

"He showed everyone," said Griffin, "that even a tough guy can show passion and hurt. It hurts Lou to lose, it's almost painful for him and he showed it by that, he showed his passion for the game. That stuck in a lot of guys' minds."

Piniella was confident that the Mariners would be celebrating soon. So soon that shortly after the season ended, he predicted the team would win the AL West the following season.

"I expect this team to win the division," said Piniella. "I'll go on record as saying that. We've got a good nucleus of veterans. What I saw evolving was a team getting some good chemistry and starting to develop leaders."

Of course, this was before the club traded away their talented shortstop Omar Vizquel to Cleveland in anticipation of bringing up an 18-year-old phenom named Alex Rodriguez, who Ken Griffey Sr., serving as an assistant to Woodward, reported wasn't yet ready for the big leagues.

Besides, with the very real possibility of a players' strike looming over the 1994 season, it did not make much sense to bring Rodriguez up in a potentially abbreviated year, thus having him gain major-league service time (in fact, his contract and that of Griffey Jr.'s would expire at the same time because of that very scenario playing out).

But in the winter of 1993–94, things were looking up for the Mariners. Major League Baseball had realigned from two divisions into three apiece, adding a wild-card team to the playoffs and a Division Series to be played before the League Championship Series, thus helping their odds of making their first postseason.

The Mariners seemed to at least have an eye on big things to come with a 21–9 record in spring training. But by midseason of 1994, they had the second-worst record in baseball and Griffey Jr. was talking trade.

In early July, the Mariners were playing their usually contentious series against the Yankees when Griffey Jr. was hit by a pitch in retaliation for Seattle brushbacks aimed at Paul O'Neill, who had played for and feuded with Piniella in Cincinnati.

After the game, Griffey Jr. went into Piniella's office and told him that if he had a problem with O'Neill, to leave him out of it.

Griffey Jr. hadn't come around to Piniella right away in Seattle. He was unhappy with his father's treatment in Cincinnati, where Piniella didn't play Senior, one of the stars on the Big Red Machine, and then management released him before he was signed by the Mariners late in the 1990 World Series season. And Junior wasn't ready to embrace his new manager in Seattle right away.

Asked if Piniella had to win him over, Junior responded, "Yeah, a whole lot. You have to understand, family always comes first. I'm thankful that it worked out for my dad, the [Reds] team still voted him a full share and he still got a ring and we got to play together [for the Mariners in late 1990]. So it worked out.

"I talked with my dad and he ended up being one of Lou's coaches [and later assistant to Woodward], so that helped."

In time, the two would grow close, Griffey once testing Piniella's ability to take a joke in legendary fashion after the manager bet him a steak dinner he couldn't get the ball out of the cage in batting practice.

The day after Griffey failed—against Rafael Soriano—Piniella came to the park to find a cow, complete with flies, squeezed into his office.

"A bet's a bet," said Griffey. "Here's your steak dinner."

Of all the teams Piniella would manage, the Mariners seemed to touch his funny bone and his heart the most. And the bond he forged with a baby-faced Alex Rodriguez endures.

In an interview with Frank Deford in March 2007 for HBO's *Real Sports with Bryant Gumbel*, Rodriguez recalled a game during that '94 season with the Mariners when, "[Dennis] Eckersley, he threw me four or five sliders. And I just kept swinging and swinging. And Lou, I mean, he comes up and goes, 'Gosh darn it, son. I mean, I wanna play you, but you can't swing at those pitches.' And I remember being 18, almost in tears.

"I remember being on the far side of the bench and man, I just felt like, 'Get me back in my senior high school uniform,' you know? And then sure enough, he comes and he gives me a big kiss on the top of my head.

"He said, 'Son, I love you. I love you. I just want you to do well.' And you know, from that day on…he was just like a father to me."

Those moments, however, would give way to more pressing concerns for the team.

In July 1994, two 26-pound tiles in the Kingdome roof came crashing into the seats before a game. Renovation would take four months and cost taxpayers a whopping $70 million ($3 million more than it took to build the Kingdome in 1976), and the team would have to move back on the road—a la the spring of 1993—for a loss of 15 home games.

But something interesting happened. The Mariners bonded on the road and actually made a run at the division lead in early August.

"We were around the ballpark lot more," Buhner recalled. "We were living out of a suitcase, so we figured we may as well go to ballaprk and we started getting there earlier and earlier. The coaching staff would be there by 1:00, we'd get there by 2:00, have lunch together before early BP. That's when, as a whole unit, we started bonding."

Until August 12, anyway. That's when the deadline for a new collective bargaining agreement expired and the players went on strike. It was the beginning of a work stoppage that would be the longest in pro sports history, wiping out the rest of the season, the postseason, and a combined 252 games at the start of the 1995 season—eight months in all.

The only positive for Piniella—in the fall of 1994, the Mariners awarded him a two-year, $1.7 million contract extension with an option to pick up a third year for an additional $850,000.

The '95 season, which would be shortened to 144 games, dawned late but bright, fans bitter, to be sure, but players glad to be back at work and Seattle players high on the idea of shooting for that new wild-card position in the playoffs.

Being the Mariners, however, there was to be more turmoil generated from ownership, this time with its proposal to build a new baseball-only stadium with a retractable roof, largely at taxpayer expense. The team's 20-year lease with the Kingdome was about to expire and they needed the profits a new stadium would produce.

The state legislature had been unenthusiastic about earlier proposals to help fund the project, the Mariners' sad state of both local and Major League Baseball no small reason. One proposal was offered up during the strike with replacement players poised to open the 1995 season.

A public-private partnership idea was finally up for public vote, one that would hike the price for an average taxpayer in King

County (site of the Kingdome) about $7.50 per year. The proposal, which drew heavy opposition, would be voted on at the primary election on September 19. Ownership threatened to move the club if the vote did not pass.

In the meantime, there was baseball to be played. And buoyed by the goal of a wild-card, it gave Woodward ammunition to go to Mariners' ownership and ask to add payroll at the trade deadline.

Given the green light, he acquired Andy Benes, a 27-year-old righthander who was 4–7 with a 4.17 ERA with the Padres, for a couple of former first-round draft picks. Two weeks later, the Mariners traded another minor-league prospect for the speedy Vince Coleman, 33, who had been batting .287 with 26 stolen bases in 35 attempts for Kansas City and had played in a World Series with St. Louis.

But hovering at a game above .500 and trailing 12½ games behind the Angels in early August, it was not just the wild-card that was at stake, but Mariners baseball. Surely, they were not inspiring anyone to keep the team.

"That was incredible, that whole stretch drive," said Buhner. "We had spent the whole season with everyone on the airplane literally looking at magazines for condos and apartments to rent and houses to buy in Tampa Bay because we were so sure the team was going to be moved there.

"Then we'd have to come back and talk to delegates, go to the capitol, meet and greets. It was almost like we were campaigning. There was always something going on every single day, sometimes an hour before the game. If it was going to save baseball in Seattle, guys were ready to do it, but now we had to play the game. For us to be able to do that and still be able to turn the switch and step across white lines and play the game every single day was incredible. We had a really special group."

The Mariners won 16 games in August, a club record for any month, and went on a run that included a three-game sweep of the Yankees. By September 1, they had cut the Angels' lead to 6½ games with their offense producing at a torrid pace, a different hero every night. Their team slogan: "Refuse to Lose."

Hardly anyone even remembered that first season, when a man in a restaurant approached Piniella and a couple of his coaches while they were having breakfast and asked when the season started. Piniella had to inform the man that they had played 14 games already.

"It had become a great baseball city," said pitching coach Stan Williams, who followed Piniella to Seattle from Cincinnati. "We were selling out every night. The dome we played in was unbelievably tough on pitchers. I didn't realize it so much until I got out of there. Ground balls shot through the infield, you'd hit the ball in the air and it would fly out of the park."

Players were still coming early to the clubhouse, and they weren't always leaving at night.

"If we had an early turnaround, a day game after a night game, guys would just hang out, sleep on couches, and stay all night," said Buhner. "There would be wiffle ball games on the field at 2:30 in the morning. We were like a bunch of little kids sneaking out on our parents.

"Obviously when Anita was in town, Lou couldn't stick around. But when she wasn't, we'd pull a cooler out there, Lou would sit down with McLaren and Lee Elia and the whole coaching staff, have a beer or two, and just shoot the shit. Lou would tell old war stories, talk about hitting, it was the greatest."

The next day, they would roll off the couches, suit up, and win again.

"Lou has as an amazing ability to get teams to play their best in tough situations," said Martinez. "It was very hard but he got the team rolling and we played the best baseball the organization had ever played in the month of September. We couldn't lose, due to his ability to have the team concentrate and focus on winning."

Benes would win seven of nine decisions the rest of the way, Randy Johnson finished the '94 season at 18–2, while Charlton was a reliable closer. And no one was talking wild-card anymore with the division title in sight.

"We had a good ballclub and they played extremely well," said Woodward, "but when you look back, people had no idea that all these distractions were going on. But they still kept playing and Lou was the one who kept them charged up. He just didn't let it get out of hand."

On September 19, the Mariners had climbed to within one game of the Angels when they defeated Texas in an extra-inning 5–4 victory on a single by Ken Griffey Jr. after pinch-hitter Doug Strange homered to tie the game in the ninth. That night, incredibly, the stadium measure barely passed.

The Angels had lost nine straight and three days later, the Mariners took sole possession of first place.

"It really was incredible timing," said Woodward. "Just the entire area, the entire Northwest, took to the ballclub. How much it played in the vote, I don't know. There had been strong baseball fans there but now, all of a sudden, we were making fans out of people who hadn't been fans before. We'd be on road and win a game, and back home in restaurants, you'd hear 'Hey, the Mariners just won in Texas,' and the word went around the entire restaurant. It was just one of those feelings the Northwest never had before."

From August 25 to September 26, the Angels had dropped 22 of 28 games, one of the worst late-season collapses in baseball history, while the Mariners lost just eight in 29 games during that span. In one month, the Angels lost 10 games in the standings.

The Mariners had not just cut the life out of the California Angels. They also, from all indications, had saved baseball in Seattle.

First, however, they would have to worry about the playoffs and the Angels. With a late rally to win six of their last seven regular-season games, Anaheim forced a one-game playoff with the Mariners, who dropped their final two to Texas. Both teams were at 78–66, and the winner would be division champs, the loser, out of the postseason.

"This is the way baseball should be," said Piniella, who would start Randy Johnson. "Winner goes on; loser goes home."

It was practically a state holiday as work and school stopped for the biggest game in Mariners franchise history. And with the noise in the Kingdome at painful levels, the Mariners defeated the Angels 9–1 behind Randy Johnson's complete-game victory to set up a matchup with the wild-card New York Yankees in the American League Division Series.

For Piniella, playing the Yankees was always an emotional experience.

"Lou wasn't afraid to let his emotions out," Buhner recalled. "And that was especially the case when we played the Yankees. You're on center stage, the East Coast and New York is always a draw for the national media, and when you're in that limelight, it's exhausting. There are a lot of emotions. We had great battles with them and when we left, we were always exhausted.

"It was one of the few times it was a little quiet when we were on the bus. When we were leaving town, Lou would be out like a light, asleep most of the time. Every time we went into New York, he was like a Jekyll-Hyde personality."

It was during those trips to New York during the regular season that his players saw firsthand Piniella's stature in the city. Never the best player on a team of superstars, he was always a fan favorite for his style of play, his clutch play at the plate, his unadulterated passion for the game.

"I remember one time in New York having dinner with Edgar Martinez at a steakhouse," Boone said. "This was during the 2001 season when we could do no wrong, and Lou comes in and sits next to us, and when he gets up to leave, the whole place is chanting his name. The whole restaurant stood up. He played 20 years ago. They could care less about Edgar and I. Not too many people have that kind of longevity."

* * *

The 1995 ALDS would begin with two games in New York and finish up with three games, if necessary, in Seattle. The Mariners were exhausted, playing their third game in three days, three cities, and in three time zones And the fans in the Bronx were in all their glory, pelting the Mariners' outfielders with coins, batteries, Frisbees, and assorted debris, which caused an enraged Piniella to pull his team off the field briefly during Game 2.

The Yankees would win Game 1, 9–6 despite two home runs by Griffey. In an extra-innings Game 2, Junior knocked out another in the twelfth but the Yankees tied it up in the bottom half. And with Tim Belcher dueling Mariano Rivera from the twelfth inning on, back-up Yankees catcher Jim Leyritz poked a walk-off homer with one on and one out in the fifteenth for the 7–5 New York victory.

The Yankees took a 2–0 series lead to Seattle amid the weird charge by Yankees owner George Steinbrenner that one of the umpires was biased toward the Mariners because he was from Portland, a claim that would eventually cost him a $50,000 fine from the league.

On the late-night plane ride back to Seattle, team chairman John Ellis and his wife, Doris, were sitting behind Piniella.

"It was the first time I'd ever been to a playoff game, this was all new to me, and my chin was on the floor wondering if we were even going to win one at home," Ellis recalled. "And Lou says absolutely confidently, 'John, we're going to win this thing.'

"Well, I thought he was just trying to make me feel good. But he said, 'No, we're going to win it,' and he laid it all out for me, how we had Randy pitching once, maybe again if he needed him.

"He was totally convinced we were going to win the series and I don't think he was putting me on. Maybe he would've ended up being wrong but by God, Piniella knew he was going to win and he wasn't going to let anyone on that team think otherwise."

The Mariners were deflated and exhausted, but Piniella's confidence was buoyed when New York manager Buck Showalter named his best veteran starter Jack McDowell as his Game 3 starter against Johnson, an indication that he was banking on a sweep.

"If they had held McDowell until the fourth game, it would have been advantageous to them," Piniella said in *Out of Left Field*.

"The mistake was matching McDowell against Randy because Randy was going to win, no matter what. We'd played very well at home, where we had a huge advantage in the Kingdome. A win would open the door."

And that it did as the Kingdome was once again deafening for its first playoff game ever and even New York–like with foreign objects flying out of the grandstand. A four-run sixth inning for the Mariners paved the way for a 7–4 win as Johnson got the win and Charlton the save.

Tino Martinez, a 1995 Mariners mainstay who batted .293 with 31 home runs and 111 RBIs during the regular season, was 3-for-4 with three RBIs, including a two-run homer off Jack McDowell in the fifth.

The Yankees jumped out to a 3–0 lead in the first inning of Game 4, and went up 5–0 in the top half of the third on a two-run homer by O'Neill. But Edgar Martinez answered with a three-run home run in the bottom half of the inning and slugged a grand slam in the eighth en route to an 11–8 victory. Griffey and Buhner also had homers.

It was only fitting that Ken Griffey and Edgar Martinez would be the heroes in Game 5. With the Yankees leading 4–2 and just five outs away from taking the series, Griffey, tying Reggie Jackson's postseason record with five home runs in a single series, hit a solo shot to make it a one-run game.

Yankees pitcher David Cone walked in a run to tie it up. In the ninth, with just a day's rest, McDowell and Johnson dramatically entered the game in the ninth in relief roles, Johnson retiring the heart of the Yankees' order—Wade Boggs, Bernie Williams, and Paul O'Neill—on a strikeout and two fly-outs. McDowell retired the side as well.

In the top of the eleventh, New York went up by a run when Randy Velarde singled home pinch runner Pat Kelly as Johnson, pitching for the third time in seven days, suddenly appeared human.

Seattle's Joey Cora led off with a bunt single on his own in the bottom of the inning, Griffey singled to put runners on first and third, and Edgar Martinez drove in the series-winning runs with a double into the left-field corner.

Griffey jumped up after sliding safely into home, scoring easily on a throw that was late and wide, but he was immediately knocked back down and buried by his jubilant teammates. Piniella's prediction had come true.

"That's when everyone said, 'Holy shit, these guys really do have something special going on,'" said Buhner. "In those days, we weren't getting the kind of coverage in the Northwest that everyone else was getting, but every day, people were picking up their papers and there was this underdog Mariner team and a kind of buzz started building.

"Once we beat the Yankees, that in itself was when we as an organization went from finishing second or third in our division to others saying, 'Hey, we have to start taking these guys seriously.'"

Two homers by Manny Ramirez in Game 2 of the ALCS against Cleveland secured a split after the first two games in Seattle. And then it was Jay Buhner's turn in Game 3, driving in four runs on two home runs—the second, a three-run game-winner in the eleventh that also to amended for an error that allowed the Indians to tie it up in the eighth.

But the Indians, trailing 2–1 would take control of the series at that point, winning the next three games while outscoring Seattle 14–2, including two shutouts, to close it out with 7–0, 3–2, and 4–0 victories.

The Mariners had been at a severe disadvantage in their starting rotation for the ALCS, thrown off by the necessity of their divisional playoff against the Angels. The Indians had swept Boston in the ALDS and were rested, their rotation set. Seattle was in such desperate need of pitching help that Piniella added rookie Bob Wolcott to the roster and started him in Game 1.

Wolcott walked the first three batters on 13 pitches, and Piniella walked out to the mound, his young pitcher expecting the worst.

As Wolcott related the conversation, "He said, 'Even if we get beat 11–0, it would be a good off-season.' That was kind of amusing."

Wolcott then struck out Albert Belle, and got Eddie Murray and Jim Thome out on a foul-out and a ground-out to second, and the Mariners went on to win, 3–2.

Surely Piniella would not have pulled his pitcher at that point, but he seemed to have treated the situation perfectly. Handling pitchers, however, is far from an exact science for managers as would bear out two games later in the series.

With the series tied at two games apiece, Piniella left Bosio in an inning too long and Thome made the Mariners pay, clubbing a two-run home run in the sixth in what would be the difference in a 3–2 victory and 3–2 series lead.

In Game 6, Piniella again erred on the side of confidence in his pitcher, this time his ace, as Johnson gave up three runs in the eighth and the game and the series was over.

In six games, the Mariners, emotionally and physically spent, scored 12 runs, a record-low for a six-game playoff series and a number that would come back to haunt Piniella in his first two years with the Cubs as his teams would total 12 runs in six games over two NLDS sweeps.

But this was surely not a case of extreme shock and disappointment as the Cubs would later feel but rather a moment of quiet reflection.

"I remember it so well," said Ellis. "I had gone into the dressing room before the game ended so that I could be there when the team came in and they dragged themselves in, not saying anything. They had killed themselves all season and lost the damn thing. So they're getting undressed, mumbling to themselves when Piniella comes in and in a breaking voice, he says, 'Fellas, they're still out there. Would you mind going out again?'

"The crowd wouldn't leave. The Kingdome was full of people on their feet, yelling at the top of their lungs for a team that lost. And out go the guys, some half-dressed, and they make a tour of the field. Lou had tears streaming down his face. And that crowd did not leave until the team came back in. I will never forget that."

It was a snapshot in Mariners history that many would never forget, a reminder, in years to come, of perhaps the last days of baseball innocence for the franchise.

The outside distractions continued as the construction of the new Safeco Field went through the usual fits and starts and threats from team ownership that it would move the franchise to Tampa.

The Mariners would endure Randy Johnson's back injury and though they won a franchise-record 85 games the following season as Alex Rodriguez won the AL batting title, they finished second and short of the playoffs.

They came back to win the AL West in 1997 as Griffey was named league MVP but lost 3–1 in the ALDS to Baltimore, before two consecutive third-place finishes the following seasons and another second-place in 2000.

The team traded Randy Johnson to Houston during the 1998 season and after the '99 campaign, the same year the team finally moved to Safeco Field, Griffey asked for and was granted a trade to the Cincinnati Reds.

The pitching—or rather the lack thereof—during that period nearly killed Piniella. So too had the task of balancing the delicate egos of his three superstars, Johnson, Griffey, and Alex Rodriguez.

Together with Edgar Martinez and Jay Buhner, few teams possessed the offensive firepower of the Mariners of the mid-'90s or the sheer talent of their three biggest stars. But Piniella had his hands full.

Though they denied it, reporters and teammates alike said there was jealousy between Rodriguez and Griffey, in particular, who were competitive regarding accolades like MVP.

As for Johnson, salary and trade demands were common as was persistent grumbling about being slighted. In the first half of 1998, it appeared to affect his pitching as he went 9–10 with a 4.33 ERA. He was ejected from one game and suspended for three others for throwing at batters.

"When he didn't get the extension he wanted, he didn't fulfill his contract, basically," said Jim Street, who then covered the team for *Seattle Post-Intelligencer.* "He just went out and went through the motions and it was horrible. Every so often, he'd get into a snit and he'd go in and talk to Lou.

"Lou said, 'Great, I feel like [then U.S. Secretary of State] Madeleine Albright.' Lou would tell him, 'If you want to get traded so badly, pitch well. You have a better chance than if you're horseshit.' But Randy never really understood that. If it looked like he was going to be traded, he'd pitch well and when it looked like he wasn't, he'd pitch badly."

In Johnson's defense, the Mariners' bullpen was consistently among the worst in the league during much of Piniella's tenure. Charlton tailed off after 1995 and they lost Mike Jackson after '96.

In '97, Derek Lowe, then a top prospect in the Mariners' system, was included in a trade with another, Jason Varitek, for Heathcliff Slocumb, a reliever who never panned out.

Johnson seethed at the lack of support and the resulting no-decisions.

"Lou would come out to the mound to get him and Randy would say, 'Go fuck yourself, I'm not giving you the ball,'" said Buhner, who considered himself a good friend of Johnson's. "The bullpen was giving away his wins and he felt, 'If I'm going to lose, let me do it myself.'

"If he caught Lou in the right mood, he'd say, 'All right, son,' but on other days they'd go to town right there on the mound. Randy

In his playing days, Lou Piniella wore jersey No. 14 for the New York Yankees. This photo was taken at spring training in 1975.
(AP Photo)

Lou Pinella's temper is well documented throughout his passionate career as a player and a manager. Here, Cincinnati Reds manager Lou Piniella tosses first base into right field during their game with the Chicago Cubs at Riverfront Stadium in Cincinnati on April 21, 1990. Piniella threw the base after being ejected from the game for arguing a call at first. (AP PHOTO/DAVID KOHL)

Lou Piniella's intricate knowledge of hitting mechanics benefited him as a player and later as a manager. In this image Piniella, then an outfielder with the New York Yankees, takes a swing during game action in 1977. (AP Photo)

Old friends: Cincinnati Reds manager Lou Piniella, right, talks with Oakland Athletics skipper Tony LaRussa as the two teams worked out for the 1990 World Series at Riverfront Stadium, on Monday, October 15, 1990, in Cincinnati, Ohio. (AP Photo/Al Behrman)

Ever the competitor, Seattle Mariners manager Lou Piniella grips a bat in the dugout in the sixth inning against the Oakland Athletics on Tuesday, June 4, 2002, in Oakland, California. The A's won the game 3–2 in ten innings. (AP Photo/Ben Margot)

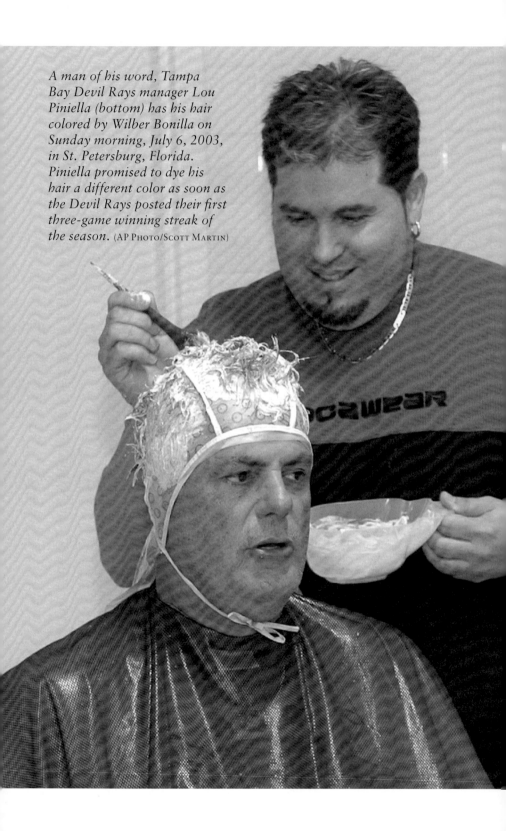

A man of his word, Tampa Bay Devil Rays manager Lou Piniella (bottom) has his hair colored by Wilber Bonilla on Sunday morning, July 6, 2003, in St. Petersburg, Florida. Piniella promised to dye his hair a different color as soon as the Devil Rays posted their first three-game winning streak of the season. (AP Photo/Scott Martin)

Go Cubs Go! Chicago Cubs manager Lou Piniella applauds after the Cubs won the NL Central title, defeating the St. Louis Cardinals 5–4 in a baseball game on Saturday, September 20, 2008, in Chicago.
(AP Photo/Nam Y. Huh)

Chicago Cubs manager Lou Piniella always thinks several steps ahead in a baseball game. Here, Piniella returns to the dugout after visiting the mound to talk with starting pitcher Rich Hill after he gave up a game-tying double to Pittsburgh Pirates' Ronny Paulino in the seventh inning of baseball action in Pittsburgh on Monday, April 30, 2007. The Pirates beat the Cubs 3–2. (AP Photo/Gene J. Puskar)

could be a real pain in the ass sometimes but tell me one person who wouldn't take Randy Johnson on their team in the 1990s and 2000s. We'd have beanball fights, and all it took was for Randy to get up on the top step of the dugout and yell out, 'I'm pitching tomorrow.'

"Lou understood that and recognized that who cares if the guy's a prick? We didn't have to all get along as long as every fifth day, he took the ball and pitched with the same prick mentality and we kept winning."

Piniella always had the reputation of being tougher on younger players. Bryan Price, the fifth pitching coach in Piniella's era, offered one reason Piniella favored veterans.

"There's no question you build credibility, you're not given credibility with Lou," Price said. "He knows the guys going out there and who have been going out there, playing hurt, grinding it out. If you knew what Buhner played through, you'd understand how someone like him would build credit with Lou."

Piniella counted on veteran players Buhner, Charlton, and Mike Blowers and his longtime coach John McLaren to monitor the clubhouse, keep the others in line, and the egos in check.

"Lou is a great judge of character and he knew who his boys were, who was going to go war for him, and he turned that [discipline] over to those guys to run the clubhouse," Buhner said.

"In the mid- to late-1990s, we had a great group of guys who were able to control that, a guy on the starting [pitching] staff, in the bullpen, on the bench, the starters. Then Lou could go manage and do what he had to do. But every now and then, he would go stick a foot up someone's ass. He didn't have to do it often but he did it."

Once, in particular, he did it with Buhner after the player was furious to find he was not batting cleanup and walked into Piniella's office demanding, "What the fuck?"

Piniella flew around the desk and was immediately chin to chin with Buhner. "I told him I was just pissed off he didn't give me a heads up, and when I walked out the door, there were no grudges," Buhner said. "After something like that, 30 minutes later he'll walk by and give you a big hug, say, 'I love you son.' His emotions are right there in front of you."

Nothing excited Piniella more, seemingly, than working with his players on hitting. Even with the offensive talent Piniella possessed during that time, there was no shortage of instruction.

Edgar Martinez, who spent his entire 18-year career with the Mariners, retired in the company of Ted Williams, Babe Ruth, Stan Musial, Rogers Hornsby, Lou Gehrig, and Manny Ramirez as the only players in history with 300 home runs, 500 doubles, a career batting average higher than .300, on-base percentage higher than .400, and a slugging percentage higher than .500.

"I learned a lot from Lou about situational hitting," said Martinez. "He was good talking about how to approach a situation. He was a great help to me when things were going bad and I wasn't swinging the bat well, just giving me tips and suggestions on how to get out of it.

"He knows hitting very well; he knows the swing. He loved it. He loved talking about mechanics, how to read pitches. He'd have other players indicate when they'd get a certain pitch and Lou would give us ideas on how to get an advantage. He gave us a lot of ideas to help us in certain situations. He'd tell us to look at the infielders and certain directions they were going, things as players we never looked at. He helped a lot to make players smarter."

Bosio remembered one spring training early in Piniella's first few days on the job when Martinez hit several foul balls in a row.

"Back then," said Bosio, "Edgar was one of the best contact, clutch, and hitters for average in baseball. He was barely hooking the ball foul, and Lou jumps in the cage and starts giving Edgar a hitting lesson. We're all going, 'What's this guy doing?'

"McLaren starts throwing the ball and Lou goes, 'No son, you've got to get your arms extended. You're getting topspin and you have to counteract that.' We were all in awe watching Lou swing a bat. Here's this 58-year-old man and he's hitting line drives. Then Edgar gets back in there and he's slicing balls down the left field line.

"Edgar goes, 'Wow, I can't believe that,' and that became, I think, a strength of Edgar's that a lot of people never realized, being able to fundamentally hit that inside or middle pitch, to keep it in play. Edgar passed Griffey, Tino Martinez, Buhner, and kind of transcended our club with his confidence and got everyone going as fundamental hitters."

A few years later, before facing Jack McDowell in the bottom of the eleventh inning with two men on in Game 5 of the 1995 ALDS, Martinez, now the consummate fundamental hitter, knew the split-finger was coming down and in, got his hands extended and rifled the ball into the left-field corner to drive in the game-winning runs.

"I look at a picture I have in my home of Griffey laying on homeplate," said Bosio, "and so many different memories go through my head—the drills Lou did with Edgar and watching Edgar rifle the ball into the corner. Then three years later, this guy is hitting that same pitch in the same place. It was amazing."

In the dugout, Piniella would quiz Price, whom he hired young (37) in 2000, without any major-league coaching or playing experience and over other candidates far more accomplished, telling him, "You never know how good a guy can be until you give him the opportunity."

"Lou always talked about guessing," Price recalled, "about figuring out patterns. As a hitter, he got more upset when he guessed wrong than anything. He'd turn to me on a 2–2 count with a runner on and say, 'What would you throw right here?' I'm thinking, 'Am I thinking the same way as he is?'

"I'd say, 'breaking ball away' or 'fastball inside' and sometimes he'd tell me what he was thinking and in his own way, he was getting an idea of what I was thinking as a coach.

"He was frustrated by those who couldn't think along, who would take a first-pitch fastball when they knew they were getting a fastball. Or if they guessed wrong but swung anyway. That would make him mad at himself as a hitter and frustrate him in others."

Buhner remembered when he was with the Yankees under Piniella as a young player, "Lou was worried I had an unhittable hitch in my swing. He told me, 'Make sure you get your front foot down because you're getting caught in between,' and he was really helpful," Buhner said.

"The beauty of Lou was that if an idea all of a sudden popped into his mind, it didn't matter where he was, you just hoped he wasn't coming out of the shower with a towel wrapped around him. He would assume your stance and say, 'Get up, hump the plate, son.'

"It was just the way he'd go about saying it, he made it so easy, it would click. Hitting is mental. You've already got it. You wouldn't have made it to the big leagues if you didn't. Sometimes you just needed those mental checkpoints."

As the Mariners tore down their team and rebuilt in lockstep with the construction of the new stadium—trading Johnson to Houston for three no-names in pitchers Freddy Garcia and John Halama and infielder Carlos Guillen—players were frustrated at taking a step back. In 1998 and '99, the Mariners won 76 and 79 games, respectively, finishing 16 games in back of Texas in '99, a season in which Piniella was ejected for arguing with umpires a career-high five times.

After the 2000 season, the contracts of both Griffey and Rodriguez were due to expire, a technicality regarding time of major-league service in the case of Rodriguez as a result of the strike settlement that caught the Mariners by surprise. Both had declined extension offers two years earlier.

Complicating matters was the fact that as Safeco Field was completed, it became apparent that it was not a hitter's park. Cold and damp, the ball didn't travel as far as the Kingdome, not exactly what a couple of sluggers with the potential of going after the all-time batting records in the game wanted to see.

The Mariners made new offers in 1999, which were at the least competitive and they thought astounding, But Griffey said he wanted to wait it out. At about the same time, a new club CEO was named, John Ellis retired, and Woodward, afraid he would be forced to trade Griffey, quit under pressure and was replaced by Pat Gillick.

Griffey's subsequent trade to Cincinnati (one of the teams he chose under his "10-and-5" status—10 years of service in the majors, including the last five with the same team) was for less money than Seattle had offered and just short of a disaster for the superstar, who also cited wanting to be near his Florida home in spring training.

On the surface, the trade was awful as well for the Mariners, who could get no better than center fielder Mike Cameron, pitcher Brett Tomko, and a couple of minor leaguers in return. Rodriguez was primed for free agency, though he promised if Seattle won the World Series in 2000, he would stay.

The Mariners made a 12-game jump to a team-record 91 wins that year; the pitching staff under the first-year Price went from second-worst in the AL to second-best, and the team won a wild-card spot in the playoffs.

After sweeping the White Sox in the ALDS, next up were the Yankees in the league championship and a rematch of the 1995 ALDS. Rodriguez played well, hitting .308 against Chicago and .409 against New York and set himself up quite nicely for the bidding bonanza that would follow after the Yankees took the series 4–2.

Rodriguez would benefit not just handsomely but historically as the Texas Rangers rewarded him with the most lucrative contract in sports history at the time—a 10-year deal worth $252 million.

The three biggest stars of their generation had shared roster space on the Mariners for five seasons and now Rodriguez, Griffey, and Johnson were gone. Including Edgar Martinez, they had had four future Hall of Famers on the team.

Piniella, who had signed a new three-year deal with the hope he could persuade Rodriguez to stay in Seattle, had a far bigger task on his hands—where to go from here.

"It always felt like we were just one player away," Martinez said of the Mariners of the late '90s. "A left-handed hitter, a left fielder, a leadoff man, it always seemed like we just needed that one player to take us to the finish line."

Ichiro Suzuki, who had actually signed three weeks before A-Rod left, would soon appear to be that guy, signing with the Mariners for $14 million over three years, including a $5 million signing bonus. A left-handed batter who was shotgun quick out of the batters' box and coming off seven straight batting titles in Japan's Pacific League, he was also a crafty center fielder with a formidable arm.

"He doesn't hit," said Piniella. "He serves like a tennis player."

One day early in spring training, Larry Stone, the national baseball writer for the *Seattle Times*, observed Piniella observing Ichiro.

"Ichiro was hitting lot of weak grounders, not pulling anything, and Lou was pulling his hair out," said Stone. "He honestly thought this guy was not any good. He said, 'I've got to see you pull the ball. Show me you can pull the ball.' And Ichiro preceeded to pull the ball five times in a row. I think that's when Lou began to see what the guy could really do."

In the 2001 season opener against Oakland, in Ichiro's first major-leage game, he laid down a perfect drag bunt for a base hit that ignited an eighth-inning rally that produced the go-ahead run in the 5–4 victory. After the game, Piniella rushed up to Ichiro in the locker room and gave him a bear hug and a kiss on the cheek, which he later laughingly described to a Japanese TV crew as "something that makes most Japanese men want to throw up."

In April, all Ichiro did was hit .336 from the leadoff spot, propelling the Mariners to a major-league record 20 wins in April and becoming an American superstar in the process. By the end of June, Seattle led the AL West by 20 games. And suddenly, the

Mariners, with acquisitions like second baseman Bret Boone and the development of post-Griffey additions John Olerud at first base, Japanese relief pitcher Kazuhiro Sasaki, middle reliver Arthur Rhodes, and reserve Mark McLemore were contenders once again.

Eight Mariners made the All-Star team (the game held at Safeco Field): Ichiro, who led the fan balloting with 3.4 million votes, Martinez, Boone, Cameron, Olerud, and pitchers Sasaki, Freddy Garcia, and Jeff Nelson.

The Mariners were 63–24, and any talk of the playoffs was almost superfluous. This was perhaps the greatest team of all time, and Piniella's crew was out to make sure generations to come would know about them.

"It wasn't a great, great team on paper," said the *Post-Intelligencer's* Jim Street. "If you look at the '95 Mariners, they had a lot more talent in its lineup than the 2001 team. But it was like all the stars were aligned, every free agent clicked."

With Bryan Price as as a cushion between Piniella and his pitchers, most of whom were usually intimidated by the manager's demanding ways, even the Mariners' pitching staff, long the club's albatross, flourished, going from the second-worst team in earned-run average in 1999 (5.24) to the best in 2001 (3.54).

"We ran a lot of guys through here; a lot of kids came up and went back down," said Price. "It's hard to get to the major-league level and anticipate you're going to do well and that can be enhanced when you know the manager is going to be pissed you didn't throw the ball over the plate.

"My rule with the pitchers was that 'Lou is going to be the best competitor you're ever going to be around, so when you struggle or screw up or walk two guys to get a rally started, he's going to be be pissed. So understand why he's upset. But when you come in tomorrow, know it's completely done and over with, no residual carryover.' He's never one to foster ill feelings toward a pitcher who struggled."

Piniella found a willing student in Price, just five months older than Mariners pitcher Jamie Moyer, who would notch the first 20-win season of his career. Price had heard the stories about how tough Piniella could be from the pitching coaches who preceded him.

"However, in my three years, I never felt the wrath of his anger, disappointment, or frustration," he said. "The thing is, you couldn't find anyone around him who wasn't prepared. You didn't want to upset him but more importantly, you really wanted to please him."

One of the things that impressed Price most, he said, was Piniella's ability to directly affect his team's play on the field.

"Lou would never be satisfied just watching a team go out and repeat the same performance," he said. "Let's say we're in a funk offensively, the guys in the middle of the order are scuffling and just can't drive in runs. Next thing you know he has guys running, he's calling a hit-and-run, squeeze. He's not going to just sit there on his hands and say, 'Well, they're big boys, they're being paid good money' and let them do their thing.

"He never thinks about what questions he's going to answer, what criticism he's going to hear. He's not going to watch the team struggle without doing anything about it."

Of course, in 2001, there did not appear to be a whole lot of struggling going on as the Mariners never lost more than two games in a row until September.

On September 10, Seattle was 104–40 with a single-minded desire to clinch the division in a matter of days, then break the single-season record for victories (116) set by the 1906 Cubs (the AL record was 114).

On September 11, the team was in Anaheim, shaken to the core with the rest of the country, as television captured the horror of the terrorist attacks.

"Everybody at that time was obviously affected," said Bret Boone, "but I remember Lou being exceptionally emotional and that was a different side of him than we really knew. We'd see him get mad and yell and scream, but it wasn't often we'd see tears in his eyes. When you break him down, he really is a teddy bear who really, truly loves his players and he let us see a different side of him that day."

The Mariners and baseball resumed on September 18, and after winning their first two games back, thus clinching the division, they dropped an uncharacteristic four in a row. There may have been some question outside of Seattle as to whether Piniella would rest his starters for the playoffs, but there was no such question within the team.

"The players wanted the record," said Martinez. "Lou was concentrating on wining in the playoffs but we wanted to play, we wanted to win, and we wanted that intensity to carry over into the playoffs."

Griffin would say later that the record chase put more pressure on Piniella than anything he had ever done. And even seven years later, Boone said he found it hard to explain.

"It started two months out, with the media [presence] so big in our clubhouse, asking, 'Are you guys going to break the record?' It was like postseason media coverage," he said.

"But, of course, we're going to run guys out there. We felt like, 'Let's go to the playoffs and do something special, too.' Lou always had the best interest of the players and the team in mind, and he did what he should do. We still got breathers and days off. Personally, I could never understand what it meant to take a day off. I've probably had three in my entire career."

When Piniella tried once to warn Boone that he was going to give him a day off later in the week, the two argued about it.

"By Thursday, I convinced him I was going to play Friday," Boone recalled. "My first two at-bats I struck out and then fouled out to the catcher. I remember Lou standing up in the dugout and going, 'Well guys, if you're waiting for Boone today, you're going to be waiting for a long time.' I went 0-for-4 and it was the last time I argued with him."

Buhner didn't recall many days off for anyone.

"He had a bunch of gamers who wanted to play every day, so he was damned if he did, damned if he didn't," Buhner said.

What Piniella may not have counted on was the inevitable letdown. The Mariners won No. 116 on October 6 against the Texas Rangers in the second-to-last game of the season, then dropped the last game 4–3 the following day.

"The night we won 116, everyone just went 'Whew,'" said Boone. "Then it was like, 'Wait a minute, we have to go to the playoffs now.'"

And it looked that way as the Cleveland Indians won the first game of the ALDS behind Bartolo Colon's six-hit, 10-strikeout performance, 5–0.

But Seattle won Game 2 and despite getting embarrassed in Game 3 by the ridiculous margin of 17–2, the Mariners recovered to win the series in five games before moving onto the matchup that everyone anticipated.

The New York Yankees, however, were on a mission of their own and it was far bigger than the Mariners' pursuit of completing the greatest season ever, far bigger than baseball at that point.

Rallying back from a 0–2 deficit to the Oakland A's in the other division series, the Yankees, behind the defensive heroics of Derek Jeter, became the first team to win a division series after losing the first two games. But more than that was the emotional momentum the Yankees were building, not just in New York but around the country.

Suddenly, they were America's team, displaying the grit and determination embodied in the spirit of their city in the days and weeks following September 11th. And when the Yankees won the first two games in Seattle by scores of 4–2 and 3–2, it appeared they would roll to the World Series.

Naturally, Piniella had other ideas.

"What I'll always remember," said the *Times'* Larry Stone, "is that after [Game2], I was in this group of writers waiting to get into the Mariners' clubhouse after the game when Lou comes stomping out and starts addressing the writers in line.

"He said, 'We're going to be back. Quote me. We're going to bring this thing back to Seattle.'

"I saw what kind of mood he was in and I forgot about the clubhouse. He was my story, I was following Lou. It was the fiery, feisty, defiant Lou."

Piniella repeated his prediction in his postgame press conference, just in case anyone missed it.

"I've got confidence in my baseball club," he said. "We've gone to New York and beat them five out of six times [this season] and we're going to do it again."

Someone asked him about his pitching and Piniella answered by recalling the 1981 World Series when his Yankee team lost to the Dodgers. "I played on a good ballclub in New York, and we beat the Dodgers the first two ballgames, and they came back to beat us four in a row. So it can happen."

It wasn't the first time Piniella had ventured a prediction. At a 1995 rally before Seattle's loss in the ALCS against the Cleveland Indians, four games to two, Piniella railed, "Cleveland doesn't know what it's getting itself into.... Believe it or not, when all is said and done, we're going to go to the World Series."

Over the past couple of seasons, Piniella would occasionally say he had mellowed as a manager. But to those who knew him best, that night in 2001 was the Piniella who looked like he wanted to grab a bat and go beat the Yankees himself. Either that or go find the nearest watercooler.

"I haven't seen them dominating anybody," Piniella said later in his office. "They're a team that's ready to get beat—if somebody would just go out and beat them.... We've just gotta go out and kick their asses."

The Mariners had won 6-of-9 regular-season games against the Yankees, which seemed to stir up Piniella even more. "I don't see any dominance," he said. "They are a team ready to get beat, if anyone would just go out and beat them. There's no mystique. They can be beaten."

Then Piniella, who called himself "not a fan of team meetings" held his first since Opening Day. But the Mariners were at a disadvantage in more than one way. Shorstop Carlos Guillen missed the ALDS with a mild case of tuberculosis he was thought to have contracted in Venezuela, and would play only three games in the ALCS. And Martinez was ineffective with a pulled groin muscle he had been nursing for a week.

When reporters asked Piniella before Game 2 about the aftermath of September 11th, he offered his deepest sympathies to the victims, saying Seattle's "hearts and our prayers and our thoughts have been on those people [in New York] and in Washington and Pennsylvania, but specifically New York, where they had the greatest devastation.

"I don't really look that much forward to going to New York," he said. "But we are going to do everything we can as an organization, as a team. If they need us to do some things to help out in any way, we're certainly going to be available for that. But as far as getting close to Ground Zero, no, I wouldn't want to.... Anything else that we can do for families or anything, yes. But to go there? No."

Shortly after arriving in New York for Game 3, that's exactly where the team went. Despite Piniella's reservations that it would be a distraction, he allowed majority to rule, and on the day before the game, a bus of about 30 players, coaches, executives, and spouses were headed for Ground Zero with a visit first to a fire station nearby.

"As soon as we walked in, these grown men, these firemen who remembered him as a Yankees player they idolized, were so excited to see him," recalled John McLaren. "And then they started crying. It was very emotional.

"When we got off the bus at Ground Zero, the ground was still smoldering, and there was a smell you never wanted to smell again, the smell of death. There was a memorial and you saw rosaries, photos, teddy bears, you name it, and then you look up, and there's the Statue of Liberty. The next night, an eagle flew into center field. The whole thing was a real tearjerker."

That night, the Mariners roughed up Orlando "El Duque" Hernandez for five runs (four earned) over five innings, scored seven runs in the sixth, and walloped the Yankees 14–3, the most runs ever scored against them in a postseason game.

Jamie Moyer earned his third straight postseason victory and Bret Boone, who had led the American League in runs batted in but had slumped in the postseason, erupted for five runs batted in.

That day, the good 'ol New York tabloids had mocked Piniella for his prediction.

"Sweep Lou," read the *New York Post*. "Yankees will make Piniella eat his words."

"I didn't think I would create that much of a stir," Piniella said coyly of the reaction in New York. "I guess when you are a New Yorker, you can say those things. But, boy, when somebody else says it, it creates a commotion."

It was Seattle's last victory of the year.

Rookie second baseman Alfonso Soriano's home run in the bottom of the ninth was the game-winner in Game 4, breaking the tie for a 3–1 Yankees victory and taking the wind out of the Mariners for good.

When Bernie Williams slugged a two-run homer against Aaron Sele as part of a four-run third inning in Game 5, the best team in baseball had nothing left. And the Yankees were moving on to the World Series for the fourth straight year.

"We won 116 games and we had a real good team," said McLaren. "We didn't have Randy Johnson but we had solid pitching. But we all felt out of sync. I think fate was on the Yankees' side."

McLaren said Piniella wasn't the same in New York, couldn't be, nor could anyone. For the Yankees, it carried them to victory. For the Mariners, to a very long off-season.

"Whenever we went to Yankee Stadium, Lou would get fired up," said McLaren. "He wanted to beat the Yankees more than anybody. He wanted to beat everybody, but the Yankees went to a different level. This was such an emotional time, it just took some of his saltiness away, he didn't have the same giddyup, the same adrenaline.

"We played hard, they were good games but it felt like it just wasn't meant to be. A bad ending to a great season. We got beat fair and square, but fate was on the Yankees' side."

In the clubhouse afterward, Piniella thanked his team.

"I remember how very emotional he was when he spoke," said Price, "how much affection he had for that group and what a special group it was. The 116 games was all great but greater was what a special, selfless group it was. We didn't have Alex Rodriguez and Griffey, we had guys like David Bell, Stan Javier, and Tom Lampkin, guys who had a real impact on our team.

"I wouldn't speak for Lou, but one emotion almost was that New York was hit hardest in 9/11, that those people needed this, they needed the Yankees to stay in this. They didn't need to walk out of that stadium eliminated by us. We came back to the realization of what the country was going through. There was so much misery and despair. It was like this Yankees win was what was supposed to happen. Most surprising was that Arizona beat them in the World Series."

As the team bus pulled away from Yankee Stadium just after midnight on October 23, Piniella slid off his 1977 Yankees World Championship ring, the one he had worn most often over the previous 24 years.

He told his wife to put it away, that he was through, that he couldn't bear to have his heart broken by the Yankees again and then look at that ring.

The hangover from 2001, some would argue, is still being felt in Seattle. Though the Mariners would win 93 games the next season, the second-best win total in franchise history, they crawled into

June with assorted aches, pains, and injuries to Edgar Martinez, Norm Charlton, Jeff Nelson, and Paul Abbott. Bret Boone and Mike Cameron were slumping.

Jeff Cirillo, who had been traded to Seattle before the 2002 season after seven full years in the big leagues and four consecutive seasons of batting .313 or better for Milwaukee and Colorado, was one of the many disappointments. And his discontent with Piniella, while not in and of itself a major story, demonstrated that at least in his case, Piniella's managerial style did not always get results from the modern-day player.

"I remember in spring training," said Cirillo, "[Piniella] brought me out of the batting cage and called me over.

"'Son, I'm scratching my head here,'" Cirillo recalled Piniella telling him. "'It says on the back on your card that you're a .311 career hitter but with that swing, I don't know how you get it done.' That was my first response from the guy.

"Some people said he questioned you to see how you would react or whatever. I had some tough managers before. Phil Garner and Buddy Bell were both very intense managers. There were a lot of variables for how and why I failed there but Piniella did not help the cause. All I know is that I felt I was on guard the whole year."

Beginning the season at 17–4, there was immediate talk of improving on 116 games, the thought itself exhausting. And despite rolling into a mid-June Interleague road trip at 41–25 and leading Anaheim by a game, by July it was evident that internally all was not well.

Piniella talked repeatedly in spring training of the need "for another bat" and in late June, his comments to a Houston writer, according to Thiel's *Out of Left Field*, angered Howard Lincoln, who had taken over as the organization's CEO two years earlier.

Piniella was talking about the trade to Houston four years earlier of Randy Johnson. The Astros acquired the Big Unit for a pennant run, and Johnson ended up 10–1 but lost two games in the first round of the playoffs as Houston was eliminated. That off-season, he was lost in free agency to Arizona. So the Astros, who had given up Freddy Garcia, Carlos Guillen, and John Halama, got three months out of Johnson and nothing in return.

"They were trying to win the World Series, and they thought Randy would be a major factor," Piniella was quoted as saying. These comments later ran in Stone's Sunday notes column for the *Times*. "I think if you have a team that's one piece short, you owe it to your fans to give it a go—and to your players. How many teams get in position that way? But you have to make darn sure that's the piece. You can decimate your farm system real quick."

Astros' GM Gerry Hunsicker agreed with Piniella's opinions, which were certainly not out of the ordinary. But Lincoln decided that Piniella was making a dig at the Mariners for their lack of action in improving their roster. Indeed, the Mariners struggled mightily with men on base and received little production from their bench.

Lincoln sent a memo to his GM, Pat Gillick, reminding him and telling him to remind Piniella, of the policy instituted the season before that trade needs and options not be discussed in the media.

A furious Piniella confronted Lincoln in his office and Lincoln told Thiel later that he, figuratively, stood toe-to-toe with his enraged manager.

"I wouldn't allow him to back me down," Lincoln said. "It was not a pleasant meeting, but it was the kind of thing that happens in organizations all the time with a very high-strung, emotional guy who lives and dies the game. I appreciated that; I appreciated how strongly he felt about things."

What upset Piniella was the idea that he had gone against club policy. After a career of treating more contentious bosses like George Steinbrenner and Marge Schott with the respect their positions demanded—despite conflicts at the end—and being what he viewed as a loyal company man throughout his years in Seattle, Piniella said he was "surprised" that he was admonished for making a comment that didn't even have anything to do with the Mariners.

Piniella told Thiel that in retrospect, he should have ignored the memo. "[But] that's not my disposition," he said. "I fought for what I thought was right—nothing more, nothing less."

Lincoln, a man of considerably strong will himself, told Thiel, "This was one of the few times in Lou's life where somebody was pissing him off and didn't back down. His point was his remarks [in Houston] had nothing to do with the Mariners. My point was 'Please.'"

For Piniella, it signaled the beginning of the end. His father Louis became seriously ill with pneumonia and circulation problems during the spring, which necessitated a trip back home. And his team was engaged in a hot race with Anaheim and Oakland and not playing the kind of consistent baseball to which the city of Seattle had grown accustomed.

After several months of observing his new skipper, Cirillo was not impressed.

"He has an approach that has been very successful for him," said Cirillo, "but I will say for me as a manager, he was like a riverboat gambler. He showed up later for a game than any manager I'd ever seen. He'd take the bus for a day game. I remember the first road game, I came in at 2:15-2:30, and there were only trainers there. Most of today's game coaches come in at noon and live at the ballpark, take all their meals there.

"For me, it was a strange concept, here comes Lou and Matt Sinatro and John McLaren coming in at 3:45 for a 7:30 game, an hour and a half after players are supposed to be there, which was really bizarre. I know he likes the track and he'd look over the game sheet like it was a stock portfolio, at the matchups like he was playing the dogs, the hunches, the deal. That said, he had great instincts for the game and I think he's a great in-game manager."

In late August, the Mariners fell out of first place, losing to the Cleveland Indians on a walk-off home run by rookie Josh Bard, the first homer of his career. In relief, Piniella was forced to go to James Baldwin, who had fallen out of the starting rotation. The next night, the Mariners lost on another walk-off homer, prompting reliever Jeff Nelson to comment that the team was playing like it was "looking forward to going home in September."

Seattle went .500 the rest of the way as the A's and the Angels zoomed past; the Angels—who finished 41 games in back of the Mariners in 2001—were on their way to a World Series championship.

With one year remaining on his contract, Piniella told Gillick and Lincoln he was thinking about retirement. The Piniellas learned that the house they had been renting in Seattle was going to be sold. And he had been away from home long enough. During the last week of the 2001 season, daughter Kristi and granddaughter Kassidy were involved in a car accident in Tampa, and though it wasn't as serious as Lou and Anita initially feared, Anita was in Seattle at the time and had to make the long flight home. That summer, Anita lost her father to ALS.

It was time to leave Seattle. But when the Tampa Bay Devil Rays and New York Mets both announced they would be looking for new managers, Piniella had a little more to think about.

On October 9, it was announced that Pat Gillick would stay for at least one more year as Seattle's general manager. On October 11, 2002, Steve Kelley, columnist for the *Seattle Times*, wrote an open letter to Piniella begging him to stay.

"You've changed the way Seattle thinks about itself," Kelley wrote. "You not only helped save the sport here, but you made this a baseball city. You helped get a stadium built but even more important, you filled that stadium. You turned the idea of the playoffs from an impossible dream to an expectation.

"Signing you gave this franchice credibility. Your Yankees heritage. The World Series ring you got managing the Cincinnati Reds. The fire you brought to the game. Seattle still needs that. All of that."

By then it was too late. Reports were circulating that the New York Mets and Tampa Bay Devil Rays were after Piniella and that the Texas Rangers, who hadn't yet fired their manager, would have interest. Of course, contact from other clubs would be tampering and Piniella denied that had taken place.

In New York, a tabloid headline read, "Go get Sweet Lou." And in Texas, speculation was rampant as A-Rod was quoted as saying Piniella was "a father figure to me." Seattle team president Chuck Armstrong was not happy about the talk.

"Lou Piniella and everyone at the Mariners have made it clear that Lou is under contract to the Mariners to manage our team in 2003," Armstrong said. "This speculation by the media and others in markets outside Seattle leads me to wonder if this is indirect tampering."

Stone urged the Mariners in his *Times* column to let Piniella out of his contract if his heart was no longer in it.

Tampa, coming off a 55–106 season in its fifth year of existence, did not appear to be the front-runner at first. But that is precisely where Piniella told his bosses he was leaning during a meeting on October 12.

When Piniella's longtime friend and assistant Stan Williams heard, the two talked. "We had a good long conversation before he left," Williams said. "He said, 'Come on in and sit down,' and we had a toddy, and he said, 'I think I've worn out my welcome here. I'm thinking about going home and spending time with my wife and family. My father's not well.' I said, 'Well, the only thing is, you might be jeopardizing your Hall of Fame managing career if you go to Tampa Bay, because you're sure as hell not going to have a winning record there.'"

On October 18, the Mariners released Piniella from his contract and the club said they wanted only "reasonable" compensation in return, but the Mets and the New York media accused the Mariners of stonewalling, and Piniella's agent, Alan Nero, was not thrilled with the Mariners either, obviously wanting more than one team bidding on his client's services.

"Regardless of who's at fault, Seattle has made a circus out of this," Nero told the *Seattle Times*. "That doesn't seem to be right. I thought Lou meant a lot more to the Seattle organization than to be treated like some kind of commodity."

Speculation was that the Mets could only deliver middle-tier players in exchange for Piniella, and the Mariners already had enough of those. Still one report out of New York opined that the Mariners were being "spiteful" toward Piniella and "deliberately manipulating" things to guide him toward where they wanted him to manage—perhaps not so coincidentally to the worst team in the league—to which Nero countered that all Piniella wanted was to "be home."

"When you listen to the New York side, you get upset and frustrated," Nero said in the *Seattle Times* interview. "Then you listen to the Tampa Bay side and see the Mariners were clear on what they wanted and were accommodated. Seattle certainly has a right to be doing what it's doing.... It's just frustrating to me that all Lou wanted to do was to talk to Tampa Bay and the Mets. I thought everything would be done by the Mariners to accommodate him."

Gillick insisted they had.

"I do not favor Tampa Bay or any other team," said Gillick. "Lou made the request to be closer to home. We've tried."

In the end, after two other "anonymous" teams supposedly entered the bidding, the Mariners said the Devil Rays were simply the more aggressive party in trying to hire the 59-year-old Piniella.

"My father [Louis Sr.] was not doing well and my daughter Kristi was going through a divorce, and it was time for me to come home," Piniella said in a 2006 interview. "I knew Seattle was going to let me go to only one place, and that was Tampa."

On the day Piniella was named the new manager of the Tampa Bay Devil Rays, he claimed not to even know who the Devil Rays gave Seattle in compensation for his negotiating rights.

"[But] if it is Randy Winn," said Piniella, "I find that somewhat ironic. In my 10 years in Seattle, the Mariners never got a left fielder for me.

It did turn out to be Winn, an All-Star, and in return, the Mariners had to give Tampa Bay Antonio Perez, a promising minor-league shortstop, while Piniella ended up with the grand prize—a four-year, $13 million contract he said would likely be his last.

"I see why Seattle didn't let me talk to anyone else when they had a chance to get Winn," Piniella told the *Seattle Post-Intelligencer*. "Everybody assumed I was going to New York. And I would have liked to talk to them. I just wasn't sure Tampa would make the financial commitment. You never know if an organization is just interested in a little publicity. But after our first meeting, it was obvious."

Jay Buhner, though upset Piniella left, understood. "He needed to get out of Seattle or else drop dead of a heart attack," said Buhner. "He wears his emotions on his sleeves and everyone has to say enough's enough and get out while you still have your sanity. Lou's not afraid to take a challenge head on. He knew what he was getting himself into and when all was said and done, he still got the last laugh."

He left a team that had won 93 games to manage a team that had lost 106. But it was the Mariners who would have to fill a void that some say they still haven't come close to filling.

"When Lou left, I lost a very good friend," said John Ellis, who remained a member of the team's board of directors after his retirement as CEO. "And as far as I'm concerned, the Mariners lost probably the one person who most epitomized our return to the living.

"I thought it was a tragic loss and I will always regret that it happened. He never should have left.... But for a guy named Piniella, the Mariners would be down in Tampa Bay."

In July of the following summer, Piniella returned to Seattle. And like always with Piniella, whatever anger or frustration there had been, had melted away.

The tears began when he drove past the lit-up stadium the night before with Anita and continued as he hugged everyone from his former secretaries to the clubhouse men to the security guards to his former players and coaches.

This had been his home for 10 years and regardless of the fact that he came back in a Tampa Bay Devil Rays uniform, he was welcomed with overwhelming love and gratitude from the people of Seattle.

The crowd enveloped the 15 pounds-lighter Piniella—"When we lose, I don't eat and I'm sure you've seen the standings," he explained to his concerned former secretaries—with standing ovations and chants of "Loooooou" every time he emerged from the visitor's dugout. This, in stark contrast to the boos that greeted the returns of Alex Rodriguez and Randy Johnson.

Piniella tried to express how he felt before the game, but it just made him tear up again.

"The important thing here is not...it's not really...it's not really the reception I get. It's how I can say thank you back.... I've managed other places; I've played baseball other places.... It's how I can say thanks for the way I was treated here for 10 years."

Finally, in a probably unprecedented pregame ceremony, his former players presented him with a poster-sized photo from the 116-win season and a framed first base autographed by every Mariners player.

The ex-manager waved to the crowd and then in an impromptu move, took the microphone.

"You made me and my family really feel at home," he said. "You made it a pleasure and joy coming to the ballpark every day. I thank you all from the bottom of my heart. God truly blessed me. I love you all and will never forget you."

CHAPTER
7

Going Home

S urely, Piniella knew what he was getting into. But as *St. Petersburg Times* columnist Gary Shelton said in retrospect about Piniella returning home to Tampa Bay as the Devil Rays manager, "It was like getting Keith Richards to perform in your band and then putting him in an oompah band in the park on Sunday. He's playing guitar to 'Love Letters in the Sand,' while old people waltz. Just absolutely the wrong place for the wrong guy."

For several years, the Devil Rays also looked very much like the wrong team for the wrong place. After all, five different major-league teams had flirted with Tampa or St. Petersburg as possible new homes before resolving whatever conflicts they had with their own locales and staying put. All of which left the Florida Suncoast Dome, built in St. Petersburg in 1990 for the sole purpose of luring a major-league team, looming like the conspicuous white elephant on the peninsula for most of the decade.

In the five seasons prior to Piniella's arrival, the team lost 99, 93, 92, 100, and 106 games under managers Larry Rothschild and Hal McRae. The franchise highlights were easy to tick off—recently acquired free agents Wade Boggs collecting his 3,000th hit and Jose Canseco getting his 400th home run, celebrated as if the two fading stars had spent considerably more than a teeny fraction of their careers in Tampa Bay.

The Rays, said Shelton, "threw a lot of money at a lot of average free agents," players like Canseco, Juan Guzman, Greg Vaughn. They traded for Vinny Castilla and called Castilla, Fred McGriff, who had been picked up from Atlanta the day of the expansion draft, Canseco, and Vaughn the "Hit Show."

"The thinking was that people would come out to see home runs and it completely blew up in their faces," said Shelton. "By the time Lou got here, he was walking into a cesspool. They had no money because they had been paying for people from two managers earlier. The owners were trying to force out the managing general partner [Vince Naimoli]. There was talk of contraction, private talk of relocation. It was just a failing franchise and I'm not sure Lou knew the depth of it. I think he heard what he wanted to hear."

Still, Piniella had known challenges before and he had conquered them. Weren't the Cincinnati Reds, after all, 75–87 and fifth-place finishers in the NL West when he walked in, led them to 91 wins, and turned the Reds into World Series champs in 1990?

Weren't the Seattle Mariners 64–98 and seventh in the AL West the year before the Great Piniella improved their record to 82–80 in 1993, if only still fourth place in the division? Two years later, they were division champs.

Okay, so this task was slightly more daunting with the Rays at a stunning 55–106 and fifth place in the AL East the season before Piniella was hired for the 2003 season. He did not appear to be intimidated at his introductory press conference.

"I wouldn't have come here if I felt I was going to fall on my face, believe me," he said.

The Tampa Bay brass, not surprisingly, were elated, with Naimoli ranking Piniella's hiring second only to the D-Ray's inaugural game and general manager Chuck LaMar placing it behind Tampa Bay being awarded a major-league franchise.

While this was supposed to be Piniella's last managing job, he also assured everyone, "The barn door isn't closed yet. That I can tell you. No, no, no. There's still a lot of baseball left in me."

Then were the words that would come to haunt and finally to doom his Devil Rays tenure. "You win with talent," Piniella said, "and this organization promised me the talent to win with."

While the Reds had the Nasty Boys and some good young players, and Seattle had Ken Griffey Jr., Randy Johnson, Edgar Martinez, and Jay Buhner when Piniella arrived, the Devil Rays still needed a major-league shortstop, a closer, some stronger bats, and on and on. They were also operating with the lowest payroll in baseball at about $19.6 million, which was down from $34 million the year before under Hal McRae.

But if nothing else, Piniella was home.

"Since I was 18, I packed for spring training," he said. "No more packing now. I like the Cuban bread and Cuban coffee. I like the idea of being home."

Joe Henderson, a respected baseball writer and columnist for the *Tampa Tribune* for more than 30 years, during which he has chronicled the baseball life and times of Piniella, said Piniella surely knew what awaited him in Tampa but may have still had his hopes a little high.

"In his own mind, he may have thought, 'I can win here no matter what, I'm good enough, I can shake the culture up and win some ballgames,'" said Henderson, who called for Piniella's hiring on McRae's last day as manager. "But it was different from Seattle, where you're not playing the Red Sox and Yankees every night. Forty percent of the Rays' schedule is against Boston, New York, and Toronto. You can't fake that. There's nothing you can do, you're just going to get killed."

After that first news conference, Piniella mentioned to Henderson that he and his wife were planning a trip to Spain and Italy with some friends after the season.

"The date happened to coincide with the playoffs," Henderson recalled, "so I made a joke like, 'What, you're not planning to be busy in October?' and he kind of winked and said, 'Well, maybe not this year but we're going to get it done.'"

Exactly five months later to the day, he had people actually believing it, or at least the 34,391 at Tropicana Field on March 31, 2003. Opening Day for the Devil Rays; Opening Night for the Lou Piniella era, which played like a smash Broadway hit.

The D-Rays had begun the game like many others, with two errors early and trailing the Boston Red Sox 3–0 after the top of the first inning. Boston's Pedro Martinez went seven innings, allowing just three hits and an unearned run, and Tampa Bay entered the ninth inning losing 4–1.

No big surprises there. But that's when Travis Lee singled and Terry Shumpert, a 36-year-old utility man whom the team picked up the day before when the Dodgers released him, hit a two-run homer to make it 4–3, Red Sox.

Piniella put in pinch runner Damian Rolls for Ben Grieve, who had singled next (the second lefthander of the inning to single against left-handed pitching), and Rolls broke up a potential double play on a ground ball by Brent Abernathy. Piniella had Abernathy steal second, leaving first open for Marlon Anderson, who squeezed out a walk. And then with two on, two outs, and two strikes on Carl Crawford, who played 63 games as a 20-year-old rookie the season before, he hit a walk-off home run into the right-center field bleachers for the 6–4 Devil Rays victory.

Five runs in the bottom of the ninth.

The poor, young D-Rays against the wealthy, veteran Red Sox, whose 11-game winning streak at Tropicana Field was snapped.

"It was pure Lou," said left fielder Al Martin, a former Mariner for whom Shumpert pinch hit in the ninth. "In Seattle, we had so many wins like this. The guy just has a way."

In the skybox where Anita and family members watched the game, the mood was described as not unlike the seventh game of the World Series.

The players showered each other with beer, and Piniella greeted reporters afterward with a happy, glassy-eyed, "What'd you think of that? Wasn't that something?"

"You couldn't write the script any better," said Henderson. "The place was going nuts, there was a massive celebration at home plate. Anita was waiting for Lou afterward outside the clubhouse and I looked over at Lou and his eyes were moist. He was really choked up at the moment, that maybe this thing has a chance."

"One game in," Gary Shelton wrote that night, "and Lou Piniella has us at hello. One comeback, and all doubts are removed. One victory, and he is worth believing in.

"Welcome home, Lou.

"And welcome back, hope."

The team had spent most of its marketing budget on erecting billboards all over the Tampa/St. Petersburg/Clearwater/Dunedin area hailing Piniella's arrival with the slogan, "It's a whole new ballgame," and for one night anyway, it was.

"It was a real nice moment," Shelton said of Opening Day, "but it was false symbolism. The new manager is in town. Now he's going to kick-start it. But he never had a chance."

The next night, 11,524 fans left Tropicana Field two-thirds empty and the Red Sox won 9–8 in 16 innings.

The Rays would lose four in a row after Opening Day, went 9–17 in April, and were 32–60 at the All-Star break.

In a mid-season interview with Marc Topkin, the beat writer for the *St. Pete Times*, Topkin counted nine "fines" in a 20-second answer when he asked Piniella how he was doing.

Anita Piniella was a little more forthcoming in a later interview. "He's having a tough time with it," she said. "Being patient is very difficult. I tell him, 'You knew it wouldn't be easy.' But he just didn't think it would be quite this difficult."

By June 18, the Devil Rays had lost their 46th game. Two years earlier, Piniella's Mariners' team lost 46 the entire season. No team Piniella had ever played on or managed had lost more than 88 games, and Topkin calculated that at the rate the Rays were going, they would surpass that by late August. No Piniella-managed team had ever finished more than 20 games out of first, and the Rays were 20 back in June and on a pace to finish 50 back.

"It was so humbling for Lou, so humbling for all of us," said Chris Bosio, the Devil Rays' pitching coach in 2003. "We had just come from this wonderful baseball town in Seattle, where they sold out every game and had talent in the minor league system and which we all felt a part of and felt we were one or two players away from having that club compete on the next level.

"The frustration of having to start over again with kids who should have been in A-ball wore on us and it was harder on Lou because it was his own backyard. He made mention of it many times—'I've got to live here.' That killed him. That humbled him. That burned like fire and you could tell it ate him up. He was so bound and determined to turn it around."

At that point, Piniella had lost 15 pounds since the season began. He had been ejected from three games, three times he had refused to speak to the media, and twice he had held his postgame press conference in the middle of the clubhouse, a favorite Piniella tactic when he wanted to make sure the players heard what he was saying and whom he was singling out.

His confrontation with Ben Grieve made all of that look like kid stuff.

In many ways, Grieve was the All-American baseball hero. His father Tom was a nine-year journeyman outfielder who played for the Washington Senators, Texas Rangers, New York Mets, and St. Louis Cardinals, and later became the GM for the Rangers, a position he held from 1984–94 before moving into broadcasting.

Father and son were both first-round draft picks, Ben chosen No. 2 overall by the Oakland Athletics in the 1994 amateur draft shortly after his 18th birthday. And when he debuted with the A's on September 3, 1997, Grieve became the youngest player in the American League that season at 21 years, four months.

The following season, Grieve made the All-Star team and was named Rookie of the Year after hitting .288 with 18 home runs and

89 RBIs. In 1999, his numbers dropped off a bit to .265, but he still hit 26 homers and drove in 86 runs despite injuries that limited him to 97 fewer at-bats than the previous year. And the next season, he bounced back with a .279 average, 27 home runs, and 104 RBIs.

After the 2000 season, Grieve came to the Devil Rays as part of a three-team deal, brought to a team yearning for a star and hoping also for a leader. But Grieve's stats dipped the next two seasons to .264 and .251 with a combined 30 home runs. He knocked in 72 and 64 runs, but his slugging percentage dropped 100 points to .387 his first season with Tampa Bay before leveling back to .432.

Worse, there was talk that the kid lacked passion, that his shortage of outward emotion reflected a player who didn't care enough. Grieve admitted he didn't have much fun the previous two seasons, but who did on a Devil Rays team that lost a combined 206 games?

In 2003, Grieve was in the last year of a contract that was to pay him $5.5 million (second-highest on the team) and at 26, he was facing the crossroads of his career. Now the team needed his abilities and some leadership more than ever.

In Piniella's first spring training as Tampa Bay manager, Grieve angered the new skipper right away with comments suggesting the Devil Rays were not a very good team. He later missed a month with an infected thumb and in late June, was hitting .229 with four home runs and 14 runs batted in.

And his demeanor on the field infuriated Piniella, who could often be heard yelling, "Ben, you play like a fucking pussy."

Grieve had expected some of that.

"When [Piniella] was with Seattle, I got to see him a lot because I was with Oakland and we played them 20 times a year," Grieve said in October 2008, "so when he came to Tampa, I had an idea of what he would be like and I thought I knew what to expect.

"One thing I remember about my first impression is that I never knew how to act around him. You never knew if he was in a good mood or mad about something. There would be days where I was like, 'Okay, we're fine,' but other days where I just never knew what to say because of his mood. I don't remember a whole lot of interaction with him, more through the coaches like [Matt] Sinatro and [John] McLaren.

"Except, of course, for that one day."

That one day was June 26, 2003, and a home game against the Yankees at Tropicana Field, the last of a four-game set against New York, who had won the prior two games. With the tying run on third base and two outs in the bottom of the ninth, Grieve, inserted as a pinch hitter, took a called third strike by home-plate umpire Wally Bell to end the game and seal a 4–3 New York victory.

"When you see it on TV, it makes me look like I'm doing something wrong," Grieve said of what followed, part of which was captured by television cameras and replayed nationally for days. "When you listened to [Piniella] talk about it after the game, it made me look bad.

"I always have to bring it up because people always question it. Mariano Rivera was pitching and it was a high strike. I remember he had struck me out before but the umpire called it a ball. The last pitch was borderline, but I almost knew the guy was going to call it a strike because he had missed the earlier pitch. But I took it for a strike and it ended the game.

"The game's over and the ump is headed for the exit and when I got to the dugout, Lou said, 'Was it high?' and I said, 'Yeah, it might have been.'

"He said, 'Well, why the bleep didn't you say something then?' And I said that it wouldn't have mattered because the umpire was walking off. [Piniella] took it as, 'It doesn't matter.'"

What transpired, said observers, was one of the uglier examples of a dressing-down from a manager of a player that they had ever seen.

"Really bad," said one of Piniella's coaches. "He undressed him in front of the whole team. They were going up the runway together and Ben was saying, 'I told the umpire after the game he missed the call, but I told him in my own way.' Then Lou veers to the left and he undresses him good.

"Ben made a statement in spring training that he didn't think we could win but things would be put in order for future years, but Lou doesn't want to hear that, he wants to win now. Ben was being realistic and the way the guy wrote it, it was like, 'We're not going to win. We don't have a chance.' Lou doesn't want to hear that shit. Plus, Ben was making $5 million, more than anyone on the team, he took a lot of pitches and struck out a lot. He was slow with no power. He just wasn't a Lou-type player."

Travis Lee, the team's first baseman and a close friend of Grieve's who shared a similar temperament, remembered the play well. "He shrugged his shoulders at the ump like, 'I can't believe you called a strike,'" said Lee. "That was Ben. He and I had the same personality. I would've done the same thing. What are you going to do, throw up your arms and make him reverse the call?

"I had this whole discussion with Larry Bowa when he was my manager. He hated me because I'd come back after I struck out and it was tearing me up inside but because I wasn't throwing my helmet, he thought I didn't care. It's probably worse for guys like me and Ben because we hold it inside, there's no release, we don't sleep, we stress. Other guys snap. Lou snapped."

Grieve said he can barely remember what was said but that he had "never" experienced anything like it.

"I don't think he really liked me to begin with, so that gave him a chance to clear his mind of everything he ripped me for," he said. "He got it all out at once. He didn't like me, and that's when he had the chance to let everyone know."

There was no give-and-take.

"He did his thing, and I didn't say anything, not a word," said Grieve. "I just kind of looked at him. If I had said anything back at all, he was so mad it probably would've led to a Rob Dibble thing, not because I would've instigated it but just because he was so mad."

Catcher Toby Hall was also fearful the two would come to blows.

"I felt badly for Ben because at that time, we always felt the other teams would get the calls because we were a young team and a losing organization," Hall said. "It was just misinterpreted when Ben said the umpire didn't care."

Grieve said the worst part was "just the fact that everyone sat there watching. It was embarrassing to be in front of your teammates and have this guy yelling at you like that."

Grieve described the young players who witnessed the incident as "wide-eyed" and one of the veterans, Al Martin, consoled him with, "Forget about it. The guy's an asshole."

"McLaren [a longtime Piniella assistant coach] came up to me after I got out of the shower," Grieve recalled, "and said, 'Hey, are you all right?' I can remember that, and I really appreciated it. I always liked him because of that."

Afterward, Piniella still wasn't finished. Meeting with reporters 20 minutes later, he angrily recounted the exchange, his demeanor described by Topkin as "eyes blazing."

"I asked [Grieve] if the ball was high," said Piniella, "and he said, 'I thought it was high,' and I said, 'Why didn't you say something?' and he said, 'It doesn't matter.'

"I said, 'What the hell do you mean it doesn't matter? It matters to me, and it matters to everybody else.'

"Rivera's a tough pitcher; I'm not expecting anything. [But] I'm expecting if you think the ball is high to tell the umpire it's high instead of walking off to the damn dugout. And then getting a response like that after we busted our asses out there for nine innings trying to win a baseball game. It doesn't matter? It matters to me, and it matters to a lot of damn people in this clubhouse.

"And when it matters to everybody, we'll start winning more goddamned baseball games around here."

When Grieve got back to his apartment, the clip of Piniella laying into him in the dugout before it continued in the tunnel and clubhouse was being played and replayed on the local news and ESPN, accompanied by his manager's remarks afterward.

Grieve watched with his wife Kathy and became more upset.

"Some managers I know choose the route where it's behind closed doors and we'll deal with it, but that's not the case with Lou," said Grieve. "He was making me look even worse through the media.

"I can remember watching him on TV and it did kind of anger me at that point because it was a miscommunication and it made me look bad to fans and everyone else watching. It just didn't seem fair. I remember calling ESPN and getting hold of someone up there and explaining what actually happened so I didn't look bad, and they gave me a chance to explain and put my quote up there because after the game, I didn't say much to reporters."

The next day, Grieve said, he was afraid to come to the ballpark.

"I didn't know if I was going to be released," he said.

On the contrary, Grieve found his name in the starting lineup. And nothing more was said.

"He's stubborn and I'm stubborn," Grieve said. "The next day, it was like it had never happened. It was never mentioned and we both left it at that."

Once again, McLaren checked on Grieve.

"Lou felt extremely bad about him," McLaren said. "He slept on it and the next day he said, 'Damn, I feel badly,' and I said, 'I'll take care of it, don't worry about it.'"

To reporters, Grieve felt the need to explain that despite his calm demeanor, he was passionate about his job.

"It's hard for people to see that when you don't throw your helmet and stuff, but I wasn't happy [over being called out]," Grieve said. "It wasn't like, 'Oh well, I'll get him next time.' That's not my attitude. But the way I carry myself, when something like that happens, I probably react the exact opposite. That's how I deal with stuff. That's the way I've always been. It looks bad. I wish I wasn't like that. It would be a lot easier, but that's how I am."

Piniella told reporters he did not need to meet with Grieve, to which the player replied, "I'm kind of scared to approach the guy right now. I don't know what to say. After all that, I don't know what to do."

A smattering of boos greeted Grieve his next time at bat and aside from a few letters to the editor objecting to Piniella's language, the local reaction favored the manager.

Piniella even received an encouraging call from fellow Tampa native Tony La Russa, who later told Joe Henderson he congratulated his old friend.

"What he said—that one line he used about how much guys care, and how there were guys in the clubhouse who cared," La Russa said, "that was a nice line. But his best line was, 'When everybody in that clubhouse cares, then we can win more games.' Lou is one of my favorites. I love watching him manage."

Outside Tampa-St. Pete, however, Piniella took some hits.

In the *Miami Herald*, columnist Dan Le Batard wrote:

"Only in baseball, where old, fat men still squeeze into the uniforms of players and the temper tantrum remains an acceptable way to show 'passion,' can a perpetually smoldering man like Tampa Bay Devil Rays manager Lou Piniella climb to a position of leadership without ever needing to understand that not everyone is built like him....

"Lou, buddy, we've seen your roster. Every player on it could believe every pitch matters more than the U.S.–Iraq war. You'd still be buried deep in last place. What we've learned, in seeing how much difference you've made in leaping to Tampa Bay, is that you don't matter..."

In the *Fort Worth Star-Telegram*, Gil LeBreton wrote that, "Back in Arlington [Texas], a dad had to watch what a jackass was saying about his son."

Tom Grieve, then TV color analyst for the Rangers, said that for Piniella to turn Ben's response that it wouldn't matter if he screamed at the umpire after he has walked out of the stadium, to the interpretation that Ben did not care, was "a cheap shot, in my opinion, of the highest order. And I would think that whether I was Ben's father or whether I wasn't."

The elder Grieve pointed out that since his son was out of the lineup, he spent most of the game swinging in the Rays' underground batting cage.

"If he didn't care," Tom Grieve said, "he would have been on the bench with everyone else, flipping sunflower seeds."

Tom Grieve said that his son was simply a "low-key guy," that he had always been that way and that it never reflected how passionate he was on the inside.

"If a manager or a school teacher, say, chews him out when he deserves it, fine," Tom Grieve said. "That's part of life. That's part of the game. But I don't like to see [Piniella] get on TV on his bully pulpit and make up a lie and try to make it look as if Ben doesn't care, because a lot of people see that and believe it...."

Lee Elia, manager of the Cubs and Phillies in the 1980s and an assistant under Piniella in Seattle and Tampa Bay, said Piniella was frustrated with Grieve but not because of what he did not say.

"He was frustrated because he saw more in Ben Grieve than Ben Grieve saw, and it bothered him that he wouldn't go to those depths to get it out," said Elia. "What we have to understand is that everyone is not like that."

But passion was Piniella's most reliable measuring stick, said Bosio. "And he couldn't understand how a player couldn't be as passionate as him at any level.... That was Lou's way of deciding whether you would be a player or not. From Day One, he tried to get more out of everybody and 98 percent of the time he did. Unfortunately for Ben, he was one guy on a long list of players I saw who Lou could not get anything out of because it was simply not Ben's way. Ben played hard, but he had his own speed and he did not show the emotion Lou Piniella wanted to see.

"It crushed Lou, and these are the things we'd talk about in the coaches' room. What's up with this kid? And John McLaren and [Tom] Foley and [Billy] Hatcher would say, 'This is who he is.' Lou is a very intelligent man, and he realized after the beating this kid took, 'Maybe I can't make this guy that guy.' You could see it."

Henderson said Grieve's name came up more than once in discussions with Piniella over the following months and even years.

"He hated himself for going after Ben Grieve," Henderson said. "I can't tell you how many times he'd sit there and go, 'I feel bad what I did to that young man. I wasn't picking on him; I was picking on the culture. I was just trying to do what I could do to change it.' And Grieve just folded like wet tissue paper. But to this day [Piniella] regrets it."

Lee understood, even if his buddy couldn't. But he knew how Grieve felt as well.

"Lou got so mad at me a couple times, I almost lost words," Lee said. "I didn't know what to say, and I really took it to heart. I don't get motivated like that. I was more motivated when I had Terry Francona in Philly and he just came up to me and said, 'You're my guy, no matter what you're going to do.'

"The great thing about Lou though, is that he'd snap at you and the next day it was, 'Hi son, how're you doing?'" It's one thing I loved about the guy. He never carried anything over. He's a man, I'm a man, we confront it, and then he supports you.

"If Bowa held a grudge against you, he's going to hold it against you all year. But with Lou, you move on. He never played politics. He didn't hide anything behind your back. He just wanted you to play for him."

Heading into the weekend following the Grieve incident, the Rays had lost 52 of 77 games, had made 22 roster moves in 48 days, had a turnover of 43 players, and had used 12 different starting pitchers.

What particularly galled Piniella is that his team did show guts, but it just wasn't talented enough to see it through—overcoming deficits of three or more runs 17 times to that point in the season but still losing nine of those games. But there were other things that drove him crazy, like the fact that in consecutive losses to the Yankees, the Devil Rays had walked 20 batters.

As tough as he made life on his young pitchers, catchers had it just as rough, and Toby Hall, a 27-year-old draft pick of the Rays playing his first full season in the big leagues, had had enough.

"McLaren said I'd better talk to Dan Wilson [who was a catcher under Piniella for most of his career in Seattle] and see what he went through," Hall said. "I spoke to Danny and he said he got yelled at all the way until he was 35, 36, but like Mac said, he told me I had to stand up for myself.

"I had bottled up a lot during spring training and for the first couple of months of the season, but when he started yelling at me all the time, I was like, 'Wait, I'm a human being. I'm trying to do my best. And I'm not pitching the ball.' I think when he realized how much raw pitching we had, it settled in on him that we didn't have what it takes."

It was not, however, without a showdown with Hall first.

"We had one blowout," Hall said. "We were in Cleveland and I finally just snapped and said, 'Lou, this isn't PlayStation. I don't have the choice to make the ball go down in the dirt, up and away. I don't know what to tell you anymore, but I'm tired of being your punching bag.'

"We went at it a little bit, and I told him to review the video to see what I'm calling and where I'm setting up. The next day he called me into his office and gave me a big hug. He said, 'Son, I just want to let you know, I love you. Everything you said was right. That was funny, that PlayStation thing. I've never heard that before.'

"Ever since then, we bonded. A lot of people thought we didn't get along, but Lou helped me grow up and realize what it takes to win."

Still, it wasn't always a healthy relationship for players or for Piniella.

"Certain players react in certain ways and obviously, young players tucked their tails in a little more and that was tough, because I could see young talent out there feel the pressure," Hall said. "I was like that the first couple months until I had my situation with him and I stopped pressing. But you always wanted to try to impress him."

The pressure took its toll on Piniella as well, and friends worried for his health as he started to look gaunt and haggard, particularly when he only shaved once every several days as he had taken to doing. In a moment of desperation, he had even promised his team he would dye his hair any color except purple if they could just string together three wins in a row.

In Bill Madden's *New York Daily News* baseball column, he wrote that Piniella said he needed $20 million over the winter to bring in new players and that he expected $12 million of that to come from the team ridding itself of the contracts of Greg Vaughn and Ben Grieve.

In a sharp bit of prescience, Madden wrote, "If Rays ownership doesn't come through with the promised payroll increase, then all bets about this being Piniella's last managing gig are off."

"For now, one thing is for sure," Madden predicted, "Piniella will impose his will to win on these Devil Rays, and passive types like Grieve and Travis Lee will be gone."

"I'm only dating these guys," Piniella told friends. "I'm not married to them."

As it turned out, Grieve's season and his career with the Devil Rays would end less than a month later when he had to have a rib removed in order to eliminate the cause of a blood clot near his right armpit. In 55 games that 2003 season, he hit .230 with four home runs and 17 RBIs in 165 at-bats.

Grieve would move on to short stints as a reserve outfielder with the Brewers and Cubs before ending his career in the White Sox's minor league organization in 2006. In retrospect, Grieve said he didn't think the money he was making or the attitude he had was the cause of Piniella's angst.

"The thing I always think about is that I struggled [with Tampa Bay]," Grieve said. "Say [Piniella] had two players with equal stats, say 30 home runs, 100 RBIs, and one guy is a hustler and one guy is nonchalant. Is he going to hate the guy who's nonchalant even though he's putting up good numbers? I think it's all performance with him, not attitude."

Billy Hatcher, who played under Piniella in Cincinnati and coached under him at Tampa Bay, said he was actually tougher on his players in Cincinnati. "He was a different person," Hatcher said. "But he says what he feels at the moment. Now if you're not thick-skinned and you're going to go run and hide, he's going to get on you every time until you stand up for yourself. He's going to teach you how to be a man. Some guys were very sensitive and could only put up with it so much. Then when they fought back, he'd say, 'That's what I'm talking about.' They'll look at him like he's crazy, but he finally got what he wanted out of them."

Grieve, like his teammates, was well aware of what all of Piniella's players passed along—that you could not gain his respect if you didn't stand up to him.

"I just didn't have any desire to do that," said Grieve. "You are who you are, and I'm sure some guys probably figured out what Lou wanted and tried to please him that way, but for the most part, Lou is smart enough to know what type of players he has."

The type of players Piniella had in Tampa were nice guys, good kids, but that wasn't restoring his appetite. Spending time with Anita, his children, and three granddaughters and retreating to the couple's beach house was therapeutic, but even that didn't take the frequently distressed look off his face.

Piniella's buddies from the neighborhood were frequent visitors in his office after games, having a beer or two and hashing out what happened for hours as they tried to lighten his mood.

"He lost so much, he was batty," said one of those old friends, Benny Lazzara. "He couldn't stand it. Day after day, week after week. You'd go see him after he lost four or five games in a row and it was like he was almost dead, clinically depressed. I'm a criminal lawyer, and I've seen people in prison less depressed."

The losing always cut deep. "I've come home from the stadium with him too many times after a loss, and it's like there's something bad in his stomach," said another friend, Mondy Flores.

Piniella had been indoctrinated to winning under Billy Martin. He was, perhaps, spoiled by his first year in Cincinnati. Surely he had his ups and downs in Seattle, but it only fueled his need to win again. In June, the Devil Rays lost a franchise-record 21 games.

"Lou was never satisfied with the way he performed; he always wanted to do better," said Elia. "He was raised on the biggest stage of all in New York, and he was with great ballclubs, great world championship clubs. And when you have a thirst to succeed, an insatiable desire to win, it's relentless.

"I enjoyed working for him, but there were days he beat the hell out of the coaching staff. But those were also days that when I look back, it's almost with fondness because those beatings made for a better relationship between us and the players. Fortunately, I had been in a World Series before I met Lou, so I could understand where we were striving to get."

Elia said when the team witnessed how hard Piniella was on his coaches, "the players knew the importance of maybe listening to us a little bit better. It made our jobs at times a little easier and did give us a sense of closeness.

"I used to wonder why players became fond of Lou," Elia said, "and one of the reasons was that it's awfully good, if you're a player who cares about winning, to play for somebody who would do everything possible to help that team win. Ballplayers like that.

"In the old days, when George [Steinbrenner] was at his zenith, his players knew he would do anything to win. It's important for players to know that and to have somebody with Lou's prestige and ability to push it to the nth degree."

Aside from the Grieve incident, the most enduring memory of Piniella's first season in Tampa Bay was finally pulling off that three-game win streak that forced the Rays' then-nearly 60-year-old manager to have his gray hair colored with blonde streaks.

The trouble was, it took them 85 games to accomplish the feat, a month after Piniella's challenge, and the three-game win streak was halted right there, scarcely before the dye in their manager's hair had dried.

Told before that night's loss that he looked younger with the blonde streaks, Piniella replied, "You know what would make me look younger? More wins. And more [than that], [I'd] feel younger."

By late July 2003, Piniella seemed to come to terms with losing, telling Pat Jordan of the *New York Times*, "I came to the realization a few days ago that I can't be concerned with losses. I should evaluate and develop talent for next year. But that's easier to say. My ego told me I could win in any situation.

"Now I've been humbled."

This was a team that confounded him. The Rays had been swept in a three-game series by the Marlins, despite giving up a total of 13 hits. And in a stat that made that preceding occurrence make more sense, they had set or tied team records for most walks in a game (12) and most men left on base (21).

Next to Piniella's hair coloring, the season's other highlight was their June 3 game at Wrigley Field, when Sammy Sosa's broken bat revealed that cork had been stuffed inside.

At the All-Star break, the Rays were drawing an average crowd of 12,981, which ranked them 29th in the majors. But you could hardly blame the fans—with 62 player transactions since Opening Day, they might not have recognized their own team.

"It was just a tough environment to play in," said Lee. "Even if you're the losing team somewhere else, you get some kind of fan support. There, you showed up for a game and there were 4,000 people in the stands and you're thinking, 'How are you supposed to get up for this?' Then the Yankees came to town and it felt like an away game with 30,000 people cheering, but we thought 'This is awesome.'"

At 32–60 and 24½ games behind first-place New York, the encouraging news, if you could call it that, was that the team had made a three-game improvement after 92 games from the season before. And better yet, 55 of those games had been decided by two runs or less.

And then something almost magical happened. By mid-August, someone doing the math realized that the Rays were 22–18 over the last 40 games. That just happened to coincide with the Grieve incident, prompting the reaction that Piniella had made losing unacceptable and had sent the message with his outburst.

Tangible evidence came in the form of the enormous roster turnover, the fact that six rookies remained, and an outstanding young outfield with Rocco Baldelli, Carl Crawford, and Aubrey Huff. There were two more three-game win streaks. After losing 10 straight one-run games from May 29 to June 26, the Rays went 11–2 in one-run games. Piniella started talking about losing games "the right way."

But make no mistake, that's not what he wanted.

"Winning is fun," he said. "That's what you put a uniform on for. You get in the habit of doing it, and it becomes just as contagious as losing does."

And just for fun, he put on a show in his first ejection at home on August 13—a 6–5 win over the Baltimore Orioles—kicking his hat five times, the final swipe landing it in the Devil Rays' dugout.

But there was no mistaking what was atop Piniella's agenda. The Devil Rays could be considerably better, he told reporters. But to do so, they needed proven players, particularly some starting pitchers, and a solid, veteran reliever. Some right-handed power would be nice, too. Though the Rays still owed deferred money, they were rid of the Grieve and Vaughn contracts and looking forward to what was being projected as one of the deepest free-agent markets in years. Grieve's contract alone represented about one-third of the D-Rays' Opening Day payroll.

"This winter is going to be very important for us," Piniella said.

On September 9, Piniella met with GM Chuck LaMar, managing general partner Vince Naimoli, and CFO John Higgins, and afterward, Naimoli said in regards to raising the payroll, "It looks good, real good."

Pressed a little further, Naimoli said there would be a "reasonable increase," which depended on money coming from ticket sales in 2004, revenue sharing, and TV contracts.

Piniella, who told reporters that $30 million would be a nice number to operate with, which would give them $15 million to retain key players and $15 million for five or six more, said he had "a good, positive feeling."

So, too, did his players. Even though they were on their way to an expected sixth consecutive last-place finish, there was an unmistaken urgency to win that had simply not been felt before.

In a September 13 contest against the Yankees in New York, a series that always raised his blood pressure no matter the circumstances, Piniella yanked his starting catcher Pete LaForest in the sixth inning when LaForest lost count of how many outs there were.

"I understand I'm hard on catchers," Piniella said. "I got that from Billy [Martin]."

The Rays finished 38–51 in a major-league high 89 games decided by one or two runs but a little more encouraging 16–13 in 29 games, second most in the AL, decided from the ninth inning on, and 10–9 in a major-league high 19 games decided on the final pitch.

Winning the final two games of the season against Boston to at least give a little poetic symmetry to his first season, Piniella's Rays finished at 63–99 and 38 games behind the Yankees in the NL East. But they were not even close to the worst team in baseball in the 2003 season as the Detroit Tigers lost 119 games and finished 47 games behind first-place Minnesota (who only won 90 games) in the AL Central.

Once again, Piniella insisted late in the season, "This is definitely my last managing job. I've never enjoyed winning 58 games so much. I think every manager should go through this once. But just once."

While Naimoli was turning down interview requests, Piniella was hoping fans would see the team's improvement and snatch up season-ticket packages at a rate that would improve the chances of increasing payroll. Attendance at Tropicana Field decreased for the sixth straight year, an American League low of little more than 12,500.

Piniella was licking his chops: "I would think if we could get a starter and two relievers, a couple of bonafide hitters—five pieces—that would be a nice scenario for us. And then help our bench out a little bit, so we can rest people a little more. That would be a nice shopping spree for us."

By the next spring, the Rays had indeed spent about $10 million—the first time since 1999 the team increased its previous year's budget—and while maybe not the spree Piniella had envisioned, he pronounced his team "vastly improved," adding 14 players to the 40-man roster.

Among the veterans he added—Ken Cloude, who famously told Piniella to "Go sit your ass down," as a Double A pitcher with Seattle, a show of defiance Piniella loved.

Piniella even took it a step further, calling the Rays "the most improved team in the division, period."

But his next prediction, at a fan luncheon, really shook things up. Or at least it seemed to shake up Chuck LaMar. "Lou said, 'We won't finish last,'" Shelton recalled, "which we took to mean, you know, next-to-last, not exactly the Promised Land. But I remember the GM gathering us around and saying nervously, 'Now remember, he's an optimistic guy.'"

Piniella certainly looked that way as a five-day exhibition trip to Tokyo to begin the season seemed to have a long-term jetlag effect on his club with the D-Rays going 10–28 through May 19.

Observing on his first few months on the job was Don Zimmer, hired to the staff as senior baseball advisor after a rift with George

Steinbrenner caused him to sever ties with the Yankees. Zimmer, a 73-year-old baseball lifer, said it was not just his previous eight seasons as bench coach to Joe Torre on a Yankees team that went to eight straight playoffs and won four World Series, that would help him help Piniella.

It was more like his years as manager of the San Diego Padres, where he suffered through 190 losses over the 1972 and '73 seasons, that taught him how to advise Piniella against having a breakdown.

And Zimmer said he felt like he had actually gotten through to Piniella during a talk before the Rays' April 23 game in Chicago, a 3–2 defeat Zimmer watched from the stands.

"I'm telling him, 'Lou, you're beating yourself up too much, you're too down,'" said Zimmer. "And he says, 'Yeah, Donnie, you're right.' And I said, 'You're too hard on yourself, you know what you've got.' And he says, 'You're right, Donnie, you're right.'

"I thought I got him over the hump. Then I come down [to the clubhouse] about 10 minutes after the game and he broke the shower door. And I'm thinking, 'I guess I really helped him.'"

On May 19, the Rays' 4–1 loss to Boston was their fifth straight and 19th in their last 22 games, prompting Piniella to raise his voice loudly enough in his postgame talk with reporters that anyone still in the clubhouse would have developed a ringing in the ears.

"You've got to battle your way out of it," Piniella intoned as his voice and temper rose. "Guys that fight and have some spunk, they get out of it much quicker than guys that accept it. I can tell you that for damn sure.

"I'm starting to feel that possibly we don't have that. How about that? That things are accepted. And that's not the way to do it. It's mind over matter, it's going out there and competing and getting it done.

"Is anybody trying to stay in a slump? Absolutely not. Is anybody trying to make outs? Absolutely not. But at the same time, sooner or later we're going to be in the middle of the summer here, and we're going to be celebrating the Fourth of July, and if we don't kick it in the butt a little bit, we're going to be in the same malaise we are now. And if we are, I hope it's with a bunch of different players, I can tell you that."

At 10–28, the worst record in the majors and the worst start in franchise history, the calculations were quickly being done each day, and the Rays would lose 119 games on the season if they kept up the current pace.

On May 30, before the last of a three-game series against the Yankees in which the Rays had dropped the first two, Piniella assessed the Yankees' usual array of stars, noting that New York's payroll was roughly $150 million more than the Rays' $29 million ($7 million of which was being paid by St. Louis to Tino Martinez). Heck, the left side of the Yankees' infield made more than the entire Tampa Bay team.

"You're not getting a Giorgio Armani suit at Filene's Basement," Piniella said. "They've paid for those type of players; they don't come cheap.... Can teams like ours afford what the Yankees can? Absolutely not. But we've got to get closer.

"The solution [is] to get much better. That's really it. But to do that, we've got to get our payroll up there where we can do those things. The answer is get better players, whether they come out of your minor-league system or wherever they come from. There are no miracles; there's no stardust or magic."

Still, the Rays won that day, making them victorious in seven of their previous 10 games, including a five-game winning streak right after his very pointed remarks at the end of their five-game losing streak.

And they kept on winning.

Beginning June 9, two days after the Tampa Bay Lightning captured the Stanley Cup, the Rays caught, well, everyone by surprise with a 12-game winning streak, blowing through the Giants and the Rockies before taking their new act out West and sweeping the Padres and Diamondbacks.

Tampa Bay became the first team to go over the .500 mark after being 18 games under, going 20–6 in June—a 30–10 run beginning May 19.

But they would drop eight of the next 10, and Piniella was banging the drum again to anyone who would listen. Specifically, he wanted to add a proven run-producer to a lineup that ranked near the bottom in every major offensive category.

They had reason to feel good about the potential of 20-year-old prospects B.J. Upton and Scott Kazmir, whom they acquired in a trade with the Mets for No. 1 pitcher Victor Zambrano, as well as the continued development of Carl Crawford, Rocco Baldelli, and Aubrey Huff. They also liked a 22-year-old kid named Jorge Cantu, whom they signed at 16 and who would play 50 games for the Rays in 2004 and hit .301.

That was mildly encouraging for an organization seemingly burned by can't-miss draft picks like Josh Hamilton, suspended for substance abuse, and Dewon Brazelton, the 2005 Opening Day starter who was demoted shortly after to Triple A but put on the suspended list for failing to report to Durham.

Like Gary Shelton said of Piniella and his gang, "It was like Butch Cassidy leading the Teletubbies."

They were scoring little (Piniella felt a team has to score about 800 runs per season in the American League to be successful, the Rays had 714 while giving up 842), leaving men on base and putting undue pressure on a young pitching staff.

His team was just not good enough to compete against the big boys [the Rays finished the season 9–29 against the Yankees and Red Sox combined].

"It's improved," he said, "but it needs more improvement."

After the 30–10 run, the Rays would go 19–42 over the next 61 games, including a 12-game losing streak that made everyone forget the good times and nullified a third-place standing.

However, when they clinched fourth on October 1, the first time the franchise had ever finished out of last place, and then won their

70th game on October 3, the last day of the season, even Piniella knew it was a cause for some celebration.

And so he broke out the champagne.

"We're going to let the kids taste some success," he said. "For us, it's not like going into the playoffs, obviously, but it's a step in the right direction, and it's a good, positive feeling for this organization."

If he had an ego coming into the job, he said, it had been beaten up and stepped on.

"Probably the biggest thing I've learned is I don't think I can just manage any team and win," he said. "I think I've been spoiled. I think you've got to have some pieces in place that allow you to [win]. Basically, good talent wins, and all you do is maneuver it as a manager."

Surely, Piniella, as every professional coach and manager, was well aware of this. But it wouldn't hurt to throw it out there—a nice way of putting in still another subtle dig at management.

Soon enough, there would be no subtlety at all.

Again, Naimoli was evasive on the subject, saying, "My expectations are that [the league-lowest payroll] is going to go up but at this point, I just can't give you a number. I don't know. I really don't know."

While Naimoli was talking about revenue-sharing and asking for the definition of payroll, it was clear that Piniella wanted it to increase to at least somewhere in the mid-$30 million range.

What he didn't know was that Naimoli would end up having little to say about it.

By the winter of 2004–05, Stuart Sternberg, a retired executive for Goldman Sachs from Rye, New York, who was the team's new general partner, having paid $65 million to buy 48 percent of the team the previous spring, was poised to take over day-to-day control. Suddenly, the foundation shifted even more under Piniella.

While the rest of baseball was contemplating the future new homes of such free agents as Carlos Beltran, Carlos Delgado, J.D.

Drew, and Carl Pavano, Sternberg was going to be prudent, take a long-term view, not throw good money after bad. And it made perfect sense. Unless, of course, you were Lou Piniella.

Publicly, Piniella was toning down his original goals of becoming a playoff contender before his four-year, $13 million contract was up. But as he headed into his third spring training, he was steaming privately over the Rays continuing to have the lowest payroll in baseball.

Tampa Bay's big off-season acquisition was Danny Bautista, who signed a one-year, $1.9 million contract. So while other managers were spouting the usual spring optimism, Piniella tried hard to strike his usual honest chord without bashing management.

"I wish I could tell you that we're going to win the Eastern Division," he said. "We're going to go out and attempt to win the Eastern Division...yeah, we're going to attempt that. But realistically, if we improve on last year's performance of 70 wins, keep this thing going in the right direction and give our kids a little more time to develop, I think that's really the job for this year.

"I wish I could say more. And we're going to do everything that we can, from the players to the staff to the front office. But it's a tough division. And improvement over last year, to me, is a step in the right direction."

Of course, he had to hope the well-worn Hideo Nomo and Denny Neagle were healthy enough to stay atop the starting rotation and that Baldelli returned by mid-season from his torn ACL the previous fall. They were also counting on 37-year-old Roberto Alomar at second base and for Alex Gonzalez to make the switch from short to third.

Spring training of 2005 was a somber time for Piniella. For more than a week, he joined his family at St. Joseph's Hospital in Tampa, spending the last days he had with his father Louis, who died on February 27 after lingering heart problems at the age of 86.

Louis Piniella was called a fierce athlete, a businessman, and a gentleman by those who knew him, from Lou's coaches growing up, to Lou's own players and coaches, to friends and relatives. He was also a survivor. In October 1980, at age 61, the senior Piniella was struck by a car crossing the busy West Shore Boulevard in Tampa and was in critical condition initially with multiple rib and collarbone fractures as well as lacerations to his head, back, and shoulder.

Over the last few years of his life, an enduring memory of many in the old West Tampa neighborhood was the sight of Lou Sr. and his wife Margaret sitting on the porch outside the house on Cordelia St., not more than 50 yards from Lou Piniella Field, watching softball games and calling out to position the outfielders.

"I played against Lou's dad in the Intersocial League [baseball] games," said Lou's high school basketball coach Paul Straub in a 2006 interview. "He was a tough competitor, a great athlete. Lou took after him. He didn't go to Lou's basketball games much because he didn't want to [lose his temper] and go on the floor."

"Lou's father was a fine gentleman," said Sam Bailey, Lou's baseball coach at the University of Tampa. "I got to know him very well. He was a nice person, good people, and very well thought of."

* * *

On May 2, Tampa Bay lost its eighth straight game, were 8–18 on the season, and drew 13,217 for a Yankees game, for crying out loud. Not that the Yankees had been impressing anyone at that point, but they generally impressed hell out of the Devil Rays. And they certainly drew the transplants.

Piniella threatened to make his players come in earlier, practice longer. But that wasn't the answer and he knew it.

On one flight to Kansas City, with his team beginning a 10-game road trip in mid-May and in the midst of losing 12-of-16 games, the coaches were having a few cocktails when Piniella announced he was going to start his bullpen and bring the starters in later.

"I had my headphones on afterward," coach John McLaren recalled, "and Lou said, 'Mac, you didn't say a word. How come?'

"I said, 'Skip, I love you and you could be the biggest, smartest guy of all time but you're going to embarrass yourself here. You have one more stop left in you, most teams can't afford you, and you can eliminate a couple more if you keep this up.'"

"The next day he asks me to come into the office, and he says 'That's why I love you, because you always tell the truth. Thank you.'"

But finally, Piniella had to do something. Or at least say something.

On June 12, the day after the Rays had dropped their seventh game in a row and 12th of their last 13—an 18-2 humiliation in Pittsburgh—Piniella broke. He was waiting for the beat writers when they showed up in the visitors' clubhouse for their normal pregame session. He had been thinking about this "all night," he told them.

He went directly at Sternberg and Tampa Bay's new ownership group, accusing them of giving up on the plan to make the team competitive and saying he would no longer take responsibility for its dismal play.

"When I came here three years ago, we were talking about a situation where we wanted to win now, and we were interested in winning now," Piniella said. "With a small payroll, we improved it from 55 [wins] to 63, and from 63 to 70. This was supposed to be the breakout year.

"The problem is we've got a new ownership group here that's changed the direction of where we're headed. They're not interested about the present. They're interested about the future. And that's their right. But when other teams are getting better presently and we're not, you're going to get your butts beat, and that's exactly what's happening.

"I'm not going to take responsibility for this. If I had been given a $40- or $45 million payroll and was getting beat like that, I'd stand up like a man and say it's my fault. Well, I'm not going to do it."

It didn't take him long to say it, but the impact was not unlike that 18–2 punch in the mouth.

"It was over after that," said Henderson. "You don't get to insult your new boss and get away with it."

None of the owners would comment on what Piniella said, but the manager strongly hinted that it was Sternberg who was calling the shots, though he had yet to gain total control of the club, and was the target of Piniella's ire and frustration.

Signed through the 2006 season, speculation began immediately that Piniella had also spoken out in a proactive attempt to get out of his contract. He was to be paid approximately $3.5 million in 2005 and $4.5 million the following season, not including about $1 million in deferred payments.

With rumors already generated that Piniella would take over for Joe Torre in New York, the question was how he could get out of his contract without too much pain, financially or public relations–wise, to either party.

The day after Piniella's comments in Pittsburgh, the team was back home, but he was not backing off.

"I've got absolutely nothing personally against anybody, they're a good group of men," Piniella said of the new ownership group. "But this is a tough business. And what I said, I said. That's all I got."

General manager Chuck LaMar said he would try to determine the direction of the organization in mid-season meetings with Naimoli and said that everyone, including Piniella, needed to take the blame for the team's current woes.

"We're all in this," he said.

Clearly, his players and the public were on Piniella's side.

"Piniella came across almost as an advocate for these poor fans who had been sold this sham of a team," said Shelton. "When he raised hell, they felt he was their hand-picked guy. Who hasn't wanted to stand up to their boss or the fat cat in the office? And what group of guys in the bleachers wouldn't want to open up a seat in the stands and buy Lou a beer? And frankly, Lou would drink it. He was Johnny Paycheck."

Although he could take his job and shove it, that would not be financially prudent. And firing him would obviously be unaffordable for a team that couldn't afford decent players. A buyout was inevitable, no real question of whether he'd go or not.

"For sure he was gone; everyone knew that," said Travis Lee. "If he would've stayed another year, he would've died. Physically, he couldn't go through it again. Emotionally, he was already dead."

The season was not yet half over, and it had been hard on everyone. On the day after the Pittsburgh throwdown, the Devil Rays reassigned Alex Sanchez, who was hitting .346 but unhappy that he was not an everyday player. Sanchez was picked up by San Francisco 10 days later, but the move was clearly lost in the shuffle, along with the baseball, which was not necessarily a bad thing.

The Devil Rays were a league-worst 22–43 after being shut out by the Brewers on June 14, would finish the month 8–18, and would lose 18 of their next 23 games. They were clearly not on a path to even accomplish their modest goal of improving upon last year's 70-game win total.

"Our defense and pitching were so bad, it was ridiculous," said Lee, "And with so many guys in and out, in and out, we never had the same 25 guys three days in a row, so it was really tough. No one knew who was staying and who was going."

If there was a rock bottom to the season, it may well have been June 21, the day the Yankees defeated the Devil Rays 20–11 at Yankee Stadium, after trailing 7–1 in the third inning, 10–2 in the fifth, and 11–7 in the eighth. That was when the Yankees scored 13 runs on 12 hits, including four home runs, three consecutively in a span of eight pitches.

Tampa Bay reliever Travis Harper took the brunt of the abuse, tying a major-league record by allowing four home runs in one inning. Harper had entered the game with the Rays still leading 11–9, faced 11 batters, and gave up nine earned runs on eight hits.

Piniella not only left the 29-year-old, six-year veteran right-hander in the game, but he didn't get anyone else up in the bullpen, which he attributed to the fact that he didn't want to use another pitcher in such an inevitable loss, and he expected him to get the last out a lot sooner. He also had no lefties left to replace Harper.

But coming as it did, nine days after Piniella spoke his mind in Pittsurgh, the questions were inevitable.

"To anyone watching the game," wrote David Picker in the *New York Times*, "it almost seemed as if Piniella was resigned to letting the onslaught run its course without intervening. He recently voiced his displeasure with how much the Devil Rays' ownership was willing to—or not willing to—spend on talent. Was he trying to demonstrate to the team's owners what could happen when he was forced to manage with the current roster? Or was he just out of decent options in a game that had turned into a rout?"

When asked after the game whether it was frustrating trying to manage a team with such a low payroll, Piniella repeated the phrase "What's so frustrating about it?" three times.

"I'm trying to win a baseball game," he said. "We have a four-run lead and we don't hold it. What are we going to do? You think we're trying to blow a baseball game?"

The next day, when the same New York writer asked if he had a chance to speak to Harper, Piniella became agitated and launched an expletive-filled tirade, ending when he pushed his chair into his office bathroom and against a wall.

"All you want to do is create headaches and problems," Piniella yelled at the reporter. "You think I did that intentionally? You think I'm going to have a pitcher beat up like that intentionally? What is wrong with you? I took that last night, and I'm not going to take it anymore.

"You think I'm going to let a guy get beat up like that? No I'm not."

Scott Kazmir, the winning pitcher the next day who would go on to become an All-Star for the Rays in 2006 and '08, said the losing wore on Piniella more than anything.

"It was hard on him, it was hard on all of us because it felt like we weren't getting help from too many places," he said. "He's a very big competitor, everyone knows that, and just losing like that, it kind of felt we didn't have a chance. It was a revolving door, everyone was leaving, it was just an uncomfortable situation we were all in."

Finally, with less than two weeks remaining in the season and fresh off a 15–2 home loss to the Boston Red Sox, the first report surfaced that he had accepted a buyout of the final year (2006) of his contract.

The *Tampa Tribune* reported that Piniella had agreed to accept half of his $4.4 million for the next season to walk away as manager of the Tampa Bay Devil Rays after three years. Later reports had Piniella also receiving $1.25 million in salary deferred from his first season. Plus, he would be free to take any job in broadcasting or with another major-league club.

And so ended the worst episode of Piniella's managing career.

"He wanted to come home at first," said Henderson, "but as he got there and he realized he had no chance to win, that's when it really started to eat at him. I called them Rays Village instead of Nation because they didn't have many passionate fans, and the ones they did have were desperately looking at Lou as the guy who was going to make it happen. As he found out that he could push and yell and scream and prod and be Lou Piniella but if the guy can't play, he can't play, that's where it bothered him the most. And it began to sink in that 'I may be costing myself the Hall of Fame here.'"

"It's bittersweet," Anita Piniella told Henderson. "I am personally sad about this. We were both home, and we had such high hopes. We wanted to finish up here with a team that would win. They're doing so well now, and I'd like to think my husband was an integral part of that."

She predicted that he would take a year off.

"This year has been tough on him," she said. "At times, I didn't see the same man I married. He just wanted to win so badly. But now that it's over, he's much more relaxed."

Piniella had privately called it the "perfect storm" of ownership, getting caught between two groups with seemingly no one accountable when he needed answers and each possessing different agendas.

In the end, as Shelton said, some managers plant and some harvest, and Piniella was "an autumn kind of guy on a spring sort of franchise."

"I think the new regime wanted him to stay on, I know they did," McLaren said. "But Lou said, 'You can't pay me enough money to lose,' and that sums it up. Nothing against the players, but [the new ownership group] knew they weren't going to put the dollars up at the beginning. They had a strategy, and it's working out for them. Lou's time frame was just much different than theirs."

The Devil Rays lost the last four games of the 2005 season to finish 67–95, a three-way tie for the second-worst record in the majors, 28 games behind first-place New York and Boston—three fewer wins than the season before, four more than the first.

"I was there Lou's first year and [after a season with the Yankees] was back in his third year, and you could tell he was just fed up," said Lee. "It was a completely different Lou.

"That first year, he really thought he could change it around and make it a winning organization. He thought the organization had his back, and by the third year when I came back, it was like he realized they were not going to do anything and it was a completely deflated Lou, not that fiery guy. He seemed like he had totally lost that passion. There was no arguing. If he did go out, it was very rare, and it wasn't even a real argument. He wasn't showing his players, but he was showing the organization, 'If this is what you're giving me, that is what I'm going to give you back.'"

Those who watched the Rays and Piniella during those three seasons said the weathering that took place during those three seasons was not unlike the photos of the president when he goes into office compared to when he comes out.

"I'm tired," he conceded as the final days wound down. "I need some time off."

But he called it a "positive parting of the ways."

"There's always disappointment," he said. "When I signed on three years ago, I didn't think it would end this way, obviously. If I thought it would, I probably would have chosen a different approach. But what are you going to do? I did the best I can. I enjoyed a lot of things about this job. I wish we won more baseball games. That's what I really enjoy the most.... Could there have been a better ending? Yeah. But it didn't work out that way. That's it."

Piniella said he looked forward to golfing and fishing, but no one who knew him believed he was ready for retirement or that he would walk away after three 90-loss seasons, including LaMar.

"For those who don't think that gentleman's not going to manage in the future, I wouldn't take that to Vegas," he said. "He's got too many years left in him. I think he's too close to being truly recognized as a Hall of Fame manager. It may not be next year, but I'd be stunned if Mr. Piniella doesn't manage in the future."

CHAPTER
8

Curses

This was not what he envisioned.

Surely not standing in a soggy clubhouse, the dull roar of another team doing a victory dance on his players' heads. Definitely not another first-round playoff sweep.

This whole curse garbage, the 100 years without a World Series win, it was not what lured him out of a nice cozy broadcast booth and back into uniform. He never bargained for the constant questions that had nothing whatsoever to do with baseball, nor the oppressiveness of a starved fan base no longer charmed by effort and personality.

This was no easy gig. But then, they never are. That much Lou Piniella did know by now.

"Listen, I don't think there's much more pressure and stress in life—other than the president of the United States—than a big-league manager," Piniella had said at home in North Tampa two years earlier, not long after being named the new manager of the Chicago Cubs. "I know how that sounds and believe me, I respect what doctors and firemen and policemen go through. But managing 162 games, if you do it the right way, it wears on you."

But that's why he vowed it would be different this time.

"I'm going to try not to let it consume me this year," he said. "I'm going to work out, play golf, try to get my mind off it a little bit. There are a lot of day games, so I can go home and have a nice dinner with my family, maybe go to the theatre, enjoy the city for what it is."

He was unshaven, not that tortured in-season look but rather beach-guy relaxed, wearing a tan and an easy smile. His friends said he had his old glow back again. You flash back to that image two years later as bloodshot eyes blaze at the reporter brazen enough to ask if he's frustrated inside that dank visiting clubhouse at Dodger Stadium.

This was not the plan. Lou Piniella went home to Tampa in 2003, and it was supposed to be for good. He'd get the young Devil Rays on the right track. With a little luck and the investment in some solid free agents that ownership promised, maybe he'd even get them to the playoffs or at least to the door. And then he'd go fishing, play golf, and walk on the beach with his wife without the constant companion of baseball demons racing through his head.

"I really thought I would retire [after 2005], but I just didn't want my career to end with three losing seasons in Tampa Bay," he said.

That was the worst, they all said. Seeing Piniella lose 90-plus games three years in a row was bad enough. But losing them at home, with his friends and family, his neighbors in the stands?

Ah, but who was kidding whom? Losing was never easy. He told that to his guys in Cincinnati like he told them in Seattle and again in Tampa, just in case they didn't get it, which they frequently didn't.

"You don't understand," he'd tell them, "I live and die through every one of you guys. I pitch through every one of you. I hit through every one of you. I play the game through every one of you."

"It was torture for him," said his former player and coach Chris Bosio of their days in Tampa Bay, "watching his guys perform."

It was that much worse when they failed to play up to their potential. And here it was, happening yet again. Twelve runs in six playoff games. Piniella kept repeating it as if even he couldn't quite believe it.

Six runs for the Cubs in three straight losses to the Arizona Diamondbacks in the 2007 National League Division Series. Six runs in another three-game sweep at the hands of Los Angeles in the 2008 NLDS.

"Give the Dodgers credit, but let me tell you this," Piniella said, his voice rising on that October night in 2008. "You can play postseason between now and another 100 years and if you score six runs in a three-game series, it's going to be another 100 years before you win here.... That's it. Period."

Later that night in the hotel bar, he would grumble about Alfonso Soriano, the guy making $136 million who insisted he was a leadoff hitter and who was good enough in his hot streaks to prevent a manager from killing him during the cold ones. But all bets were off in the playoffs, where Soriano went 1-for-14 against L.A. after going 2-for-14 against Arizona in 2007.

And then there was Kosuke Fukudome, the Japanese import with the great credentials and a swing that had become so annoyingly steeped in bad habits that Piniella simply gave up waiting and gave up on Fukudome after Game 2 in Chicago against the Dodgers.

"The kid is struggling, and there's no sense sending him out there anymore," Piniella told reporters, demanding that they stop asking about him.

That said, there were a few whispers that the old man was turning soft, that at 65 and managing his fifth team over 21 years, "He's not the old Lou" as one talk-show host put it in the days after the Cubs' elimination, "not the Lou the Cubs thought they hired."

The so-called "old-school" guy who once went after Rob Dibble physically and Ben Grieve mentally, the guy who only 16 months earlier had treated the Wrigley Field faithful to a good old-fashioned dirt-kicking of the third-base umpire, was now seemingly allowing Soriano and Aramis Ramirez to continue their habit of admiring fly balls at home plate and in Soriano's case, loafing in left field.

Ironically, that was one of the draws of this job for Piniella. Taking over another reclamation project, albeit with a seemingly much bigger upside and a $300 million budget, Chicago didn't appear to necessitate as much ass-kicking as Cincinnati, Seattle, or Tampa Bay.

Though the 2006 Cubs had lost a league-worst 96 games, one more than the Devil Rays in Piniella's dismal last season there, the Chicago clubhouse was stocked with veteran leadership, they were poised to add quality free agents, and for the love of God, were due for some breaks.

Piniella, who was assumed to be headed to the Yankees until George Steinbrenner decided not to fire Joe Torre, beat out former Cubs favorite and recently fired Florida Marlins manager Joe Girardi; team broadcaster and former World Series–winning manager for the Diamondbacks, Bob Brenly; and the still-employed San Diego Padres manager, Bruce Bochy.

The continual rumors that Piniella was going to be hired by New York embarrassed him, he said, and prompted a phone call to Cubs general manager Jim Hendry to assure him that "there's nothing to it."

"Lou told me the first night we got together that this was the job he wanted," said Cubs general manager Jim Hendry. "He had a good relationship with George, but he didn't have any interest in doing that. He had too much respect for Joe [Torre]. But this was the job he wanted anyhow.

"He was doing the playoffs for FOX and called me—I was actually on the road interviewing someone else—and said, 'I know there's stuff coming out about the Yankees but I wanted you to know I had nothing to do with it, and that if you want me, this is the job I want.' He cleared it up right away and never played one against the other."

Hendry had admired Piniella for a long time, almost 50 years, actually, to 1961, when as a six-year-old, he saw Piniella play high school basketball and baseball at Tampa Jesuit, where Piniella starred.

"I grew up in Dunedin, and we made the commute," Hendry said. "My older brother was two years younger than Lou, and he was a good guy and took me to games. We didn't know him, but Lou was the kind of athlete everybody looked up to."

Other than that, however, Hendry had little contact with Piniella, other than a few chance meetings during spring training.

"But I always admired the way he managed, and I knew a lot about him during his Cincinnati and Seattle days," said Hendry, who also had a mutual friendship with Ron Guidry, a former Yankees teammate of Piniella's who spoke highly of him, and also consulted with Cubs pitching coach Larry Rothschild, who was on Piniella's staff in Cincinnati.

Hendry met with Piniella in Tampa in what he called "a great evening."

"He had a good handle on our club and ideas of what to do right away, and he wasn't really concerned with how high the payroll was going to go," Hendry said. "I told him at least $100 [million dollars], and that satisfied him. I'm sure he did some work on me too and thought even though we were coming off a rough, rough year, that I was capable of getting it turned around.

"I just remember coming out of there thinking how refreshing it was that he still had a lot of passion, he was still all about winning, that he hadn't lost that because he's older or because he spent a couple tough years in Tampa. I really got the sense that he really still had a burning desire to win, and I think he was really intrigued by the challenge to win here.

"I gave everyone I interviewed consideration, but my gut kept going back to Lou."

John McDonough, who just a month earlier had been named to replace Andy MacPhail in a memorable press conference in which the former Cubs VP of marketing uttered the word "World Series" nine times in 11 minutes, loved Girardi and barely knew Piniella. But he said the urgency the club had to win it all matched that of Piniella's.

"Lou was the perfect fit because of the direction we were headed," said McDonough in October 2008, 11 months after resigning from the Cubs to become president of the Chicago Blackhawks.

"I certainly went out on a limb in stating our goal was to win the World Series. For better or worse, people had previously talked about things like playing meaningful games in September. World Series is difficult for people to say. But I wanted to say it, and I needed Cubs fans to know that was our objective. It was not a prognostication, it was where we wanted to go. And when we said that, Cubs fans were like, 'Okay, now that we've heard that, this means we're really going to try to do it.'

"There was a strong sense of purpose, and with that mission articulated, Lou no doubt was the right guy at the right time, with dagger-in-the-heart instinct to put 'em away and put 'em away now.

"Down the road, I do believe Joe Girardi will manage the Cubs. But Lou was the perfect guy for that time."

The Cubs clearly wanted Piniella's experience and his superior baseball acumen. In style, he was a contrast to prior Cubs manager Dusty Baker, the consummate player's guy (who was not offered a contract extension after the 2006 season), and they could use someone to shore up fundamentals and remind players not to loaf. With a huge free agent market beckoning, payroll was not going to be a problem, nor was generating a fan base, though suddenly more people in Chicago were watching the Sox on TV than the Cubs. The time frame for winning couldn't be more pressing.

In other words, these weren't the Tampa Bay Devil Rays.

It took 15 days from Baker's departure to announce the hiring of Piniella and as always the case in Chicago when you're talking about the Cubs, it meant a fresh start.

"Long-suffering Cubs fans, we're going to win here," Piniella vowed upon being introduced as the 50th manager in Cubs history after signing a three-year, $10 million deal with an option for a fourth year in 2010. "And that's really the end of the story."

More like the beginning. And Piniella was already being indoctrinated into the new world of Cubdom, beginning with that morning of the press conference.

"I did what I always did whenever we hired a new manager," recalled then-Cubs media relations director Sharon Pannozzo, who was breaking in her 17th new Cubs manager in her 24 years with the club. "I'd always pick them up at their hotel for their [introductory] press conference and go over some important facts they needed to know, a little prep course, in the short time period I had [on the limo ride to the park].

"I think Lou thought because he had been in New York that this would be nothing. And I think he was totally blown away when we got to Wrigley and there, in the middle of the day in the middle of the week, was a welcoming committee of like 30 fans there ready to greet him.

"He said, 'What's that?' And I said, 'They're there for you.'"

She chuckled. "Say what you will about New York being a tough town, but they don't have direct contact with the fans like you get at Wrigley," she said. "They're right in your face right away. Even Ronnie Woo-Woo was there."

Ronnie "Woo-Woo" Wickers is a longtime Cubs fan and fixture at Wrigley Field whose cheers "Cubs Woo, Cubs Woo, (insert any name) Woo" had punctuated Wrigley Field for the better part of the last 50 years and surely pierced the air that morning.

"They all waved to him, and Lou was very gracious and signed a few autographs," said Pannozzo. "But he was totally taken aback. And that was his first indoctrination to Wrigley Field."

Most first-time Cubs managers are eventually asked about the curses that have haunted the Cubs, like Billy Sianis' billy goat in 1945 and the famous black cat in Shea Stadium in 1969. But Piniella seemed to catch all the questions at once, at one point turning to Pannozzo after being told the legend of the billy goat (Sianis put a hex on the Cubs after he was supposedly told to leave a World Series game because his lucky goat was bothering fans), and asking her what he was supposed to say.

"I don't think any of them really know the particulars," said Pannozzo of past Cubs managers. "They're all aware of this long drought. I remember telling Lou about this concept of a curse [on the ride to the park] but not getting into too much detail with him. I didn't get into the whole billy goat thing because to me, I didn't think he needed to know at that point. Otherwise, it was too big of a deal.

"I got the impression from Lou that he had been around the block many times and was the kind of guy that didn't take any shit and would just as soon not deal with it and move on, that it wouldn't bother him; whereas some other [managers] through the years, it did get to them."

Very quickly on, however, Piniella learned that as Cubs manager, there was also more than the usual amount of schmoozing and hand-shaking. With marketing guru McDonough at the helm and the sale of the Tribune Co. appearing imminent, there was that much more selling to be done—and much of it to which he was not contractually bound but rather expected to do for the good of the franchise.

"I don't think he realized the internal demands that would be made of him," said Pannozzo, who resigned that December. "The Cubs are a marketing machine. They have the Cubs Caravan (a whistle-stop bus tour with players and manager through outposts in rural Illinois and Indiana, meant to connect with Cubs fans) and the Cubs Convention (also conceived by McDonough) and all these other internal programs going on that demand his participation."

And it all began immediately. Right after the press conference, on his way to take a tour of the clubhouse and see his new office, Piniella was intercepted by a Cubs marketing person with 12 dozen balls for him to sign.

"Lou was dumbfounded," said Pannozzo. "He said, 'Do I have to do this now?'

"They had Soriano sign them too [after he arrived], and they ended up using those baseballs for the employee Christmas gift."

In the middle of January, Piniella found himself on the Cubs Caravan bus for two days, followed by three days at the Cubs Convention, where 15,000-strong wearing passes adorned with their new manager's face smothered their usual brand of affection on all things Cub.

Piniella was so worn out that he arrived late for his Q&A on Day 2 of the convention, complaining of a stiff back from the caravan. By the next day, it had to be aching even worse as he felt the pressure of 99 years of anguish weighing down upon the organization.

When one fan demanded of Hendry, "I'd like to know what facts you have, as opposed to what-ifs, that make you think this is going to be a success when it hasn't been a success the past three years?" Piniella reacted with some amazement.

"Jim, this is a tough crowd," he said.

Piniella himself played cheerleader.

"Look," he told the audience, "the perfect example of what we're talking about here is the New Orleans Saints. They were 3–13 last year, and on Sunday they're playing for a trip to the Super Bowl. That's how quickly things can turn around in sports, and that's what we're going to look forward to in Chicago this summer with the Cubs."

He had reasons to be optimistic.

The team had already re-signed Ramirez to a new five-year, $75 million contract a month after Piniella's hiring. And a week after Ramirez was back in the fold, the Cubs would sign Soriano for $136 million over eight years, the richest deal in team history.

The club had also come to terms with pitcher Kerry Wood on a one-year incentive-laden $1.75 million deal in the hopes that a move to the bullpen would resurrect a career beset by injury and picked up free agent infielder Mark DeRosa, who agreed to a three-year, $13 million contract.

Hendry would later sign free-agent pitcher Ted Lilly to a four-year, $40 million deal (the identical offer Toronto proposed), while hooked up to a heart monitor after experiencing chest pains during the winter meetings in Orlando. Finally, Hendry added pitcher Jason Marquis to the mix with a three-year contract worth $21 million.

They also signed Cliff Floyd and Daryle Ward to one-year contracts.

"When the bosses are behind you like they are here, it makes things a whole lot easier," said a pleased Piniella.

The new skipper was looking forward to his first spring training, eager to get back on the field. The summer before had been his first out of uniform since 1989, the year he was fired as both general manager and then, for the second time, manager of the New York Yankees. He worked that season for the MSG Network, primarily as an analyst for the pre- and postgame shows, but also did some color work on the game broadcasts with Greg Gumbel.

Once, Piniella said he disagreed with a lineup decision made by then-Yankees manager Dallas Green. "And for all practical purposes, [Green] stopped doing interviews for the pregame show," recalled Gumbel. "But I can't remember anyone ever saying a negative word about Lou Piniella. Dallas Green didn't like what he said, but he never said anything about Lou."

Returning to the broadcast booth in 2005 and 2006, where Piniella partnered with Joe Buck, Tim McCarver, Thom Brennaman, and Steve Lyons on FOX Sports, Piniella received generally positive reviews for his work, though he admitted to a case of nerves at first.

"It was good for me, it lightened me up some," Piniella said. "It made me realize it's entertainment. I enjoyed eating a hot dog and having a couple beers at the ballpark, which I had never done, then leaving the park early and seeing families in the parking lot playing catch. It was a different perspective and I liked it, I really did."

Lyons, who worked the 2006 ALCS with Piniella, remembered trying to loosen him up in the booth.

"He felt what they wanted in him was to give his perspective as a manager, to just sit there and watch the game and tell everybody what he thought was going on," Lyons said. "To his credit, I think he wanted to do more than that, and he had notes, studied stats and figures. He had a ton of stuff in front of him, though he spent too much time doing that and the real Lou didn't come out.

"It was the main reason I joked with him, and I got myself in trouble for it."

Working Game 3 of the series, the night before he accepted the Cubs' job, Piniella talked about the A's Marco Scutaro and his unexpected offensive production, saying it was like "finding a wallet." Later, Piniella said Oakland needed Frank Thomas to get "en fuego" [hot] because he had been "frio" [cold], earning a compliment from Brennaman for being bilingual.

Lyons then joked that Piniella was "habla-ing Espanol" and quipped, "I still can't find my wallet. I don't understand him and I don't want to sit too close to him now."

That night at dinner, shortly after Piniella had remarked how funny their give-and-take had been, Lyons, a former big-league utility player who had worked for 11 years and had won three Emmy's for FOX, received a call telling him he was fired for making racially insensitive remarks.

"Lou and Thom got on the phone, and neither one of them could understand it," said Lyons. "The following day was Game 4 and Oakland was going for the sweep, and we were instructed to say nothing, so Lou couldn't say anything. The next day, he accepted the Cubs job."

Later, however, Piniella was asked about the incident and defended Lyons. "It was overblown, and he meant absolutely nothing by it, except a funny line," Piniella was quoted as saying. "I certainly didn't even give it a second thought. Probably, if I had been a little sharper or a little quicker, I would have come up with a good rebuttal."

* * *

It was one more good reason for Piniella to get back on the field where he belonged, and by the spring of 2007, his message to his new team was simple.

"Have fun," he said. "Forget the negativity. What happens in the present is what's important, not what's happened in the past."

If it was his attempt to release years of angst with one speech, only time would tell. But in his first days with his new team, his intentions were met with as much admiration as incredulity.

Here was a man claiming he never heard of billy goats and curses, suggesting instead a concept rarely considered among a fan base convinced that anything that could go wrong, and even a lot of things that couldn't always did.

Three years removed from one of the bigger meltdowns in modern baseball history, Piniella came up with "Cubbie Swagger."

"By that, I want a nice quiet confidence about them that we're going to go out and compete every day and play good games and win a good majority of them," he said. "You do that by being prepared; you do that by working hard. You do that by having a little passion for what you do, having a little pride in what you do, and by going out and believing in your teammates."

He made it sound so simple.

"That's something that doesn't happen overnight," Piniella allowed. "But all the good teams that I've managed have had a real quiet confidence about them. I like the word 'swagger,' so we'll call it swagger. It's not a cockiness. It's just a confident demeanor that you'll go out there and compete and play hard and play to win.

"And if you do that over and over again, with the talent level that we have here, we're going to have a very successful season here, believe me."

Believe him?

"It might take a while for [Piniella's] enthusiasm to become contagious," wrote *Chicago Tribune* Cubs beat writer Paul Sullivan. "People in Chicago have seen too much Cubbie *stagger* over the years. Hendry would prefer that everybody stop looking back at the great maw of bad Cubs seasons, but it's sort of hard when Game 6 of the 2003 National League Championship Series is still fresh in the mind."

Even three years later, the trauma of 2003 lingered. Five outs away from their first World Series appearance since 1945 and leading the Florida Marlins 3–0, the Cubs allowed Game 6 and their collective psyche to crumble, arguably on one foul ball.

In reality, it was a group collapse, precipitated, perhaps, by a fan's lunge at Luis Castillo's pop-up in the stands but exacerbated by the antics of left fielder Moises Alou, who admitted years later he could never have caught the ball anyway; a botched double-play ball by shortstop Alex Gonzalez, and a series of hard-hit balls and eight runs off Mark Prior and relievers Kyle Farnsworth and Mike Remlinger, all in the same inning.

Was it a sense of doom that made Game 7 an exercise in futility the next night, as a hushed Wrigley Field crowd watched the Marlins defeat Cubs ace Kerry Wood and win their second National League pennant in their 10-year existence with a 9–6 victory?

Piniella would get a taste of that mentality in his first spring training when Wood bruised his ribs in a fall climbing out of his hot tub. For the nine-year veteran about to begin what the Cubs hoped was a second career as a relief pitcher, this was no big deal. "It's almost funny," Wood said.

But for pessimistic Cubs fans quite familiar with the history of a former phenom who had been on the disabled list for all or parts of six of his previous eight seasons, this was always a big deal. Hence the "Here we go again" nature of the questioning from reporters, much to the irritation of Piniella.

"Let's not get into that," Piniella said. "This has nothing to do with ['Here we go again'] or anything else. Things happen, that's all."

As spring training got underway, Piniella seemed intent to make a fresh impression on the Chicago media, insisting he had changed over the years and that at 63 he had lightened up a little.

"Old-school managers have to adjust, and if they don't, they're not very successful," he said. "You have to adjust to today's game and today's player. I don't think that old-school managers would have all that much success in today's game.

"I consider myself very contemporary. I enjoy players. I don't like too many meetings, but I do like communication and I let guys play. I don't really bother people. I like to challenge them, get the best we can out of them.

"But I'm not old-school. With the things that go on in today's game all the time, an old-school manager, he'd be mad all the time, right? He'd have something to complain about. You just accept things, and what's important is how you play on the field and how you conduct yourself when the game starts. Play hard and play to win.

"Curses," he told reporters, "are for people without self-confidence."

Still, if he was going to transform a 96-loss team, he was going to do it the only way he knew how, with a mixture of the old Lou and the modern Lou.

"I remember I didn't get a sign or didn't execute a play the way he wanted me to that spring," DeRosa said a year later, "and he was really yelling, I mean more than I have been yelled at as a professional. And you take it and it kind of takes you back a little bit, and five minutes later he comes up and is like, 'I hope you didn't take that personally. I'm just trying to make a point.'

"I actually think sometimes it makes you play better if you're playing to impress your manager, rather than just going out there knowing if you make a mistake, your manager is not going to really say anything."

Longtime Piniella assistant and Cubs first-base coach Matt Sinatro had to smile to himself whenever he heard that Piniella had changed.

"In spring training, everyone said, 'Oh, he's mellowed,'" said Sinatro. "I said, 'Oh yeah, he's mellowed—until the third inning when the guy drops the ball.'"

The Cubs had a problem with dropping balls—to the tune of 19 errors in the first 16 Cactus League games.

While Piniella was generally pleased with his new club, telling Hendry when the GM asked if there was anything else he needed,

"No, we have all the ingredients," he was surprised at the lack of fundamentals, despite what he had been told.

Running into longtime Chicago TV and radio personality David Kaplan at a golf outing in June 2007, Piniella declared, "Now I know why you guys haven't won. It's just everything here. Guys don't take pitches; they don't learn how to slide step in the minors. It's crazy, I'm reteaching things guys should know. I've had to completely change the mentality. Any time something goes wrong, it's 'Oh well, it's just the Cubs.' That shit has to stop."

It frustrated Piniella to no end, just as it did his staff when the Cubs went through a streak of base-running gaffes. Generally, they all agreed that not as much emphasis was placed on the fundamentals when players were young and first learning to play the game and that some things were beyond coaching at the big-league level.

"Tram [Alan Trammell] and I and Lou covered everything in the spring we needed to cover," said third-base coach Mike Quade. "And then we come out and it's a different deal once the season started. I mean, what the heck is going on? There's a routine ground ball to short and the guy on second is running to third? We don't have a drill for that. Just don't do that."

Piniella was also quickly losing patience with some of the questions and the manner in which he was being questioned by the Chicago media. They were too consumed with the day-to-day conditions of former phenoms Mark Prior and Kerry Wood. They wanted timetables on Alfonso Soriano's center-field experiment.

And after just the ninth game of Piniella's Cubs managing career, they wanted to know "What isn't working?" after a 6–5 Cubs loss to the Reds in which starter Carlos Zambrano imploded in a six-run fifth inning. "What the hell do you think isn't working?" Piniella snapped. "You saw the damn game."

It was the Cubs' fourth loss in a row, and that sense of urgency was already showing. "I can start to see some of the ways this team has lost ballgames," Piniella said. "I can see it."

That Piniella was so worked up on April 13 was not necessarily unprecedented in his career, but it was testimony to the unique nature of his new job. "It's part of the seismic culture that is the Cubs," said McDonough. "You're looking from afar at this franchise that hasn't won in 100 years as lovable and cuddly, and then you get here and there's this epiphany that 'Oh my God, I never realized it was this big.' And not just on June 23 against the Cardinals, but on April 5 against the Pirates and January 16 at the Hilton and March 1 in Mesa. And everywhere you go, there are Cubs fans across the country and I don't think [Piniella] realized it.

"I do think before someone becomes manager of the Cubs, they really need to take a Cubs 101 course to understand how big it is."

Piniella certainly had to be getting the general idea after a spring that did not let up marketing-wise, with almost nightly get-togethers and meet-and-greets with the sponsors. "But I just saw these people last night," was a common refrain from Piniella, who would occasionally skip them altogether.

Then as the season started, he was the face of a new photo campaign for the team, "Play Like There's No Tomorrow." McDonough said Piniella "never pushed back. He was very friendly, very personable. I don't think we overused him."

But on top of that, there were also the unusual demands of day baseball, which did not necessarily include, as Piniella imagined, a lot of nice, relaxing dinners and theatre afterward.

There were dinners when friends from Tampa, whom he could never disappoint, would visit Chicago, but they did not end up being relaxing. "They want to go out and have dinner at night and have a few pops, and I enjoy it," he remarked the following season. "The only problem is I've got to be at the ballpark at 8:30 the next morning."

And that was hardly the end of it.

"Day baseball just makes more demands on players and managers—on their time, their exposure on a daily basis," Pannozzo said. "For a night game, there's the 4:00 [TV and radio news] hits, and you're done. There's not so much after the game.

"For a day game, there's all morning, the noon [newscasts], the game, and then there's the 5:00 and 6:00 news. It just keeps at you all day long, and there's a different level of exposure that goes along with it."

Piniella got it, at one point saying to an acquaintance early in his Cubs tenure, "What is it with the media in this town? I don't shave and it's a fucking news story."

Piniella was asked if managing the Cubs was "different," and he didn't hesitate. "It's so different than any other job in baseball, it's not even funny," he said. "The scrutiny here is just different, the 100-year thing, the day baseball, the enormity of what we're trying to do. Unless you're in it, you don't get it."

Lee Elia tried to tell his old friend. Elia was the manager of the Cubs in 1982-83 and had taken and given the worst to Cubs fans, his infamous 1983 tirade—"Eighty-five percent of the fuckin' world is working. The other fifteen come out here."—the stuff of legend.

"I don't know if I tried to warn him," said Elia, a trusted coach and friend for more than 30 years to Piniella, "but I told him about my first experience as a major-league manager, and I thought it was as difficult an arena as you could get put into and I was not one who dwelled on the negative. But I got tired hearing it, and I didn't have the experience or the moxy to let it be. The only way to beat it is with success.

"I think it got to Lou a little early when he felt like, 'My God, I just walked in the door, I do have some credentials here.' He told me one time [in 2007], 'Doggone it Lee, I can almost feel what you went through 25 years ago.'"

* * *

The Cubs carried a 22–29 record into June 2007 and were riding a four-game losing streak when Derrek Lee called a players-only meeting in an attempt to turn things around.

Instead, scarcely two months into his first season, it led to an ESPN report that Piniella had "lost the team." Piniella asked Lee directly if that was the case and was told only that some players had complained about playing time. In fact, there had been some grumbling about Piniella, others said privately, but it fell far short of a team revolt.

But things were about to get a lot hairier.

The Cubs' starting pitcher the next day against the Atlanta Braves was Carlos Zambrano, whose agent-imposed Opening Day deadline for a new contract had been extended into the season (he was eligible for arbitration after the season), but nothing had yet been resolved.

Zambrano had predicted a Cy Young for himself and a World Series for the team in 2007, but thus far had struggled in first innings and carried a 5–4 record and a 5.24 ERA into the game. And against the Braves, the day of his 26th birthday, he got into trouble again, walking the leadoff hitter in the fifth and allowing a single to the next hitter. One out later, both runners scored on a double by Jeff Francoeur.

Zambrano then allowed a walk to Scott Thorman, a single to the .189-hitting Pete Orr and a double to the pitcher, Kyle Davies, a .067 hitter following a run-scoring passed ball by catcher Michael Barrett, who followed with a throwing error to third.

When he was finally given the hook by Piniella, Zambrano had allowed 13 hits and seven runs (six earned) in five innings as the Cubs trailed 7–1.

After the inning ended and with the television cameras pointed toward the Cubs' dugout, Zambrano approached Barrett, pointed to his head and shouted about the pitch Barrett missed. Barrett responded by pointing to the scoreboard and to his own head. Zambrano then lunged at his catcher, and the two exchanged blows before being separated.

Piniella ordered Barrett to have a seat, then walked Zambrano to the clubhouse. But a short time later, after Piniella returned to the dugout, Barrett slipped into the clubhouse also, resulting in another fight with Zambrano and a black eye and bloody lip for the catcher, who was sent to the hospital for six stitches.

While Piniella did not condone the fight, he had certainly experienced it before over the course of his playing and managing career. Worse was the current state of his team.

"You don't like to see the silliness on the field," he said, his voice rising in anger after the game. "I only have so many guys I can play. It's about time some of them start playing like major-leaguers or get somebody else in here who can catch a damn ball and run the bases properly."

The public perception was of a club in turmoil. An "overpriced, slapped-together mess," in the words of *Chicago Tribune* baseball writer Phil Rogers.

"Another ugly snapshot from a sorry season," wrote *Chicago Sun-Times* baseball writer Chris De Luca.

Meanwhile, pressure was also building in favor, it seemed, of a Piniella tirade of some sort, preferably against the umpires. On the day of the Zambrano-Barrett altercation, there was a *Sun-Times* article addressing the fact that Piniella had not yet been ejected from a game. And after Friday's game, when more questions arose about his relatively calm demeanor, Piniella went so far as to predict his ejection drought would end "soon," despite the fact that he thought games were being umpired well.

The next day, in Saturday's *Tribune*, it was noted that even the mild-mannered Cubs Class A rookie manager Ryne Sandberg had already been booted three times and suspended once for giving an umpire a forearm.

Piniella acted like he'd rather avoid it, saying, "When I argue, I usually present a better argument than most guys, a little more demonstrative. And they'll play it over and over."

The next day, after his players expressed regret over the fight and love for each other, Piniella gave the media and the Wrigley faithful what they had been waiting for with his dust-up with third-base umpire Mark Wegner and subsequent ejection in the eighth inning of the Cubs' sixth straight loss.

The play that precipitated Piniella's outburst had the Cubs' Angel Pagan called out at third. But it hardly mattered. Kicking his hat and covering Wegner's shoes with dirt, Piniella was going to make it count. The fans reigned debris onto the field in a modern-day show of support.

"I think it was time," Piniella said afterward. "But I really did think the guy was safe."

Laughs all around.

He joked that he felt he had gone "through my freshman and sophomore years in two months" of managing the Cubs.

And suddenly, despite the fact that the Cubs' were nine games below .500 and already seven and a half games behind first-place Milwaukee and in fifth-place in the NL Central; despite the fact that they had just lost for the tenth time in their last 12 games, things seemed, well, to be back on course somehow.

"That changed the whole outlook of the Cubs season when that took place," Barrett said of the fight in a 2008 interview. "[Piniella] told me to sit on the bench and not go anywhere, and I disobeyed him. He knew how to protect me, but I don't think he wouldn't have cared whether I got off the bench or not. I'm sure he liked when I went [after Zambrano] into the clubhouse.

"He didn't bench me for it. He knew it made us a better team. That day, he knew it. When you look at the Bronx Zoo and the teams he came up with, those things happened a lot more. That's what gets me—with today's media, those things are frowned upon. But when you play the game with passion, on edge, with intensity, those things are going to happen. You don't encourage it; you don't dwell on it. But that's why Lou's so good, he didn't dwell on anything as long as you came to play."

But more than all of that, said Barrett, was what Piniella accomplished with his actions the next day.

"What he did that day, and I thanked him for it, was he put all the attention on himself," said Barrett, who had received a 10-day suspension the previous season after punching White Sox catcher

A.J. Pierzynski. "He did what a good manager does. Here we have this Zambrano-Barrett issue and so many others, and Lou said, 'I'm sick of this, I'm going to put it all on me.'

"When he did that, he told everyone, 'This is my team, and if you don't like it, buzz off.' And from that day on, we were a different team."

They would also soon be a team without Barrett. The catcher was caught on camera getting into another heated discussion with a Cubs pitcher, Rich Hill, two weeks later, and a week after that, Barrett was traded to the Padres for catcher Rob Bowen.

The Cubs, meanwhile, continued the momentum that had begun to build after the Piniella ejection, winning 16-of-24 games and a major-league best 30-of-45 [encompassing his subsequent four-game suspension]. Zambrano, meanwhile, also went on a mini-roll, going 5–1.

Not unlike the Seattle Mariners, whose epic June brawl with the Orioles in Piniella's first season there signaled they were tired of being pushed around, the Cubs were still not through creating tough-guy headlines in June.

On June 16, the usually tranquil Derrek Lee, on his way to first after being hit on the hand by a pitch from the Padres' Chris Young in the fourth inning, charged the mound and took a swing at Young before both benches cleared. Though Young denied it, the Cubs felt he was retailiating for the actions of Soriano the day before, when the Cubs' slugger did a pseudo-Moonwalk out of the batter's box after popping a home run off David Wells.

Zambrano, the starting pitcher that day, had been in the clubhouse changing jerseys in the bottom of the fourth when he emerged from the clubhouse, belt in hand and looking like he was ready to rumble. He was in the midst of a gem, and fans had to worry the mercurial pitcher would lose concentration.

Though the Cubs lost 1–0, Zambrano pitched seven and a third no-hit innings before giving up the game-winning, solo homer in the ninth, and it did nothing to disrupt the team's sudden mojo.

The Cubs finished June with a sweep of the White Sox at U.S. Cellular Field, then swept the Rockies in another three-game series, and took 2-of-3 against the division-leading Brewers—winning the first game on a walk-off two-out, two-run home run by Aramis Ramirez.

They would head into the All-Star break on July 9 a game over .500, four and a half games out of first place, and with a newfound confidence despite a nine-game home-run drought. They would also do it with Derrek Lee going more than a month without a home run and hitting just six in the first half after slugging 46 in 2005 (he missed 59 games due to a broken wrist in 2006).

On July 24, closer Ryan Dempster returned after missing a month with a strained muscle in his rib cage to earn the save in the Cubs' 4–3 victory over St. Louis, the same day Lee returned from serving his five-game suspension and hit a key two-out RBI single in the ninth. Zambrano earned his NL-leading 13th victory to put the Cubs six games above .500 and in second place, three games behind Milwaukee in the NL Central.

Piniella pulled strings throughout his roster, going to a three-man closer rotation of Dempster, Bob Howry, and Carlos Marmol. The Cubs were getting stronger and younger with a starting lineup in mid-August that featured five players who had played together in the minor-league system.

One was shortstop Ryan Theriot, slotted behind Cesar Izturis until Piniella fell in love with him in spring training. "That little so-and-so is going to end up being my shortstop," Piniella told a friend in the spring of Theriot. "He understands how hard you have to play. He gets it."

Theriot was now hitting .286 and ranked third in fielding percentage among major-league shortstops with 60 or more games.

With Zambrano signing a five-year, $91.5 million contract on August 17, the Cubs were poised for that meaningful September they had been talking about and were alone in first place for the first time since April 2004. They were also getting ready for a pennant run with a healthy Soriano, without whom the Cubs had gone 8–11.

While Cubs fans and the media debated whether Soriano, who had been out with a torn quadriceps, should return to the leadoff spot, thereby bumping the effective Theriot, and Zambrano closed out a 0–4 August, emotions swung wildly with each victory and each loss. It was a phenomenon that did not escape Piniella as he tried to avoid the bouts of tightness that so frequently plagued Cubs teams past.

"In Chicago, people get real excited when the team is playing well, and they get down when the team isn't. We've got to find a little equilibrium somewhere," he urged.

The Cubs won two of three games against Milwaukee to take a 1½-game lead into September. And when the Cubs came back from a 5–1 deficit to Houston on September 2 to win 6–5, Piniella called it the biggest win of the year.

But things were back to Cub normal the next day as Zambrano allowed eight earned runs, seven hits, and five walks in four innings in an 11–3 loss to the Dodgers. Zambrano, who also ran through third-base coach Mike Quade's stop sign trying to score from first on a double by Soriano and was easily thrown out at home, was booed as he left the field, then ripped the fans afterward.

"I thought these fans were the greatest in baseball, but they showed they just care about themselves," Zambrano said. "That's not right. When you're struggling, you want to feel support. I'll remember that."

Piniella tried to get his enigmatic pitcher to lighten up. "He just came unglued after that run through the streets of Pamplona," Piniella cracked of Zambrano's running through Quade's stop sign.

The Cubs would drop nine of 15 games from August 25 through September 9 but would rebound with 11 victories in their next 14, at which point they had opened up a three-and-half game lead over

Milwaukee with just six games left. And for all the pressure that Wrigley Field had brought to bear, Piniella could not help but enjoy the enthusiasm of the home crowd.

As the Cubs were in the process of sweeping the Pirates at Wrigley, the latest scoreboard display showed that Atlanta had taken a lead over the Brewers, at which point Cubs fans began their own impromptu version of the Braves' tomahawk chop.

"That was unique," Piniella said. "This is a baseball environment, unbelievably exciting. When the game is over and the home team wins, it's special. I can see why players want to play here. I don't think there's an environment like this in baseball."

Despite following that with a three-game sweep at the hands of the Marlins in Florida, the Cubs completed their worst-to-first journey, clinching the division title with a 6–0 victory in Cincinnati, coupled with a Brewers loss an hour later.

Zambrano got the win with seven dominant innings while Soriano hit his 13th homer in September, equaling Ernie Banks' club record.

"Everybody roots for the underdog," Reds right fielder Ken Griffey Jr. said of the Cubs' turnaround. "But I wouldn't consider Lou an underdog."

Piniella acknowledged the season was much tougher than he thought it would be for all of them, deflecting attention from himself. "This is not about the manager," Piniella said. "This is about the team, the city, and the fans."

* * *

The celebration would turn out to be short-lived as the Cubs were swept by Arizona in the first round of the playoffs, Piniella roundly criticized for his decision to pull Zambrano with the score tied 1–1 in Game 1 after 85 pitches and six innings.

On the first batter he faced in the seventh, Cubs reliever Carlos Marmol gave up the go-ahead run on a solo homer to Mark Reynolds and another later in the inning in the eventual 3–1 loss.

Choosing to go with the three-man playoff rotation of Zambrano, Ted Lilly, and Rich Hill (and bypass Jason Marquis), Piniella said he wanted to save Zambrano, who would have had just three games' rest before pitching Game 4, a game, obviously, the Cubs would never get to play in the best-of-five series.

Piniella and Zambrano later said Zambrano told the manager he could have gone another inning, and in the days and weeks after the game, Piniella said if he had known what would happen, he would have left his ace in for another inning and then gone to Bobby Howry. But Piniella also said that in the same situation, he'd do the same thing again.

Piniella has rarely been worried about taking an unconventional approach. St. Louis Cardinals manager Tony La Russa said that's what he likes about his old pal.

"I don't think he's mellowed, but I do think he's smarter," La Russa said in a September 20, 2008, pregame interview, the day the Cubs clinched their second division title under Piniella. "Some guys think of the right thing to do, but they worry about the second guess. I thought he did a great job of pulling his lineup in the fifth inning [the day before, when Piniella left in only one starter, Mike Fontenot, with the Cards leading 9–0]. Some guys wouldn't do that because they'd be worried how it looked. Lou doesn't care, and I thought he was very smart doing it.

"One thing Lou does, if he figures out that X is the right thing to do, he doesn't worry that might result in criticism, and I think that makes an effective manager. Lou just has a feel for the game, he trusts his gut."

The debate over whether Piniella is more of an instinctive or analytical manager differs, depending on the source. Piniella said in the spring of 2007 that he tends to be more analytical.

"I believe in numbers," he said. "Baseball is a strict percentage game. That's why they keep [statistics].... So you might as well utilize those things. If I had to go with pure gut or pure numbers, I'd take the numbers."

Big on matchups, Piniella said he would consider resting a pitcher in a series if the numbers proved he had struggled against that team. He would consequently never rest a hitter on a day he was going against a pitcher he had hit well. And he would almost always play a faster lineup against a team with poor defensive catchers or susceptible pitchers.

But there are still plenty of gut moves, said his coaching staff, that Piniella has made as the Cubs manager.

"One thing he has done several times [in 2007 and '08] is starting runners at first and second, playing the hit and run, with nobody out," said Cubs third-base coach Mike Quade, in his first seasons under Piniella.

"That's something a lot of managers won't do, and I've seen him do it often. The whole thing is, you start runners on first and second and with a line drive out, it's a triple play and you're out of the inning. But in reality, how often is that going to happen as opposed to the ground-ball double play?

"There are things that that he won't think twice about. If he's got the right hitter at the plate, it's, 'Screw it, let's go.' It keeps everyone guessing."

Piniella called for a squeeze play four times during the 2007 season.

"We were run-challenged, we weren't hitting a lot of home runs, and he adjusted accordingly," said Quade. "That's something I've always been impressed with—being able to adjust and understand your club. Let the game come to you. He does that as well as anybody. He has a good knack and instinct for when to push and when to back off."

But the idea that Piniella is making decisions on the spur of the moment can be misleading.

"He is always thinking three, four innings ahead before he has to make a move," said first-base coach Matt Sinatro, who has been with Piniella since 1994 in Seattle, when Sinatro was an advance scout and later on Piniella's coaching staff.

Former Cubs great and team broadcaster Ron Santo offered an example from a 2008 game in which DeRosa came to the plate with men on first and second, no one out, and the Cubs leading 3–2 in the eighth inning against Philadelphia. Santo and broadcast partner Pat Hughes discussed the likelihood of a DeRosa bunt with Santo discounting it because DeRosa had been hitting so well.

DeRosa did bunt, advancing the runners. Then, with the infield in, No. 8 hitter Ronny Cedeno struck out swinging, and Santo and Hughes debated whether Piniella should pinch hit for catcher Henry Blanco, with strong hitters Mike Fontenot and rookie catcher Geovany Soto on the bench.

Blanco grounded out to end the inning, but the Cubs ended up holding the lead and winning.

"Afterward, I talked to Lou and said, 'You've got to explain that to me,'" Santo said. "He said, 'I thought with the infield in, Cedeno had a very good chance of just making good contact or taking a base on balls [he swung on what would've been ball four].'

"As for Blanco, he said the Phillies had two of their top runners in Shane Victorino and Jimmy Rollins coming up in the ninth. He said, 'I kept Blanco in the game [a very good defensive catcher] because they're not running on him. If I brought in [the left-handed] Fontenot [to hit for Blanco], they'd have probably brought in their lefthander from the bullpen, then I would've brought [right-handed] Soto in there. But we had a one-run lead, and I didn't want either of those guys to steal a base with a one-run lead.'

"He's not one step ahead; he's three steps ahead."

Of course, critics would argue that Piniella got lucky and that he out-thought himself when he pulled Zambrano in Game 1 of the 2007 NLDS. But his bench coach and former Detroit Tigers manager Alan Trammell said Piniella continually tests players in certain situations and "figures out how comfortable they are, better than anyone I've seen, whether this guy is more cut out for that role."

One of Piniella's favorite parts of managing is making out his lineup card, which he often does in three versions, bouncing the options off coaches, broadcasters, and team executives.

"I've been around a lot of managers," said team broadcaster Len Kasper, "and Lou, to me, more than anyone, seeks other people's opinions. He'll ask me my thoughts about certain guys, and you don't know how good that makes you feel, as someone who didn't play the game but watches the games every day, for a manager of his stature and someone who has been in the game that long.

"He'll give his opinion about something and then say, 'What do you think?' I think that's pretty rare in this game, but I also think it speaks to his comfort level with himself. He's confident, he's been through this so many times, but he doesn't feel the need to tell everybody what he knows. He's just constantly thinking the game and thinking of ways he can improve the team and thinking of different ways to tweak things."

During a game, however, the flow of input is greatly reduced. And Piniella's first-time coaches had to learn how their skipper wanted it dispersed.

"One of the biggest jobs I had was to figure out Lou's style—do you need to back off or do you need to give input?" Trammell said. "And the best thing I learned quickly was to back off. Lou is thinking ahead, and he's not a guy who wants to be cluttered by me making three and four suggestions. He also gives me a couple of keys, things he wants me to remind him of, and that's what I do. If he wants my question or opinion, I give him a quick response. That's what he likes."

While some managers live by computer reports, Piniella wants his staff to have the research at his disposal, but he prefers to simplify what he has in front of him so that he can be free to make what most would consider a gut decision. That should not, however, be mistaken for an inability to process the information by someone more than one friend called "math professor brilliant."

"Some managers are overly scientific and too smart," said Gene Michael, senior vice president and special advisor to the Yankees. "Lou is up to speed with all the statistics, but he has a great feel. Billy Martin had that feel and so does Lou, and that's why he's one of the best managers in the game."

Chris Bosio, a former player and coach under Piniella, said Piniella evaluates players like he handicaps horses.

"He can look at either and just know how that person or animal is going to perform, and that's a gift," Bosio said. "He can just tell by his actions, and Lou will play a hunch based on that every time because it's in his belly. He doesn't care what the numbers say.

"He'd talk to Matt on plane flights and say, 'Look, this guy is hitting .368 on the road and .325 at home. But he didn't hit .325 hitting inside pitches. We're going to throw him in, try to intimidate him.' That's how he felt we could get to Paul O'Neill. Pound it inside, get him to move his feet. We learned so much from Lou."

The Cubs' starting pitchers say they like to sit near Piniella on the bench, not just to joke with him when the time is right or to catch his one-liners, but to "hear" him manage.

"I've learned more about baseball being around him these last two years just because he thinks out loud," said Ted Lilly. "He's always thinking about all these options he has. He's trying to be ahead, and that's part of the tactic.

"From a managerial perspective, nothing is set in stone, he tries to do anything, and he picks his spots well."

Ask pitchers how it is to have Piniella as a manager and most give the same answer, whether with a smile or a grimace. Just throw strikes, they all say, and he'll have no problems with you.

While teaching hitting comes naturally to Piniella, he has had to learn the intricacies of pitching over the years. But it is as a hitter that he approaches most things on a baseball field. And it is as a hitter that his pitchers have discovered some of the most useful bits of information.

For Ryan Dempster, a 31-year-old with solid years behind him as a relief and starting pither as well as an All-Star season in 2008 when he went 17–6, talking pitching with Piniella has revealed simple ways of approaching his craft that had not occurred to him before.

"Like facing a guy who's hitting .330," said Dempster, repeating some of what Bosio learned more than a decade earlier. "Well, that's a guy you probably have to pitch inside a little bit more because he's handling the ball away so well. If you think about it, the hardest pitch in baseball to hit is the fastball down and away. If you're hitting .250, you're probably not handling that pitch down and away because guys are throwing it there and you're not getting your hits.

"But a guy who's hitting .330, he's hitting that pitch, he's covering that pitch away, so you might need to pound him more inside. Whereas a guy who's hitting .250, why come inside when that's probably the only pitch he can hit?

"When Lou said that, I was like, 'Yeah, you know, you're right.' You can't just sit there and throw the pitch down and away or inside all the time, but just the general philosophy of it really made a lot of sense to me."

For a manager who has had the reputation of being especially tough on pitchers, he can actually be quite the opposite, said Sinatro.

"I love the way he manages," he said. "I've seen him give pitchers every opportunity to win the game, and that's nice. I've seen him take care of pitchers' arms. I've seen him think of a player first instead of the 'W,' and in the long run, that's going to turn into more 'W's.'"

Coaching under Piniella, however, can be exhausting.

"He always keeps the pedal down, good, bad, or indifferent," said Sinatro. "When we're going good or when it's bad, everything's the same, he keeps on grinding. We might have 10-run lead, but he's always on guard. That's why he has made all of us coaches better, because we all have the same feeling that you never let up. It's fun to be that way, but it's also draining. It's a relief when the game's over with a win."

Piniella can also be very hard on himself when his judgments are off.

"He never makes excuses," said Sinatro. "I've heard him say, 'I blew it.' He asks Alan or me what we think, and we're not around to make him feel good; we're here give him a true answer. Then there are definitely times when it's not his fault and I'll go, 'Why are you letting that eat you up, because you don't deserve that.' But that's him, that's why he's such a winner."

Kasper agreed it is one of Piniella's more admirable traits.

"Some managers put on this front that they always knew what they wanted to do," he said. "Lou will tell you if he wasn't sure. It's so disarming, and you can just see the wheels spinning. That's how life is. You're not always sure about what the answer's going to be.

"Or he'll change his mind. He'll make a decision, and if someone comes around with a better idea, he's willing to go back and say, 'Maybe this isn't the best thing right now.'"

That candor, however, while sometimes endearing to his coaches and players, can be misunderstood.

"He's super smart about the game of baseball," said Kerry Wood. "He walks out to the mound slow and waddles and all that, but he's got everybody fooled."

Certainly, Piniella might have tried harder to assuage the "Grandpa Lou" image that he himself had fostered by, well, calling himself "just an old grandpa" in 2007 and admitting to "senior moments," like the time he removed Mike Fontenot for a pinch-hitter in the same inning he had homered during the 2008 season.

Barely two months into Piniella's first season, following the dirt-kicking, hat-throwing display that got him ejected, *Sun-Times* columnist Rick Telander called him "Lost Lou" and "essentially a befuddled near-senior citizen."

Cubs pitching coach Larry Rothschild, who was Piniella's bullpen coach with the Cincinnati Reds during the 1990 season, said that characterization comes from those who simply don't know Piniella well enough.

"That's the way Lou is," Rothschild said. "There are times when he's walking out to the mound and you kind of have to tell him where the mound is because he's thinking while he's doing it. He knows what he's doing, and he's always done that. But people look at stuff like that and say he's getting older or whatever.

"When I hear stuff like that, it's actually comical because being around him both 15 to 20 years ago and now, he's every bit as sharp, every bit as passionate."

In his WGN radio show with host Steve Cochran, Piniella said he used his press conferences—an uncomfortable exercise for him with the formal nature of the Cubs interview room as opposed to the casual chats he used to have in his office in other jobs—to "have a little fun" with the media.

"I play a little Columbo with the media from time to time," he said of the '70s TV show, probably not a helpful reference. "You know, I play the dumb role. Like I have senior moments, throw 'em off track a little bit, and you know what? They're pretty easy to throw off track."

Adding to Piniella's image were his unique phrasings—the malaprops that, in his first season alone in Chicago, had him being compared to the city's king of the malaprop, the late Mayor Richard J. Daley.

Lists were published of "Lou-isms" and "Lou Glossaries." What he said: Ivory. And what he meant: Ivy. He called pitcher Scott Eyre "Steve," "Stevie," and "Ire" (it's pronounced "air") for an entire season. He referred to Chicago's "Magnificent Mile" as the "Michigan Mile," which was close because at least it refers to Michigan Ave.

But Piniella also coined the brilliant "Cubbie Occurrence" to explain things that seemingly only happen to the Cubs, a phrase quoted time and time again and one that will no doubt reference him for years to come.

And he is a man that friends say is so adept at numbers, the stock market, crossword puzzles, and current events, that he could probably rake it in on Jeopardy.

"He is a very smart guy; don't let anybody tell you he isn't," said John Ellis, former chairman of the Seattle Mariners, former CEO of Puget Sound Energy, and a brilliant man himself. "And he isn't just street smart, he's smart-smart."

There were laughs aplenty the day Piniella and first-base coach Matt Sinatro got lost driving from Chicago to Cincinnati (Sinatro was driving; Piniella fell asleep) and the two nearly ended up in Cleveland before arriving at the ballpark three hours late.

But the laughs came just as much from Piniella, the eternal great sport, making fun of himself, "The sad part about it is we had a wonderful GPS system in the car," Piniella said, "and I didn't know how to use it."

"I don't think anything gets by him," said Chicago TV and radio sports show host David Kaplan, a lifelong Cubs fan. "He gets lost going to Cincinnati, and everyone thinks it's cute. When he first took the job, he used OnStar turn by turn and still couldn't find his way to Wrigley Field. It all feeds into that perception. But he is one of the sharpest managers around.

"I didn't always feel we had an advantage over the guy in the other dugout, but with Lou, the Cubs are never out-managed. There is just not going to ever be a move by the other side he wouldn't have anticipated or have a reaction to. If there is some kind of advantage to be had, Lou is going to find a way to have it. It's not always going to work out, but it's always a decision grounded in some sound reasoning."

The same players who affectionately tease the "waddling," defend him just as zealously.

"I think sometimes people don't think he's all there, but they never say it after a win," said Ryan Dempster, "they only say it after we lose because he's scratching his head trying to figure out what we could have done differently to win the game."

In the winter following the 2007 season, there was certainly some head-scratching, and Piniella still stung from the criticism over the Zambrano decision. But he tried to focus on the positive of the Cubs' turnaround.

"The amazing thing about baseball," he said, "is unless you win a world championship, you're going to be disappointed. It's sad in a way, but it's a reality.... But to go from last place to first, to have a 19-game differential and win a division, I think you should be pleased."

Over the next three months, the Cubs would trade left-handed hitting center fielder Jacque Jones, who was to earn $5.5 million in 2008, and cash to Detroit for utility infielder Omar Infante and sign 30-year-old Japanese free agent Kosuke Fukudome, a left-handed hitting right fielder to a four-year, $48 million contract.

They also signed Kerry Wood to another one-year deal for $4.2 million; made Mark Prior a free agent when they non-tendered him after he refused to sign a one-year, incentive-laden deal; and brought back pitcher Jon Lieber after a six-year absence with a one-year contract. They would decline options for Cliff Floyd and pitcher Steve Trachsel and tell Dempster to get ready to move into the starting rotation.

But Fukodome was by far the biggest news, a two-time Japanese Central League MVP with a lifetime .305 average, who hit 31 homers and had 104 RBIs in 2006 [he missed the final two months of the 2007 season following elbow surgery].

The Cubs beat out the White Sox and the Padres for Fukudome, and across town, Chicago's South Side team was not pleased. "We out-bid the Cubs," said White Sox chairman Jerry Reinsdorf, nearly a year later. "The reason Fukudome didn't come here was that he wanted to play right field because he felt it was his best position, and there was obviously nothing we could do about that [with Jermaine Dye in right]. And he wanted to be the first Japanese player on the team."

Fukudome was the Cubs' first Japanese player, though they did later sign former White Sox reliever Shingo Takatsu, 39, to a minor-league contract.

Having managed Ichiro Suzuki, reliever Shigetoshi Hasegawa, and closer Kazuhiro Sasaki, Piniella felt like, in a way, he knew what he was getting. "These young men are well prepared, they play hard and are respectful of the game," he said of Japanese players.

Piniella especially liked Fukudome's short, compact swing on first inspection and was envisioning batting him No. 2 in the order, though as likely the only lefty in the lineup, Piniella conceded he might want to drop him down to No. 5.

Fukudome had a translator with him, as he would all season, and naturally one of the first questions was whether the new Cub believed in curses. He doesn't.

As for Piniella, he had been thinking about his first speech to his team in spring training since January. "My message first and foremost to my team, and I've been thinking about that, is don't put the load of 99 years of not winning on you," Piniella said. "Don't put any pressure on yourself. Let this team stand on its own merit."

The 100th anniversary of the Cubs' last World Series appearance was looming large, and there wasn't a thing he could do to make it go away. This anniversary was as much about vindication as it was celebration.

While Zambrano vowed not to make any more predictions after his World Series/Cy Young forecast the year before fell flat, Dempster picked up the slack by guaranteeing the Cubs would become world champions.

"Enough with the B.S., the curse this, the curse that, the goat this, the black cat, the 100 years—whatever it is," Dempster said on his first day of spring training. "We've got a better team than last year—I truly believe—and last year we made it to the playoffs."

If Piniella minded, he didn't let on.

"I like the confidence our players have," he said. "As a team, we were disappointed the way our season ended abruptly last year in the playoffs. I remember when I played for the Yankees in '76 and [Cincinnati swept us] in the World Series. To a man we vowed we would do better, and '77 and '78 turned out pretty well [with back-to-back world championships]."

Looming in the background was also the impending sale of the team by Tribune Co.'s new ownership group headed by Sam Zell after management spent $120 million on payroll and raised ticket prices by 15 percent.

A nice World Series run would come in handy.

All Piniella wanted for the moment was to avoid the slow start of 2007, when the Cubs dropped the opener and were 22–31 on June 2, the day of his only ejection of the season and a day many considered the turning point of the year.

After a spring that was not exactly uneventful but featured only one real blowup (with Piniella admitting he "overreacted" to Jason Marquis' comment that he'd rather be traded than go to the bullpen by saying, "Then go.... How's that?"), the Cubs approached Opening Day optimistically.

The decision to move Dempster to starter looked like a positive one. Kerry Wood was entrenched as the team's closer as was rookie Geovany Soto as the starting catcher. And Felix Pie, he of the enormous expectations, started in center field.

Mark DeRosa was completely recovered from minor surgery for an irregular heartbeat, while the persistent rumblings surrounding a potential trade for Baltimore second baseman Brian Roberts had finally died.

Of course, the glad tidings were promptly quashed in a 4–3 loss to the Brewers on a chilly, rainy Opening Day, along with the would-be heroics of Fukudome, who went 3-for-3 including a double and a ninth-inning home run that tied the score. Zambrano failed to win his fourth Opening Day start for the fourth straight year as a hand cramp forced him out of the game in the seventh. Wood was dinged for three runs in the ninth, and Bob Howry took the loss.

Still, Piniella had reason to be pleased. Chicago media was already speculating that Fukudome's contract was the best money the Cubs ever spent and wondering if the team's crafty No. 5 hitter had been purposely holding back in spring training as was theorized with Ichiro.

Piniella had Theriot batting leadoff with Soriano batting second, which pleased most fans. For exactly two games. That's when the Cubs lost their second game in a row and Piniella moved Soriano back to leadoff after he went 0-for-9.

From the beginning, Piniella had acknowledged that while Soriano might not be the prototypical leadoff man, trying to convert him would be "like buying a Rolls Royce and trying to get Volkswagen mileage out of it."

Though everyone knew this and knew Piniella's propensity for playing with his lineups, the questions began in earnest and would continue for much of the season, making the Cubs' manager increasingly irritable.

"You know what's amazing?" Piniella asked. "If I don't change the lineup, I get asked, 'Why aren't you changing it?' And if I do change it, [the media says], 'You're tinkering.' Hopefully, it works out and we don't have to change it."

But Soriano, symbol of the Cubs' commitment to win and win now when he was signed, would continue to be a lightning rod for much of the season.

An easygoing, affable man by nature and, by all accounts, a good teammate, Soriano was also a highly paid athlete who most believed was getting his way by continuing to remain in his comfort zone of leadoff man, despite claiming he would do whatever Piniella wanted him to do.

While no one denied he was a gifted hitter and highly productive—he had freaky hot streaks during which he could carry the team offensively all by himself—he was also prone to cold spells. And for a leadoff hitter, he swung at too many first pitches, drew few walks, and more often than not, took home run swings.

It was maddening.

In 2007, Soriano missed five games in May with a hamstring injury and went on the 15-day disabled list in August with a quad strain. When he returned, he had the best September in team history with 14 (of his 33) home runs and 27 (of his 70) RBIs while batting .320 (.299 for the year) and leading the Cubs into the playoffs. Once there, however, he continued his career-long postseason struggles by going 2-for-14 as the Diamondbacks swept the Cubs.

Defensively, while he has a strong arm, Soriano was below-average as a fielder. And worse was his exasperating habit of hopping when he caught fly balls, which seemed to lead directly to a calf injury when he landed awkwardly on a routine pop-up by Ken Griffey Jr. on April 15, 2008.

At that point, Soriano was off to his second slow start, hitting .175, and again, the debate raged. If, as coaches said, he had lost a step to the injury, why would he be returned to the leadoff spot where now he couldn't even steal bases as that role demanded?

Fueling the criticism was the appearance that the Cubs knew they needed a new leadoff man, or why else would they have pursued Brian Roberts as they did?

Piniella didn't want to hear it.

"Every time I make a lineup change, I'm not going to sit here and be making explanations for it," he said. "That's what I get paid to do, and that's what I'm going to do."

Not helping the matter was that the left-handed Pie, whom the Cubs envisioned as their leadoff man of the future, was continuing his bad habits at the plate and off to a slow start with a .154 average.

The good news was that the Cubs shook off their 1–3 start and didn't seem to miss Soriano, turning in their best April in club history with a 17–10 start and good for first place in the division.

Even better was the fact that Dempster was 4–0 in five starts, Wood solid with four saves in six tries, and three players (Lee, Ramirez, and Soto) had 20 RBIs or more.

But with Soriano's return came Piniella's temper. Back on May 1, Soriano went 0-for-4 without hitting the ball out of the infield and let a fly ball in the ninth sail over his head, paving the way for a two-run Brewers rally that carried them to a 4–3 victory.

It was the Cubs' fifth loss in seven games and allowed the Cardinals to retake first place. Afterward, Piniella was asked if he considered inserting Reed Johnson into left as a defensive replacement.

"You're damn right I thought about it. You think I'm stupid or something?" he snapped, cursing under his breath as he walked out.

The next day, Piniella explained his anger.

"You don't take superstars out of the lineup," he said. "It's a long, long season. I have confidence in Soriano, and when I was asked a question, I probably should've responded a little different, but I was hot under the collar. And if you can't get hot under the collar as a major-league manager losing a two-run lead against a division rival that you're competing with for a championship, then you shouldn't be managing."

That night against St. Louis, Soriano misjudged two fly balls that he said occurred while trying not to hop. He homered in the ninth to send the eventual Cubs loss into extra innings but not before he was booed by disgruntled Cubs fans who had made the journey to Busch Stadium.

Soriano's fielding woes continued. Another dropped fly ball allowed the tying run to score in a eleventh-inning loss to Pittsburgh on May 25, a play that prompted WGN analyst Bob Brenly to remark that "you could throw a dart" in the Cubs dugout and hit anyone who could play outfield better.

Meanwhile, new acquisition and former St. Louis Cardinals star Jim Edmonds, whose pick-up in mid-May sent Pie back down to Triple A, was off to a slow start, going 3-for-24. Kerry Wood had blown four saves in his first 16 chances. And as usual, Cubs fans psyches, like their beloved team's play, were shifting like the lakefront breeze.

On June 3, the Cubs won their ninth-straight game with a 9–6 victory at San Diego and their 19th victory in their previous 25 games. They were 17 games over .500, their best start since 1977, and they had a three-and-a-half-game lead over the Cardinals in the NL Central.

It was hard to ignore the dramatic turnaround from exactly one year before, a weekend in which the Cubs were at their low point—nine games under .500 after the Zambrano-Barrett brawl and Piniella's dirt-kicking spectacle and ejection the next day—before turning the season around.

But as Piniella had beseeched of everyone after the Cubs' quick start and occasionally repeated early in the 2008 season, "Let's not get all giggly yet."

They were reminded of this on June 11, when Soriano left the lineup again, this time for six weeks with a broken left hand after being hit by a pitch. After his rough start, Soriano was hitting .283 with 40 RBIs and a team-leading 15 home runs. During his absence, the Cubs swept the White Sox at Wrigley and were swept in three at U.S. Cellular Field the next week.

They picked up Rich Harden and Chad Gaudin in a trade with Oakland for Matt Murton, Sean Gallagher, and two minor leaguers, prompting Aramis Ramirez to say, "We have enough to make the playoffs, but a guy like Harden is going to get you to the World Series."

But they would lose Kerry Wood on July 11 for an eventual 20 games with a blister on his pitching hand. And Carlos Zambrano would go on and come off the DL with a shoulder strain.

Piniella appeared tired and more than a little cranky, warning reporters again during a road trip to Tampa, "I don't want to hear anymore when I get back to Chicago and when we get Soriano back, about [the leadoff spot] or anything else...I'm not going to put up with it anymore. I think we know what we're doing here."

The week after that, Piniella was ejected from a game for arguing a checked swing, his first since the dirt-kicking episode the year before. And the week after that, the Cubs sent a franchise-record seven players and their manager to the All-Star Game behind a National League–best record of 57–38 and in sole possession of first in their division for the previous seven weeks.

The Cubs would go 16–18 in 34 games without Soriano and were immediately sparked by his return on July 23, defeating Arizona 10–6 as Soriano doubled and had an RBI. In their next 35 games with him, the Cubs went 26–9.

It was typical of Soriano. The Cubs seemingly couldn't live without him, even at his most exasperating, and fans knew it.

He would hit .333 in 39 at-bats in July and .283 in August. On September 6, with the Cubs riding a six-game losing streak, their division lead shrinking ever so slightly (to four games ahead of the Brewers) and their fan base teetering on utter panic, Soriano hit three home runs and drove in five runs in a 14–9 win at Cincinnati.

But on August 13, Soriano apologized to Piniella and his teammates after his career-long habit of pausing at home plate to admire an apparent home run nearly got him killed in the first game of a doubleheader with Atlanta.

The move backfired on Soriano in the eighth inning of the eventual Cubs victory when the ball he thought was a home run instead bounced off the left field wall. A sure double was reduced to a single, and Soriano was booed by Braves fans. He also had a fastball thrown at his head by rookie pitcher Francisley Bueno the next inning in retaliation.

"I said [to Piniella and teammates], 'That's not going to happen again,'" Soriano said.

At least one longtime Cubs observer had seen enough.

Steve Stone, the former big-league pitcher and for 25 years a television and radio analyst on both sides of Chicago, was astounded that Piniella was seemingly allowing Soriano to behave as he had. Stone was equally astonished later in the season when Zambrano, rocked for eight runs in an inning and two-thirds in his first start after throwing a no-hitter, walked off the mound before Piniella arrived to remove him from a game, a move that drew an immediate rebuke from Piniella.

Throughout his eight years as a Cub, Zambrano had had bursts of brilliance peppered with displays of erratic behavior both on the mound and in the dugout, such as the August 26 game in which he attacked the watercooler after giving up three runs in the first inning to Pittsburgh. It was not the first watercooler to pay for his frustration. Earlier in the year, Zambrano had also thrown a gum tray, broken a bat over his knee, and punched a hole in the locker room wall.

Piniella said that given his own history with watercoolers, he understood. But he also said that as a pitcher, Zambrano had to channel his emotions more constructively.

As for how Zambrano felt about his manager, it was hard to tell, as he often ducked the question. "Lou is in some ways a hard guy to deal with," he said once. "He's very quiet. He's not like Dusty Baker. But he's a good man. He talks when he has to talk. He tells you what he has to tell you. He's a good manager. As a human, he makes mistakes also. But he's human. That's basically all I have to say about him."

On his radio show and in a subsequent interview, Stone said Zambrano was becoming the new Sammy Sosa of the Cubs clubhouse. Stone was referring to the former right fielder's temperamental behavior, eventually resented by his fans and teammates. And Stone, now a broadcaster for the White Sox after turning down an extension offer from the Cubs following a 2004 season in which he clashed with players who felt he was too critical, said it was further evidence that Piniella had grown too soft.

"I don't think Lou today is the same manager he was when he was tackling Rob Dibble," Stone said. "I don't think he's mellowed in terms of intensity. I think he realizes there are ways to do things now maybe he couldn't before. And there are things he did before he can't do now. But one thing I disagree with—he said you can't handle players today the way you did in 1990. I posed that same scenario to [Atlanta Braves manager] Bobby Cox, and he said that's a bunch of horseshit. He said you make a set of rules, they apply to everybody, and you live with that set of rules. Players will get used to whatever set of rules you implement. And I do know there are certain things Lou tolerates that most likely Bobby Cox, and Tony La Russa wouldn't.

"Can you imagine a guy in left field walking after the ball in the corner [as Sorianao did in 2008] for Tony La Russa?" Stone continued. "Bobby Cox was a guy who stopped a game in the sixth inning, got up out of the dugout and pointed out to center field and then-rookie Andruw Jones, who dogged it after a fly ball that dropped in front of him. And [Cox] said, 'Come on in,' in the middle of the inning, and only when Jones got in did he take somebody from the dugout and run him out to center field. Then he told Jones, 'Go in and sit down in the lockerroom. You obviously don't want to play.'"

"[Tampa Bay manager] Joe Maddon did the same thing twice with B.J. Upton. And [Angels manager] Mike Scioscia went up to [GM] Bill Stoneman toward the end of a pennant race in September and said, 'Get Jose Guillen off my team.' He was his leading RBI man and he said, 'He can't play for me any longer. I want him off my team.' [Guillen was suspended just before the 2004 postseason after being openly angry about being lifted for a pinch runner, the last in a series of me-first incidents, and never played for the team again]."

Upon his first introduction to Chicago media and fans, Piniella acknowledged his managerial style has evolved over the years.

"You appeal to people's pride," he said. "That's where it starts. You can't be a hard-ass as a manager, and I'm not a hard-ass.... When I came up to the big leagues...boy, you had to respect the manager, because if you don't, you're not going to play on that team. Now the manager basically has to earn the respect of the players, and that's my job—earn their respect, so I can expect respect back at the same time.

"That's really the way I operate. These are the guys with the longer-term contracts. And they're the ones who are the most important cogs because they're the talent."

In an August 29 interview with the *Tribune*'s Paul Sullivan, Piniella's players compared him to their former manager, Dusty Baker. "Dusty cared about his players so much, and he'd do anything in the world for us," Theriot said. "That's probably a trait that sometimes isn't a great one."

Ramirez also paid Baker a backhanded compliment. "I didn't see him like a manager; I just saw him like a friend," he said. "He's a players' manager. Lou is a little different. Lou is all about winning the games and playing good ball."

Soriano, who speaks primarily Spanish with Piniella as most of the Cubs' Latin players do, said he felt a common bond with Piniella when the two met in Florida in the fall of 2007. Hendry and Piniella had met Soriano to sell him on the Cubs, and Soriano said Piniella made an impression on him that day that only continued.

"The only thing I know is he loves to win and he hates to lose," Soriano said in September 2008. "That's what I know. He is a very happy man when we win, but he's very mad when we lose. That's good. I'm the same way. That's why we get along.

"The first year was complicated for everybody because we didn't know him so well, but now we know how he feels so we respect him and give 100 percent every day. I like him. I joke with him all the time."

While there's a fair amount of joking, however, Piniella has always tried to keep a healthy distance from his players.

"He told us, 'I'll treat you guys the way I wanted to be treated as a player,'" DeRosa said. "He's very rarely seen in our clubhouse. He keeps his distance from the players. He doesn't get too close because as a player, that's how Billy Martin treated him, and that's how he liked it. He said, 'I didn't want a manager moseying through the clubhouse every day.' It makes you feel uncomfortable. You've got to be on your best behavior.

"He's played the game for a long time. He knows what makes players comfortable and what doesn't. But he's also not going to sit there and let the players police themselves to a fault. He makes his presence known quite often through the course of the year."

Players insist that behavior such as not running the bases hard or committing mental errors are dealt with by Piniella immediately and not always so subtly.

"Oh yeah, if you make a mistake, you don't want to come in the dugout, not because you're embarrassed—people are going to make mistakes—but because you know you're going to hear it from Lou," said DeRosa. "But you're also going to hear it if you do something good."

But handling athletes is a constant evolution, say those in the coaching profession, and today's players simply do not respond to criticism the same way their predecessors did.

"Those kinds of things I'm sure he takes care of privately, and without sitting in Lou's office, that kind of criticism is short-sighted," said Jim Hendry, when given Soriano's actions as an example and told of Stone's comments. "I don't think Lou has any problem with discipline in the clubhouse. At the same time, I'm sure in the NFL today, coaches don't grab guys by the face masks like George Halas or Vince Lombardi did."

Indeed, the day of Soriano's apology, the same day he took another purpose pitch behind his head, Piniella told reporters, "He's a wonderful young man. I told him, 'You're a leader here. If I don't say something to you, how can I say something to someone else?'"

On his WGN show, Piniella elaborated on their discussion about Soriano admiring his handiwork at the plate. "I said, 'There's no need for that,' and he recognized it right away.... He overestimates his power sometimes."

Cochran remarked that in the era of modern-day athletes, if a player apologizes, it is "a breath of fresh air," and Piniella agreed. "That's exactly the way I handled it," he said. "There's no other way. He felt bad about it. He said so. He showed contrition and that's the end of it. Nobody's perfect."

Those close to the team said Piniella knew exactly what he was doing in his treatment of Soriano.

"Even though he may not seem it, Soriano's an insecure kid who wants people to love him, and he would go into a shell and never hit .150 again if a manager kicked his ass and Lou knows that," said one observer.

Cochran likened Piniella to "the best teacher you ever had. He doesn't coddle anyone, but he has a way of knowing just how to take care of the temperamental kid, the slacker he knows has potential, the emotional kid. Some of us are just blessed with the ability to read human behavior, and Lou has that gift. I really think that's his legacy, that's his brilliance."

Friends say that while he considered Billy Martin a mentor, Piniella also recognized Martin's many flaws in relating to people and was determined to get it right. But Jeff Cirillo believes that like Martin, Piniella has the power to make or break players, and while he had seemingly gone easy on Soriano, he has demoralized others who may not have deserved it.

Cirillo, a career .296-hitting third baseman who chafed under Piniella's direction in his two seasons playing for him in Seattle when he hit .249 and .205, was doing the broadcast for a Brewers-Cubs game during the 2008 season when he made this private observation, related a few months later:

"Bobby Howry walked a guy on four pitches," Cirillo said of the Cubs' reliever. "Howry had a great year last season but struggled some [in 2008]. So instead of [Piniella coming out and] patting him on the butt and accepting that baseball is a cyclical game and sometimes it's there and sometimes it's not, he gave him a two-hand backhanded sweep, like 'Get out of here, I sweep you away.'

"What happens is, the fans pick up on those things, and then it's free reign on Bobby Howry. After all, 'If the captain and chief is disregarding this guy, why shouldn't we?'"

But others observing Piniella's body language saw different expressions of his authority. "I saw him when he called to Zambrano, 'Get back on the mound,'" said McLaren. "It's his best pitcher, and he made a statement right there. Lou knows when to pull the trigger. He's smart. He does things in his own way, and he knows how to get the message across."

But McLaren also contends that Piniella does treat Latin players differently, and that it's a smart move. "He knows some are very temperamental, very sensitive, and he knows if he screams and hollers at them, that's the worst thing you can do," he said.

However, after Game 2 of the 2008 NLDS, it was reported that Piniella had yelled at some of his Latin players in Spanish, including Soriano and Ramirez, who were laboring through another poor offensive postseason. Piniella acknowledged that the word "cojones," a slang for, take your choice—balls or guts—was used more than once as the manager and a few players gathered in the clubhouse kitchen. One TV reporter interpreted the message to mean his players needed to show some, and the report was talked about on Chicago radio the next day.

Piniella was still annoyed two days later as the series shifted to Los Angeles, insisting that he was merely telling his players to "throw it right on the line now. That's it. That's all it was.

"It's upsetting to me in that I haven't yelled at any player here in two years," Piniella continued, oddly defensive. "I don't yell at players. I respect them. I respect them, and sometimes I have meetings with them in my office. Outside of that it's been very positive.

"I was giving them a little pep talk, and when you give a little pep talk in Spanish, you get a little animated. Plus, I'm not a stoic-type character anyway, so I do get a little animated. But it was just a little pep talk, a nice, friendly pep talk with Soriano and Ramirez, because they're two of my key people."

Edgar Martinez, who played under Piniella in all 10 of the manager's seasons in Seattle, said he admired Piniella's ability to connect with his players in any language.

"It's very rare to see a manager be able to communicate with players on different levels," Martinez said. "He is very smart guy, and he knows what to say at the right time. Sometimes he talks to the Latin players in Spanish to send a message because he knows he will get his message across better to certain players that way. But he knows how to get his message across in English, too."

Often over the course of his career, Piniella has chosen the media to deliver a variety of messages. After a 4–3 loss in St. Louis on September 9, the Cubs' eighth loss in their last nine games, he employed one of his favorite methods—the angry postgame interview given within earshot of his players.

"If we had played ball like this all year, we wouldn't be here playing for a championship," he bellowed. "We'd be playing a spoiler role for somebody else. We can talk about having fun. We can talk about relaxing. You have to get your damn shirt [sleeves] rolled up and go out and kick somebody's ass. That's what you have to do, period."

The next day, the Cubs beat the Cardinals 4–3 to keep their lead over the Brewers at four-and-a-half games and reduce their magic number to 10 for clinching the division. But more notable was the way the Cubs played, as winning pitcher Ted Lilly set the tone by slamming into St. Louis catcher Yadier Molina while being thrown out at the plate in the second inning.

Afterward, Lilly was coy when asked if Piniella's speech had motivated him and the team, quipping, "You know, he might be over 100, but he still has a lot of fire. He hasn't lost that, especially when we've lost tough games."

Asked again about it a few weeks later, Lilly said, "He expects us to play hard. If Lou was a pitcher, he would have run over him."

"He's still very intense," Trammell said of Piniella, "he's just a little wiser, so he picks his spots here and there. In St. Louis, he made it a point for the guys to hear it, no doubt about it. He did it on purpose. He just hasn't had to do it very much with this club."

Kerry Wood said Piniella keeps his players guessing. "There were a couple days where we lost some games in a row," said Wood, "and I thought, 'Okay, we lost again, he's going to let us have it,' and he'd come in and be the complete opposite, saying, 'Guys, relax. Man, this is supposed to be fun.'

"I'm thinking, man, we could really use a good chewing right now. And he comes down and cracks a joke and walks by you and says, 'We'll get 'em tomorrow, man that guy did a good job over there today.' And then there are days where you think, 'Okay, we just let that slip away from us but we played good baseball,' and he'll let you have it. So it's kind of different. We've all been around the game long enough to know, 'Okay, we're probably going to get yelled at today.' But he mixes it up on you."

As for corralling certain players specifically, most agree simply that times have changed.

"You just don't meet Reggie Jackson on the top steps [of the dugout], like Billy Martin did, in the modern baseball world," said Lee Elia. "For what reasons, I don't know completely. But that year and a half up in the [TV] booth, Lou probably realized you can entertain some toughness and get things done in the same way without being so visual about it in front of your fans."

Dempster compared it to Stan Musial having to hit a Brad Lidge slider. "No one was throwing an 87-mile-per-hour slider then," he said. "Times have evolved."

For better and for worse.

"Going back 20 years ago, 50 years ago, even 10 years ago," Dempster continued, "guys hustled a little bit more. Guys just don't hustle for ground balls; they don't hustle for fly balls. How many times do you see pop-ups and the guy is standing on first base? And before, you'd pull that guy out of the game or you'd say, 'Go sit on the bench if you don't want to hustle.' It's hard to do when all of us are making millions of dollars and the team is saying, 'You can't sit that guy on the bench, he's making [X-amount of money].

"Maybe early on, maybe not being too far away from being a player himself, [Piniella] got on guys a little bit more because he still had that side to him. But as you get older, I think you realize that it's not your responsibility as a manager, it's the guys in the clubhouse. Whether it's not running out a ground ball or not backing up a position or a pitcher not covering first base, that's our responsibility to go over to your guy."

Piniella's former players agreed.

"Lou is smart enough that he's not going to go nose-to-nose with one of his best players," said Tim Belcher, who played for Piniella with the Reds and Mariners. "That's not being soft or granting special favors; that's managing."

Jay Buhner, one of Piniella's favorite players in Seattle, was almost incensed at the idea that Piniella should be criticized for not being tougher on Soriano. "He has 24 other guys on that bench, a whole bench full of veteran guys," Buhner said. "Zambrano beat the crap out of Barrett. Why can't someone else grab Soriano on the top step of the dugout and say, 'Enough with this shit, knock it off. You do it again, and I'm going to embarrass your ass.' He didn't have to worry about that stuff with us. We policed ourselves."

In Seattle, Piniella had a core group of good veteran players who could do that. It's also useful to note that Alex Rodriguez was not a high-priced free agent when Piniella first had him but an 18-year-old baby. Griffey, too, had come up through the Mariners' system. Teams were able to grow up together, and leaders to develop naturally unlike the constant transition of teams 10 years later.

In Tampa, Piniella had an entire pitching staff making the minimum salary and simply did not have to deal with the issues he had on the Cubs.

In addition, Piniella was extremely conscious of the image that has played out publicly throughout his career, seen over and over in recycled clips, and in his final stop he was simply trying to maintain some sense of control over it.

"Temper has always been a little bit of a problem for me," he said early in his Cubs tenure. "Probably expended way too much energy when I played, and early in my [managing] career, I was probably more confrontational. I'm not any longer.

"I think it has been more of an evolution than anything else. At the same time, everybody wants to be liked. It's human nature to want to walk into the clubhouse and everybody says, 'Boy, what a nice guy,' and all 25 players like you."

While they may not have loved him the last month of the 2008 season, which felt a lot worse than 12–12 after August's torrid 20–8, they did listen. Or at least they tried to listen.

Piniella liked to teach, and at one point or another with every team he had managed, he had gone into the cage, picked up a bat or simply assumed a batting stance to show his players exactly what they were doing wrong.

He demonstrated to Matt Murton the proper way to stride into the ball on an elevator during a stop on Piniella's first Cubs Caravan. He worked closely with Felix Pie earlier in the '08 season when the young outfielder was struggling.

"He said I drop my hand a lot," said Pie. "I appreciate that. This is a great guy. He likes to joke, he likes to smile and play, but when he's serious, he's serious."

And now he was being serious with Fukudome, whose production had dropped steadily throughout the season, from .327 in March and April to .293 in May, .264 in June, .236 in July, and down to .193 in August.

Piniella and hitting coach Gerald Perry worked with Fukudome one morning in late August specifically on shortening his stride and tried to correct a recent tendency of pulling off the ball. His two-run, pinch-hit homer that afternoon was a cause for wild celebration in the Cubs' dugout.

"He's a good hitter," said Piniella. "He just got in some bad habits."

Unfortunately for the Cubs, Fukudome was not quite over the bad habits yet. But fortunately for Piniella, he had other reasons to be optimistic about the stretch run, like his rookie catcher Geovany Soto and newly acquired castoffs Reed Johnson and Jim Edmonds, who had made key contributions. Rich Harden shook off shoulder soreness to turn in an ERA of 1.77 in 12 games.

When the regular season had concluded and the Cubs had been crowned division champs for the second straight year under Piniella—their first back-to-back titles of any kind for the franchise since the 1907–08 World Series victories—they had five players with 20 or more home runs, four with 80 or more RBIs, and three pitchers with at least 14 wins. Wood had successfully converted to a closer with 34 saves and Dempster to a starter with 17 victories.

Players tried to be somewhat subdued the Saturday they clinched at Wrigley, saying all the right things about wanting to save themselves for more important celebrations ahead. But Piniella knew what they had accomplished. And when Mike Quade told him in the clubhouse afterward, "The fans are yelling for you, Lou," the Cubs skipper grabbed Jim Hendry and returned to the field in his stocking feet, waving to the crowd.

Piniella understood how hard it had been, how much it had taken out of him personally, how much it always did to get through a major-league season. He was proud of accomplishing at least one hurdle that had not been cleared in 100 years.

As he headed back down the tunnel, he found himself walking next to 26-year-old pitcher Randy Wells from Lebanon, Illinois, who made his Cubs debut—a 1-2-3 ninth—just two days earlier after seemingly a lifetime in the minors. Wells would be gone again in a matter of days, but for now, he was covered in champagne and alone with Lou Piniella, an opportunity that did not escape him.

"I was like, 'I'm in the tunnel with Lou,'" said Wells, grinning days later.

And then he blurted out the first thing he could think of.

"It sure beats Iowa," Wells said.

Piniella laughed. "Pitch well tomorrow, and you might go to the next round," he replied.

Back inside, Mark DeRosa was asked about those first moments after the victory that only the team was privy to, a private and precious couple of minutes to reflect on what they had accomplished, and DeRosa focused on their manager.

"The media and all the fans, you don't see what we see out of him on a daily basis, how much he cares about us and how much he cares about getting this done," DeRosa said. "To see his reaction after the game was just special. He was just excited, you could see it in his face.

"He keeps things in perspective; he keeps us even-keeled, but at the same time he realizes we worked hard to put ourselves in this position. That's the thing, you work so hard for six months to get to this position, you don't want it to go away."

That morning, the pressure had reached still another boiling point with Piniella during his pregame chat when a reporter raised the premise that the Cubs were "built for the World Series."

"Let me tell you this," Piniella said. "This team has played hard all year. They've treated the people in Chicago to a damn good season of baseball. And believe me, they all want to win as much as I do. But the problem is there's only one team that can win. And for people to say this team is built for the World Series and if it doesn't win the World Series, it's not a successful year? I just don't buy that, period.

"It's not fair to put all the expectations of all the past failures here and all the past successes here on the 2008 team. You let this team stand on its own merit and you let them do what they can do and as well as they can do, and let them go as far as they can."

It was the first message he had delivered to his team that spring, almost to the word. "Don't put the load of 99 years of not winning on you," he had told them. "Don't put any pressure on yourself. Let this team stand on its own merit."

And then, three days after the Cubs announced they had picked up the $4 million option on Piniella's contract for 2010, they were done. Three and out. Again.

The night before the Cubs opened the best-of-five Division Series with the Dodgers, one of the hottest teams in baseball at the time, a team that had added Manny Ramirez and Casey Blake and had a resurging Rafael Furcal who had pitched the Cubs tough in earlier meetings, Piniella went out to dinner with White Sox chairman Jerry Reinsdorf.

"He called it," said Reinsdorf of the first-round disappointment. "He was really worried about whether they'd be able to score runs. Fukudome wasn't getting the job done. And they really needed left-handed hitting."

Piniella's worst fears would be realized. They were outscored in those three games a combined 20–6. Soriano and Ramirez were a combined 3-for-25 from the plate with no RBIs. Fukudome was 1-for-10.

As with his decision to pull Zambrano in Game 1 of the 2007 NLDS, Piniella made some decisions sure to be second-guessed, such as why start Fukudome in the first two games when he had been hitting so poorly? Reliable Mike Fontenot had been starting at second with the versatile DeRosa in right since early September.

Piniella felt he had to play DeRosa at second because of a calf pull that limited his mobility. But couldn't he have played Reed Johnson in right instead of Fukudome, fans and media asked, when Johnson, albeit a righty, had batted .303 in 109 games during the season?

Clearly, Piniella still had faith in Fukudome's left-handed bat as well as his defense, and a clutch grab in the Dodgers bullpen in Game 1 validated the latter. But a strikeout in the seventh that showcased Fukudome's awkwardness at the plate would make a stronger impression with fans.

"You know, this is basically a lineup that has played a lot this summer and helped us get here," Piniella said after Game 1. But he also acknowledged, "I've had as much patience with [Fukudome] as I've had with anybody I've ever managed."

Then there was also Piniella's decision to keep Dempster in Game 1 as long as he did—when Dempster walked seven batters, including three in the fifth, before James Loney launched a grand slam to silence the Wrigley Field crowd, seemingly for good.

With Dempster's pitch count at 100, no one was warming up in the bullpen. "We were going to let him get himself out of trouble," said Piniella. "Their guys threw strikes and ours didn't. It hurts."

Still, Piniella appeared relaxed before Game 2, scooping up a piece of pizza in the cramped makeshift press room under the Wrigley Field stands and gobbling it up during his pregame press conference—that is, until he was told that DeRosa had called the game "a must-win" for the Cubs.

"If we lose tonight, well, we might as well just stay home and forfeit the game in Los Angeles then," a suddenly edgier Piniella said. "You've got to win three ballgames in these things."

You could almost hear the heartburn starting to churn.

Game 2 would feel like two losses as the Dodgers walloped the listless Cubs in a tomb-like Wrigley Field, 10–3. Zambrano, allowing three earned runs on six hits while walking two and striking out seven in six and one-third innings, was hardly the culprit as the Cubs committed an NLDS-record four errors, one by every member of the infield.

And Fukudome struck out three times.

"From now on, I don't want to hear about Fukudome anymore as far as whether he'll play or not," Piniella said. "I'll play Fontenot or Reed Johnson or someone, and that's the end of that."

And so it was.

The Cubs were never in Game 3, just like they were never really in the series after the Dodgers took their first lead in the fifth inning of Game 1. Rich Harden, who was supposed to regain a little of that

Cubbie swagger, gave up two runs in the first inning, and that was that. Period, as Piniella would say.

He couldn't explain his team's sudden tightness, this organizational defect, any more than he could cure it. But he couldn't put himself above it either. All he could do was rely on his own 44 years in the majors.

"It's a game," he said before Game 3. "It's a game. That's really what it is. It's a game. You've got to have confidence in yourself. That's the most important thing. And you've got to have confidence in your teammates. And you can't try to overdo.

"I remember in '81, we played the Dodgers in the World Series, and we beat them two in a row and came here and Fernando [Valenzuela] was pitching Game 3 and I was hitting [fourth] that day. I came up with two runners on base in the [first] inning. I was ahead 3–1 in the count. I wasn't a home-run hitter; I was more of a gap hitter. I said, 'I'm going to crowd the plate and hit a home run.' Well, he threw me a screwball, and I hit a nice double-play ball, where if I had just done what I had done all year and stayed within myself and hit the ball to right-center field, we probably would have scored a couple of runs and given our pitchers a couple runs to work with.

"That's what I'm saying. You can't overdo...you've got to stay within yourself."

His voice trailed off.

"They say sometimes the last game is the hardest to win," he said. "Let's hope it's so."

The last game is also the hardest to lose, and this one was no different.

In anger, someone on the Cubs bench, the *Sun-Times* later reported, apparently took a bat to a metal water pipe in the dugout that leads into the locker room, nearly flooding the area, a mishap for which the team apologized and paid $4,000 to repair.

In the clubhouse, players hugged and consoled each other, reporters wearing the sort of solemn game faces reserved only for the most crushing defeats.

Piniella showered and dressed quickly, but he was still hot. "I'm not making excuses, but you have to score some runs," he said as reporters mobbed him just outside his office in the tiny visitors' clubhouse. "This team here is in the postseason for whatever reason, but I haven't seen it."

"As frustrated as you are..." the next question began but got no further.

"I'm not frustrated sir; I'm not frustrated," Piniella said, his words clipped. "I'm just stating facts which are obvious and true. I'm not frustrated. I congratulated the team on a fine season. I thanked them for their hard work and their preparation, and I told them to enjoy their families this winter."

"Are you still excited about the next two years now?" he was asked.

"Well, sure I'm excited," he said. "But I want to do more than play the part of the good loser, you know, I really do. I want to do more than play the part of congratulating the other team in the first round of the playoffs."

In the hotel bar afterward, several people heard Piniella grumble about Soriano's ineffectiveness as he went 1-for-14. Some players had theorized that Piniella had given Soriano his word when the Cubs signed him that he would be his leadoff hitter. But after two years, it sounded as if Piniella had seen enough and was finally ready to move him down. The lingering question, of course, would be if not Soriano, then whom?

As for Ramirez, who went 2-for-11 in the NLDS, Piniella told friends that unlike Soriano, he was confident he could tap into an inherent toughness in Ramirez that he admired and could somehow bring him around.

But there was little analysis in the immediate aftermath of the playoff loss.

One Cubs coach said he could "never have imagined a more awkward flight home, to be that devastated. Nobody even felt like talking. It was silent." There would be changes in the off-season.

Gone were Mark DeRosa, Kerry Wood, and Jason Marquis. In was Milton Bradley and another temperament to massage.

Back home in Tampa days later, Piniella said he didn't even want to watch the playoffs. "I'd rather watch an NFL game," he said on his WGN radio show. "I'm still hurting from the damn thing."

Three weeks later, said his buddies, Piniella had finally begun to unwind, and they had their customary first lunch of the off-season, Lou and Mondy and Tony. The stone crabs had just come in October 15 and so they gathered as they always do, "with lunch starting at 1:00," laughed Tony, "and finishing about 6:00."

They each nursed a glass of wine or two, caught up, laughed, relaxed. They talked about the Rays, and Lou insisted he was happy for them. They also talked about fishing and about horses. Lou and Anita had been looking for one to buy for their granddaughter, an accomplished equestrian.

They talked about how much more patient they had become as they had gotten older. And they teased him about the little talk in Spanish he had with his Latin players after Game 2.

"I was just giving them an Ybor City pep talk," Lou teased back, referring to the town where they had played ball, a tough section of Tampa where many Latin immigrants settled and where many of their families were from. And then Lou made that scrunched-up face they know and love, and they all had a good laugh.

People stopped by the table periodically with a "Hey Lou, how're you doing?" People he knew, many he didn't. Didn't matter, it never did. He was back in his element, "where he's just one of the guys from Tampa," said Tony, "where we don't expect anything out of him."

The three made plans. Before he knew it, Lou told them, it would be the holidays, and then in another couple of months, he'd be back at it. "Another couple months and he'll be itching for baseball," said Tony.

If there was any doubt, said Steve Cochran, he recalled the phone conversation he had with Piniella about a month after the season ended. "One of the last things he said before we hung up was, 'You know, we're going to get this done,'" Cochran recalled. "It was out of context to what we were talking about, and so I paused and he said, 'You know, win the World Series.' He didn't want me hanging up the phone without knowing it was still ever-present on his mind."

References

Bass, Mike. *Marge Schott: Unleashed*, (Sagamore Publishing).

Browning, Tom, with Dan Stupp. *Tom Browning's Tales from the Reds Dugout*, (Sports Publishing LLC).

Jacobson, Steve. *The Best Team Money Could Buy: The Turmoil and Triumph of the 1977 New York Yankees*, (Signet).

Madden, Bill, and Moss Klein. *Damed Yankees: A No-Holds Barred Account of Life with "Boss" Steinbrenner*, (Warner Books).

Pepe, Phil. *The Ballad of Billy & George: The Tempestuous Baseball Marriage of Billy Martin and George Steinbrenner*, (The Lyons Press).

Piniella, Lou, and Maury Allen. *Sweet Lou*, (Bantam Books).

Shannon, Mike. *The Good, The Bad, & The Ugly: Heart-Pounding, Jaw-Dropping and Gut-Wrenching Moments from Cincinnati Reds History*, (Triumph Books).

Thiel, Art. *Out of Leftfield: How the Mariners Made Baseball Fly in Seattle*, (Sasquatch Books).

Index

A

A's, xiv, 60, 78, 139, 141–43, 192, 202, 243
Abbott, Paul, 189
Abernathy, Brent, 200
AL Central, 217
AL East, 92, 105, 151, 198
Al Lopez Field, 6
AL West, 161, 173, 180, 198
Albright, Madeleine, 174
ALCS, 138, 171, 185–86, 242
ALDS, 169, 171, 173, 177, 179, 184, 186
Alexander, Doyle, 59
All–Star Game, ix, 145, 267, 273
Allen, Maury, 63
Alomar, Roberto, 37, 223
Alou, Moises, 245
Altobelli, Joe, 98, 106
American League, xi, 37, 46, 55, 57, 59,
    76, 85–86, 97, 105, 133, 154–55,
    168, 87, 202, 218, 221
American League All–Star, 101
American League Championship, 67, 78,
    157
American League East, 106
American Legion, 139
Anderson, Dave, 109, 112
Anderson, Marlon, 200
Anderson, Sparky, 58–59, 92
Appel, Marty, 54
Argyros, George, 151
Arizona Diamondbacks, 188–89, 220,
    235–36, 256, 270, 273
Armstrong, Chuck, 151, 193
Armstrong, Jack, 130
Atlanta Braves, 144, 147, 250, 256, 273,
    275

B

Babe Ruth, 143, 176
Babe Ruth League, 125
Bailey, Sam, 10, 24, 224
Baker, Dusty, 238, 274, 276
Baldelli, Rocco, 216, 221, 223
Balderson, Dick, 150
Baldwin, James, 191
Baltimore Orioles, 15–17, 24, 27, 51, 62,
    64, 76, 78, 82, 159–60, 173, 216, 268
Banks, Ernie, 256
Barnett, Larry, xi, 36–37
Barney, Smith, 81
Barrett, Michael, 40, 250–253, 272, 282
Baseball Writers Association, 20
Bass, Mike, 146
Bates, Billy, 132, 142
Bauer, Hank, 15
Bautista, Danny, 223
Belanger, Mark, 15
Belcher, Tim, 32–33, 35, 147, 169, 282
Bell, Buddy, 189
Bell, David, 188
Bell, George, 102
Bell, Jay, 133
Bell, Wally, 204
Belle, Albert, 172
Beltran, Carlos, 222
Bench, Johnny, 58–59
Benes, Andy, 165–66
Benzinger, Todd, 130, 137
Berkow, Ira, 95
Berra, Dale, 91
Berra, Yogi, 79, 82–86, 93, 95, 101, 105
Bibby, Jim, 47–48
Big Red Machine, 58, 122, 162

Birtsas, Tim, 125
Blackman, Marty, 71
Blair, Paul, 62, 67
Blake, Casey, 286
Blanco, Henry, 259
Blowers, Mike, 175
Bochy, Bruce, 236
Boggs, Wade, 170, 197
Bonds, Barry, 138
Bonds, Bobby, 55–56
Bonilla, Bobby, 134, 138
Boone, Bret, 156–58, 168, 181–84, 187, 189
Bosio, Chris, xiv, 156, 160–61, 172, 176–77, 202, 209, 234, 261–62
Boston Red Sox, 56, 62, 64, 72–73, 75, 138, 171, 199, 217, 219, 200, 229–30
Bouton, Jim, viii, 23
Bowa, Larry, 210
Bowen, Rob, 252
Braggs, Glenn, 133, 138
Brazelton, Dewon, 221
Bream, Sid, 138
Brenly, Bob, 236, 271
Brennaman, Marty, xii, 123, 130, 142
Brennaman, Thom, 242–43
Brett, George, 57–58, 67
Browning, Debbie, 141
Browning, Tom, 32, 122–23, 125, 130–31, 142, 144, 147
Buck, Jack, 136–37
Buck, Joe, 242
Bucknor, C.B., 39
Bueno, Francisley, 273
Buhner, Jay, 155–56, 158, 160, 164–66, 170–71, 173–78, 184, 195, 199, 282
Burke, Michael, 49
Burleson, Rick, 74–75, 94
Busch Stadium, 145
Bush, Laura, 137
Bush, President (George), 137

C
Cactus League, 246
California Angels, 114, 157, 165, 167–68, 171, 192, 275
Cameron, Mike, 179, 181, 189
Canseco, Jose, 139, 197–98
Cantu, Jorge, 221
Carew, Rod, 45, 66
Carlton, Steve, 20
Carolina League, 24
Castilla, Vinny, 198
Castillo, Luis, 245

Cedeno, Ronny, 259
Cey, Ron, 68
Chambliss, Chris, 58
Charlton, Norm, 125, 138, 155, 166, 170, 174–75, 189
Chass, Murray, x, 61
Chicago Blackhawks, 237
Chicago Cubs, xvi–xvii, 7, 25, 30–31, 39–42, 97, 139, 145, 155, 172, 182, 209, 212, 233, 235–41, 243–59, 261, 263–74, 276, 278, 280, 282–89
Chicago Sun–Times, 251
Chicago Tribune, 41, 77, 139, 244, 251
Chicago White Sox, vii, ix, 20, 25, 40, 42, 47, 72, 77, 90–91, 105, 114, 161, 179, 212, 252, 254, 267, 272, 274, 286
Cincinnati Enquirer, 127
Cincinnati Post, 128, 132, 135, 141
Cincinnati Reds, xi–xii, xiv, 6, 32–33, 35, 42, 58–59, 97, 106, 118–19, 121–36, 138–39, 141–45, 147–49, 151, 162, 173, 192, 198–99, 247, 256, 264, 267, 282
Cirillo, Jeff, xii, 159, 189, 191, 278
Cleveland Indians, 11, 13, 17, 19, 24–25, 69, 73, 89, 161, 171, 184–85, 191
Cloude, Ken, 159, 218
Cochran, Steve, 264, 278, 290–91
Coleman, Vince, 165
Colon, Bartolo, 184
Colorado Rockies, 159, 189, 220, 254
Comiskey Park, 161
Cone, David, 170
Connor, Mark, 86
Cooney, Terry, 28, 37
Cora, Joey, 171
Cowens, Al, 58
Cox, Bobby, 120, 147, 275
Crasnick, Jerry, 128, 132
Crawford, Carl, xv, 200, 216, 221
Cy Young Award, 69

D
Daley, Richard J., 264
Dark, Alvin, 19–20, 45
Darling, Ron, 145
Dauer, Rich, 27
Daugherty, Paul, 143
Davies, Kyle, 250
Davis, Eric, 125, 130–32, 134–35, 140–41, 147
Dayett, Brian, 82
De Luca, Chris, 251

Deford, Frank, 30, 140, 163
Delgado, Carlos, 222
Dempsey, Rick, 51
Dempster, Ryan, 254, 262, 265–268, 271, 281, 284, 287
Denkinger, Don, 102–3
Dent, Bucky, 74
DeRosa, Mark, 241, 258, 268, 285, 290
Detroit Tigers, 106, 217, 259
Dibble, Rob, xi, xii, 33–34, 125–26, 130, 133, 138, 145, 205, 235, 274
DiMaggio, Joe, 49
Dodger Stadium, 234
Doran, Bill, 145
Downey, Mike, 77
Drabek, Doug, 102, 134
Drew, J.D., 222–23
Duncan, Mariano, 125, 133
Duque, El, 187
Dye, Jermaine, 266

E

Eckersley, Dennis, 126, 163
Edmonds, Jim, xv, 271, 284
Elia, Lee, 30, 166, 209, 214, 249, 281
Ellis, John, 151–54, 169, 172, 179, 195, 265
ESPN, xvii, 29, 36, 39, 127, 207, 249
Evans, Dewey, 56
Eyre, Scott, 264

F

Farnsworth, Kyle, 245
Fenway Park, 62, 73–75, 82, 94
Ferlita, Paul, xvii, 5–7, 22–23, 43
Fernandez, Tony, 102
Ferraro, Mike, 100
Ficcorotta, Joe, 4
Finley, Charlie, 60
Finley, Chuck, 157
Fisk, Carlton, 56, 91
Flood, Curt, 60
Flores, Mondy, xvi, 2–3, 40, 43, 214, 290
Florida Marlins, 215, 236, 245, 256
Florida State, 11
Floyd, Cliff, 242, 266
Fontenot, Mike, 257, 259, 263, 286–87
Fort Worth Star-Telegram, 208
Foster, Steve, 33
FOX Sports, 236, 242–43
Franco, John, 125, 147
Francona, Terry, 210
Frey, Jim, 97
Froemming, Bruce, 40–41

Fukudome, Kosuke, 235, 266–67, 269, 283–84, 286–87
Furcal, Rafael, 286
Furman, Andy, 121–22, 129

G

Gaetti, Gary, 157
Gallagher, Sean, 272
Garcia, Anita, 18
Garcia, Damaso, 102
Garcia, Freddy, 178, 181, 190
Garner, Phil, 38, 189
Gaudin, Chad, 272
Gehrig, Lou, 49, 83, 176
Gillick, Pat, 151, 179, 190, 192, 194
Girardi, Joe, 236–38
Gonzalez, Alex, 223, 245
Gonzalez, Tony, 2–4, 6, 21, 43, 150
Gossage, Rich (Goose), 69–70, 74, 76, 100
Gray, Dorian, xvi
Green, Dallas, 113–14, 117, 242
Green Monster, 74
Grieve, Ben, xiii, 31–32, 200, 202–10, 212, 214, 216, 235
Grieve, Tom, 208–209
Griffey, Ken Jr., vii, 36, 155, 82, 101, 160–63, 169–71, 173–74, 177–79, 188, 199, 256, 270, 282
Griffey, Ken Sr., 162
Griffin, Rick, 155–56, 158–61, 183
Guidry, Ron, 68, 72–73, 75–76, 101, 105, 237
Guillen, Carlos, 178, 186, 190
Guillen, Jose, 275
Guillen, Ozzie, vii–viii, 42
Gumbel, Bryant, 30, 140, 163
Gumbel, Greg, 242
Guzman, Juan, 198

H

Halama, John, 178, 190
Halas, George, 277
Hall, Toby, xiii, xv, 206, 211–12
Hall of Fame, 16, 193, 229, 231
Hamilton, Josh, 221
Harden, Rich, 272, 284, 287
Harper, Travis, 227–28
Hasegawa, Shigetoshi, 267
Hatcher, Billy, xiii, 125, 127, 131, 138, 143, 210, 213
HBO, 30, 140, 163
Heisman Trophy, 79
Helms, Tommy, 118, 125

Henderson, Joe, 139–40, 148, 199, 201, 208, 210, 226, 229
Henderson, Rickey, 105–7
Hendry, Jim, 236–37, 241, 244, 246, 276–77, 284
Hendry, Ted, 37–38
Higgins, John, 217
Hill, Rich, 252, 257
Hillsborough High School, 18
Hirschbeck, John, 37
Hirshbeck, John, 39
Hornsby, Rogers, 176
Houk, Ralph, 49
Houston Astros, 114, 145, 173, 178, 189–90, 255
Howry, Bob (Bobby), 254, 257, 268, 278–79
Howser, Dick, 72, 77, 79, 93, 99
Hrabosky, Al, 71
Huff, Aubrey, 216, 221
Hughes, Pat, 259
Hunsicker, Gerry, 190
Hunter, Catfish, 51, 54–55, 57–61, 65, 68, 73

I

Iavarrone, Carmine, 23, 40
Infante, Omar, 266
Iorg, Garth, 102
Izturis, Cesar, 254

J

Jackson, Bo, 161
Jackson, Danny, 130, 138
Jackson, Reggie, ix, x, 60–64, 67–72, 74, 77, 79, 101, 170, 281
Jacobs Field, 36
Jacobson, Steve, 53, 72, 118, 137
Japanese Central League, 266
Javier, Stan, 188
Jesuit High, 6, 8, 18, 23, 140, 236
Jeter, Derek, 184
John, Tommy, ix, 68, 76
Johnson, Cliff, 76
Johnson, Davey, 137, 154
Johnson, Mike, 174
Johnson, Randy, 160, 166, 168, 171–75, 178–79, 187, 189–90, 196, 199
Johnson, Reed, 271, 284, 286–87
Jones, Andruw, 275
Jones, Jacque, 266
Jordan, Pat, 215

K

Kane, Bill, 67, 88
Kansas City Royals, 20, 26, 45,–48, 57–59, 67, 71–72, 76, 78, 86, 96–97, 99, 165
Kaplan, David, 247, 265
Kasper, Len, 260, 263
Kauffman, Ewing, 45–48
Kazmir, Scott, 221, 229
Kelley, Steve, 192
Kelly, Pat, 171
Kelly, Roberto, 133
Kelly, Tom, 159
Kemp, Steve, 82
King, Clyde, 79, 86–87, 89, 93–94, 106
Kingdome, 163–65, 168, 170, 173, 178
Klein, Moss, 61, 69–70, 79, 90–92, 108, 111
Kubek, Tony, 50

L

LaForest, Pete, 217
LaMar, Chuck, 198, 217–18, 226
Lampkin, Tom, 188
Larkin, Barry, 125, 147
La Russa, Tony, 4–5, 9, 91, 137, 139–140, 143, 208, 257, 275
Lau, Charlie (Charley), 46, 85–86
Lavoy, Bob, 9
Lazzara, Benny, 213
Le Betard, Dan, 208
Lebreton, Gil, 208
Lee, Bill, 56
Lee, Derrek, 249, 254
Lee, Travis, 200, 205, 212, 227, 230
Lemon, Bob, 26–27, 45, 72, 76, 79, 81, 84
Leonard, Dennis, 58, 67
Leyland, Jim, 137
Leyritz, Jim, 169
Lezcano, Sixto, 55
Lidge, Brad, 281
Lieber, Jon, 266
Lilly, Ted, 241, 257, 261, 280
Lincoln, Howard, 189
Lipon, Johnny, 17
Littell, Mark, 58
Lombardi, Vince, 277
Loney, James, 286
Lopez, Al Jr., 4
Los Angeles Dodgers, 17, 67–68, 76, 78, 85, 119, 131, 185, 200, 235, 255, 286–88
Lou Piniella Day, 83, 96

Lou Piniella Field, 224
Lowe, Derek, 174
Lyle, Sparky, 67, 69–70, 73
Lynn, Fred, 75–76
Lyons, Steve, 242–43

M

Madden, Bill, 63, 65, 79, 111, 212
Maddon, Joe, 275
Maddox, Elliott, 51
Magadan, Beñina, 1
Magadan, Dave, 2
Magadan, Mac, 13
Magadan, Marcelinno, 1
Magadan, Mike, 2
Mahler, Rick, 130
Major League Umpires Association, 145
Marmol, Carlos, 254, 256
Marquis, Jason, 241, 257, 268, 290
Martin, Al, 200, 206
Martin, Billy, ix, xi, 30, 37, 55–59, 62–64,
    67, 70–72, 76–79, 84–89, 92–93,
    95–96, 103–4, 107–113, 117, 119,
    137, 214, 217, 261, 277–78, 281
Martinez, Buck, 102
Martinez, Carmelo, 138
Martinez, Dave, 147
Martinez, Edgar, 155, 160, 166, 168,
    170–71, 173, 176–77, 179–81, 183,
    186, 189, 199, 280
Martinez, Pedro, 200
Martinez, Tino, 155, 170, 177, 220
Mattingly, Don, 85, 89, 105, 107
May, Carlos, 20
May, Pinky, 13, 14
May, Milt, 13
McCarver, Tim, 36, 134–35, 137, 142, 242
McDaniel, Lindy, 48
McDonough, John, 237, 240, 248
McDowell, Jack, 170, 177
McEwen, Tom, xvi, 23, 139–40
McGriff, Fred, 198
McGwire, Mark, 139
McKeon, Jack, 45, 47–48
McLaren, John, 166, 175, 176, 186–88,
    191, 204, 206–07, 210–11, 224, 230,
    279
McLemore, Mark, 181
McNally, Dave, 27, 60
McRae, Hal, 67, 197, 199
Meacham, Bobby, 91
Messersmith, Andy, 60
Metro, Charlie, 45

Mexican League, 52
Miami Herald, 208
Michael, Gene, xv, 27, 52, 67, 79, 86, 89,
    95, 99, 100, 114, 261
Miller, Marvin, viii
Milwaukee Braves, 119
Milwaukee Brewers, 38, 51, 64, 119, 212,
    227, 253, 256, 268, 270, 273, 278,
    280
Mitchell, Kevin, 155
Molina, Yadier, 280
Monahan, Gene, 66, 90
Moore, Jackie, 123
Morris, Hal, 125, 130, 135–36
Morris, Jack, 105
Moseby, Lloyd, 102
Moyer, Jamie, 182, 187
Mullin, John, 120
Munson, Thurman, ix, 49, 55–56, 59–60,
    62–64, 67, 74, 77–78
Murcer, Bobby, 36, 49, 51, 55, 76
Murray, Eddie, 172
Murton, Matt, 272, 283
Musial, Stan, 176, 281
Myers, Randy, 125, 130, 138, 145, 147

N

Naimoli, Vince, 198, 217–18, 222, 226
National League All-Star, 145
National League Central, 41
National League Championship Series,
    106, 132, 244
National League Division Series, 235
National League West, 118
Neagle, Denny, 223
Nelson, Jeff, 181, 189, 191–92
Nero, Alan, 193
Nettles, Graig, 29, 56–57, 67, 75
New Orleans Saints, 241
New York Daily News, 63, 212
New York Giants, 59
New York Mets, 46, 192, 202, 204
New York Post, 187
New York Times, x, 61, 71, 95, 98, 107,
    109–111, 215, 228
New York Yankees, viii, ix, x, xv, xvii, 15,
    17, 25, 27–29, 32, 36, 48–64, 66–74,
    76–79, 82–106, 108–115, 117–19,
    121, 125–26, 132–133, 147, 149–51,
    157, 160, 162, 165, 168–71, 178–79,
    184–88, 192, 199, 204, 211, 215,
    217, 219–21, 224, 227, 230, 236–37,
    242, 261, 268

Newark Star–Ledger, 61, 108
Newman, Jeff, 29
Newsday, 54, 72, 91, 118
Newsweek, 58
Niekro, Phil, 99
Nixon, Richard, 56
NL Central, 252, 254, 271
NL East, 217
NL West, 122, 144, 198
NLCS, 58, 133, 138, 140–41
NLDS, 172, 235, 244, 259, 279, 286–87, 289
Noble, Marty, 91
Nomo, Hideo, 223

O

O'Connell, Jack, 8
O'Neill, Paul, 35, 125–26, 128–29, 133, 135, 137–38, 147, 170, 261
Oakland A's. *See also* A's, 54, 125, 138, 184
Oakland Athletics, 202
Oester, Ron, 128, 132, 134
Ohio State, 79, 120
Olerud, John, 181
Oliver, Joe, 124, 126, 129, 134, 136, 142, 147
Orr, Pete, 250
Otis, Amos, 45–47, 57

P

Pacific Coast League, 25
Pagan, Angel, 252
Pagliarulo, Mike, 107
Palermo, Steve, 29
Palmer, Jim, 15
Pannozzo, Sharon, 239–40, 248
Parker, Rob, 127–28
Patek, Freddie, 45
Patterson, Bob, 134–35
Paul, Gabe, 20, 52–53, 67, 69
Pavano, Carl, 223
Pepe, Phil, 99
Perez, Antonio, 195
Perez, Ron, 18
Perez, Tony, 123, 133
Perlozzo, Sam (Sammy), 123
Perry, Gerald, 283
Phelps, Ken, 160
Philadelphia Phillies, 58, 209, 258–59
Phillips, Dave, 26–28, 30
Picker, David, 228
Pie, Felix, 268, 270–71, 283
Pierzynski, A.J., 253

Piniella, Anita (Garcia), xi, 18–19, 31, 35, 47–49, 69, 77, 79, 83, 91, 108, 121, 127, 148, 153–54, 166, 192, 195, 200–201, 213, 229–30, 290
Piniella, Derek, 31, 39, 83, 153
Piniella. Kristi, 83, 153, 192, 194
Piniella, Lou, vii–xvii, 1–11, 13–43, 45–115, 117–31, 233–90
Piniella, Louis, 2–3, 83, 191, 194, 223–24
Piniella, Louis Jr, 83, 153
Piniella, Margaret, 1–4, 8, 21–23, 25, 83, 224
Piniella Park, 1
Pittsburgh Pirates, 132–39, 248, 255, 271, 274
Plummer, Bill, 154
Pony League, 4
Power, Ted, 137
Price, Bryan, 175, 177, 179, 181–82, 188
Primero, Carlos, 80
Prior, Mark, 245, 247, 266

Q

Quade, Mike, 247, 255, 258, 284
Quinn, Bob, 34, 111, 118–21, 125, 133, 139, 145, 147
Quinn, John, 119
Quinones, Luis, 138
Quisenberry, Dan, 101, 104

R

Rader, Doug, 154
Ramirez, Aramis, 235, 241, 254, 271–72, 276, 279–80, 289
Ramirez, Manny, 171, 176, 286
Randolph, Willie, 56, 90, 105, 107–8, 137
Razutto, Phil, 103
Reed, Jeff, 134–36
Reinsdorf, Jerry, ix, 266, 286
Remlinger, Mike, 245
Remy, Jerry, 74, 94
Rennert, Dutch, 130–31
Reynolds, Mark, 256
Rhodea, Arthur, 181
Rhoden, Rick, 105
Rice, Jim, 62, 75
Richards, Keith, 197
Righetti, Dave, 28–29, 82, 85, 100–4, 110, 113
Rijo, Jose, 125, 133–34, 142–43
Ripken, Cal, 15
Rivera, Mariano, 169, 204, 206
Riverfront Stadium, 124, 141
Rivers, Mickey, 56, 62, 75

Roberts, Bip, 147
Roberts, Brian, 268, 270
Roberts, Robin, 15
Robinson, Jackie, 55
Rodriguez, Alex, 162–63, 173–74, 178–80, 188, 196, 282
Rogers, Phil, 251
Rollins, Jimmy, 259
Rolls, Damian, 200
Rose, Pete, 97, 119, 121–23, 145
Rosen, Al, 69, 75–76, 95
Rothschild, Larry, 123, 197, 237, 264
Royko, Mike, 139
Ruskin, Scott, 147
Ruth, Babe, 49, 125, 143, 176

S

Sabo, Chris, 125, 129, 133–35, 142–43, 145, 147
Safeco Field, 173, 178, 181
Salas, Mark, 106
San Diego Padres, 131, 165, 219–20, 236, 252–53, 266
San Francisco Giants, 29, 55, 227
Sanchez, Alex, 227
Sanchez, Celerino, 52
Sandberg, Ryne, 251
Santo, Ron, 259
Sasaki, Kazuhiro, 181, 267
Schott, Marge, ix, 34, 118, 121, 123–25, 128–29, 144–48, 190
Schottzie, 128–29, 148
Schuerholz, John, 147
Scioscia, Mike, 275
Scott, Dale, 113
Scutaro, Marco, 243
Seattle Mariners, xiv, 32, 36–38, 114, 151, 153–65, 167–74, 178–88, 190–96, 198–201, 253, 265, 278–79, 282
Seattle Pilots, viii
Seattle Post–Intelligencer, 75, 150, 174, 195
Seattle Times, 180, 192–94
Sele, Aaron, 187
Selkirk, George, 14
Selma Cloverleafs, 13
Shea Stadium, 51, 239
Sheets, Andy, 38
Shelton, Gary, 197–98, 201, 218, 221, 226, 230
Showalter, Buck, 169
Shulock, John, 38
Shumpert, Terry, 200
Sianis, Billy, 239
Sims, Duke, 20

Sinatro, Matt, 191, 204, 246, 258, 263–65
Singleton, Ken, 82
Skinner, Joel, 106
Smith, Zane, 137
Solomon, Larry, 150
Soriano, Alfonso, 187, 235, 240–41, 247, 253–55, 270–74, 276–80, 282, 286, 289
Soriano, Rafael, 163
Sosa, Sammy, 215
Soto, Geovany, 259, 268, 270, 284
Sport Magazine, 60
The Sporting News, 20
Sports Illustrated, 56–57
SportsCenter, 36
St. Louis Browns, 119
St. Louis Cardinals, 5, 86, 165, 202, 248, 254, 257, 271, 280
St. Pete Times, 201
St. Petersburg Times, 19, 197
Stanley, Fred, 25–26, 31, 52, 54, 65, 68
Steinbrenner, George, vii, ix, 30, 49, 53–55, 58–60, 62–67, 69–74, 76–77, 79, 81, 84–89, 94, 96, 99, 101–109, 117, 119–21, 132, 138, 143–44, 147, 150–51, 155, 169, 190, 214, 219, 236
Steinbrenner, Hank, 103
Stengel, Casey, 58, 76, 119
Sternberg, Stuart, 222–23, 225–26
Stewart, Dave, 141
Stone, Larry, 180, 184, 190, 193
Stone, Steve, 25, 274–75, 277
Stoneman, Bill, 275
Stottlemyre, Todd, 151
Strange, Doug, 167
Straub, Paul, 6–8, 23, 224
Straub, Steve, 8
Street, Jim, 174, 181
Suarez, Ken (Kenny), 4, 9
Sudakis, Bill, 51
Sullivan, Paul, 244, 276
Suncoast Dome, 197
Sutter, Bruce, 101, 104
Sutton, Don, ix
Suzuki, Ichiro, 38, 180, 267
Swindell, Greg, 147

T

Takatsu, Shingo, 267
Tallis, Cedric, 20, 46, 48
Tampa Bay Devil Rays (D–Rays), 30–32, 192, 194–203, 208, 211–12, 214, 216, 218, 221, 223–25, 227, 229, 230, 234, 236, 238

Tampa Bay Lightning, 220
Tampa Tribune, xvi, 23, 139, 148, 150, 199, 229
Telander, Rick, 263
Texas Rangers, 179, 184, 192, 202
Theriot, Ryan, 255, 269, 276
Thiel, Art, 150, 153–54, 189–91
Thomas, Frank, 243
Thomasson, Gary, 70
Thome, Jim, 172
Tiant, Luis, 20, 76
Tidrow, Dick, 76
Tomko, Brett, 179
Topkin, Marc, 201, 206
Torborg, Jeff, 86, 88–90, 92, 137
Toronto Blue Jays, 101, 105, 114, 117, 121, 151
Torre, Joe, 219, 226, 236
Torrez, Mike, 62, 68, 74
Trachsel, Steve, 266
Trammell, Alan, 41, 247, 259–60, 281
Trebelhorn, Tom, 154
Tropicana Field, 200–201, 204, 218

U

U.S. Cellular Field, 40, 254, 272
University of Florida, 18
University of South Florida, 18
University of Tampa, 9–10, 19, 24, 224
Upton, B.J., 221, 275

V

Valenzuela, Fernando, 288
Van Slyke, Andy, 133, 138
Vaughn, Greg, 198, 212, 216
Veeck, Bill, 72
Velarde, Randy, 171
Veritek, Jason, 174
Victorino, Shane, 259
Virdon, Bill, 49, 55–56
Vizquel, Omar, 155, 157, 161

W

Wagner, Leon (Daddy Wags), 19
Walker, Wildman, 127
Ward, Daryl, 242

Ward, Gary, 105
Washington Senators, 14–15, 23–24, 202
Weaver, Earl, xi, 15–16, 24–25, 27, 37, 45, 51, 92, 97–98
Wegner, Mark, 40–42, 251–52
Weiss, Walt, 139
Wells, David, 253
Wells, Randy, 284–85
Western Division title, 131
White, Bill, 145
White, Roy, 56, 58, 71
White House, 137
Whitson, Ed, 92
Williams, Bernie, 170, 187
Williams, Stan, xi, 17, 114, 121, 123, 127–28, 141–43, 166, 193
Williams, Ted, 176
Wilson, Dan, 211
Winfield, Dave, 79, 82, 85, 100–101, 113
Winn, Randy, 194–95
Wohlford, Jim, 47–48, 54, 58
Wolcott, Bob, 172
Wood, Kerry, 241, 245, 247, 263, 266, 268, 272, 281, 284, 290
Woodward, Woody, 86, 93–94, 108–9, 112, 114, 150–54, 162–63, 165, 167, 179
Wright, Ken, 48
Wrigley Field, 256, 287
Wynegar, Butch, 88–89

Y

Yankee Stadium, 99
Yastrzemski, Carl, 74–75
Yelding, Eric, 145
Young, Chris, 253
Young, Cy, 250, 267

Z

Zambrano, Carlos, 31, 40, 247, 250–57, 259, 266–68, 272, 274, 279, 282, 286–87
Zambrano, Victor, 221
Zell, Sam, 268
Zimmer, Don, 218–19